I0795007

THE AMERICAN CENTURY SERIES

KEYPORT

IN THE TWENTIETH CENTURY

The 26th Anniversary

OPENING *of this Store we celebrate on* Saturday, June 25th

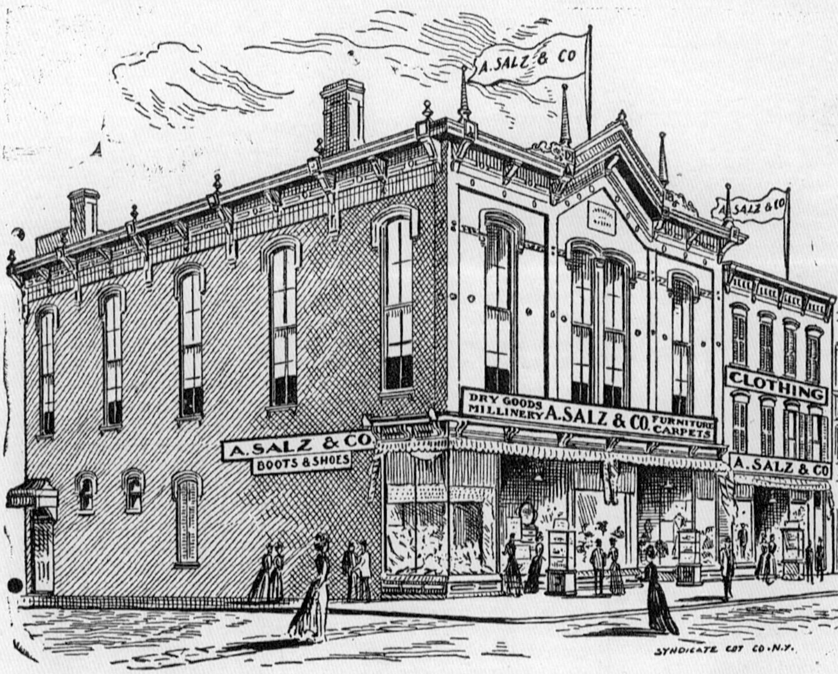

With MUSIC, SOUVENIRS and Gala Attractions.

Every floor and every section of this Establishment will be filled with an "Exposition" of Extraordinary Bargains.

MUSIC by the Famous NEW YORK ORCHESTRA and MILITARY BAND and also Other Celebrated Artists.

All other Anniversaries are to be surpassed and EVERYBODY is expected—Everybody Welcome.

A. Salz & Co.

KEYPORT. N.J

A. Salz's Store, 1911. In 1911, Adam Salz proudly celebrated his 26th anniversary at the corner of Broad and Front Streets. The store was touted as the largest general mercantile store in Monmouth County during the turn of the last century and remained open well after the death of Mr. Salz.

THE AMERICAN CENTURY SERIES

KEYPORT

IN THE TWENTIETH CENTURY

Timothy E. Regan

ARCADIA PUBLISHING

Copyright © 1998 by Timothy E. Regan
ISBN 978-0-7385-0016-4

Published by Arcadia Publishing
Charleston, South Carolina

Printed in the United States of America

Library of Congress Control Number: 98-87870

For all general information, please contact Arcadia Publishing:
Telephone 843-853-2070
Fax 843-853-0044
E-mail sales@arcadiapublishing.com
For customer service and orders:
Toll-Free 1-888-313-2665

Visit us on the Internet at www.arcadiapublishing.com

This book is dedicated to my parents, Gene and Betty

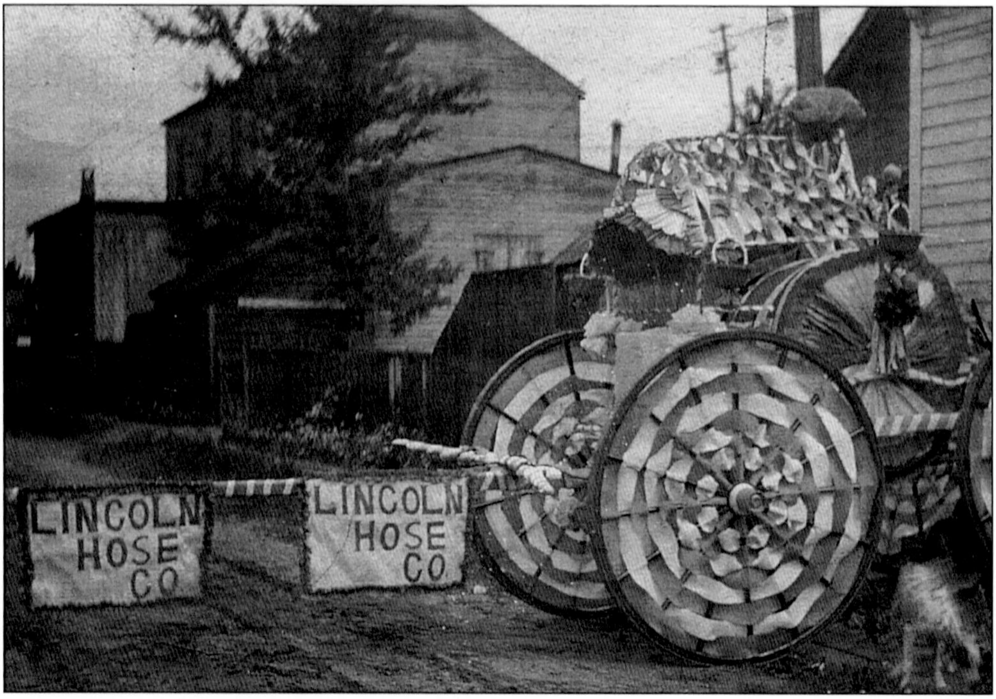

LINCOLN HOSE COMPANY NO. 1, 1900. The members of Keyport's finest hose company have gone all out to decorate their hose carriage for the big parade. This scene is from Waverly Street, in front of the first hose house.

CONTENTS

Acknowledgments

The following people donated their time, memories, and photographs to the author and without them this book would not have succeeded. Thank You.

To my parents, Betty and Gene, who took the time to answer my sometimes long and obscure questions on Keyport's past, for feeding me late-night dinners, and for their constant inspiration.

Once again my heartfelt thanks goes out to my friend Bert Morris. Bert always set the time aside to answer questions while donating some of the best images for this third volume on Keyport.

To local historian and author Tom Gallo for loaning the great railroad photographs of Keyport and allowing me access to his extensive postcard collection.

A big thank you to John and Jackie Brandauer, who donated the rarest of the images in this book and provided some of the much needed information on the Lockport Stores.

Thanks to Dorothy (Dot) Poling for the photo of Luke Slover Jr. and the many unique images of the town between 1930 and 1960.

Thanks to James "Luke" Poling for his information on Luke Slover, as well for his fine contribution of photos.

Also, a special thanks to Norrine Schanck, Frank Currier, Dick Currier, Remsen Straub, Elmer Beck, The Keyport Historical Society, Jim McTernan, Dorn's Photographic Studio, and Les Horner. The very special cover photograph was loaned courtesy of Mrs. Luker. Thank You.

I would like to thank all the people who refrained from calling 264-0706 on me for my flashlight-beamed, nighttime graveyard and landmark patrols.

Finally, to my wife, Patricia, who still finds the patience to assist and sometimes avoid me while I'm running around the house for information, missing dinners, or spending countless hours on the Mac. Thanks Patti.

INTRODUCTION

In just a few short months the town that we now know as Keyport, New Jersey, will begin to embark on its fourth century of existence as a permanent settlement in North America. In that time of over three hundred years, no other century impacted or shaped the town and its people as much as the 20th century. Let's take a trip and look at where "We" went and what "We" did in the 20th century.

We welcome the new century. We go to the Pavilion Hotel for the New Year's Eve dance. We catch a horse car. We work extremely long hours for little pay. We don't go to college. We respect our elders. We welcome electricity to the town. We go to theaters like the Surf and the Armory where live orchestras provide music and narration to those great silent films. We go off to fight a war against the German Empire. We organize American Legion Post 23 to assist and honor those who served in the armed services. We plant nine trees in Beach Park to honor those who give their life in the war. We go to work for the Central Railroad of New Jersey, or drive delivery trucks for West Furniture. We dedicate our new beautiful new high school. We eat lunch at the Palace Diner on Broad Street, and catch up on the latest news in the *Weekly*. When we are sick we go to Dr. Van Walker and then to Hopkin's drugstore for some medicine. We wonder about Prohibition. We find plenty of moonshine. We worry when the stock market crashes but we stick together and stay afloat throughout the Depression. We vote for Roosevelt and say goodbye to Prohibition. We buy a new Hudson sedan at Buhler and Bitter and we watch as our first-aid squad races to the scene of the Hindenburg crash. We listen to the radio play Glenn Miller and hear about a man named Hitler and his fascist ways. We wave goodbye as our sons and fathers leave the Broad Street Station to fight for our freedom. We ration gas. We wonder who Kilroy is. We celebrate when our sons and fathers arrive home and we honor and erect memorials to those who don't. We welcome peace. We build backyard barbecues, and with some extra money we saved, we buy used boats from Kofoed's yard. We build a new post office. We buy televisions from a place called Colfax's up town. We fight another war and lose more Keyporters. We spend Saturday's at the Strand and watch as Mr. Homer Gerlufsen leads the marching band in every parade. We go to work at the Armstrong Cork Company and join the Yacht Club. We shop for Christmas presents at J.J. Newberry's and wait for Stultz to deliver our fuel oil.

We vote for Kennedy and page through *TV Guide* for our favorite show, *Gunsmoke*. We fly the library flags at half-staff for our beloved President. We go to Wetsons for hamburgers and listen to the Beatles in our Mustang that we bought at Tom's Fordland. We go off to yet another war in a far-away place called Vietnam. We say goodbye to our passenger trains. We learn from teachers like Frank Stockel, Ed Burke, Thaddeus Krensavage, and Ethel Reilly. We dress in bell-bottoms and flowers and head to Goody and Em's to drink. We say goodbye to those who never come home from Vietnam. We wonder about this thing called counterculture. We watch man walk on the moon. We vote for Mayor Billy Ralph. We watch as the foundation of Keyport, the Key Grove Mansion, is destroyed. We celebrate peace. We welcome the country's bicentennial, watch *Roots*, and live through the "Me Generation." We worship at the new St. Joseph's Church. We play softball at Cedar Street Park. We join the fire company and work at the annual fair. We make our kids cross the street when walking by the Strand. We vote for Reagan and celebrate the Clearwater Festival on "Ring Road." We go to Dr. Olini and when were really sick he comes to us. We hang out at the Chowder Pot or the "Bulkhead." We go to Phasor Video for movies. We visit our grandparents in the American Legion Apartments. We fish. We head to 7-11 for Slurpees. We fight another war, but everyone comes home this time. We march in the Halloween Parade. We watch as houses are restored and the town becomes a Mecca for antiques. We get older. We live in Keyport. We welcome the new century.

One

1900–1910

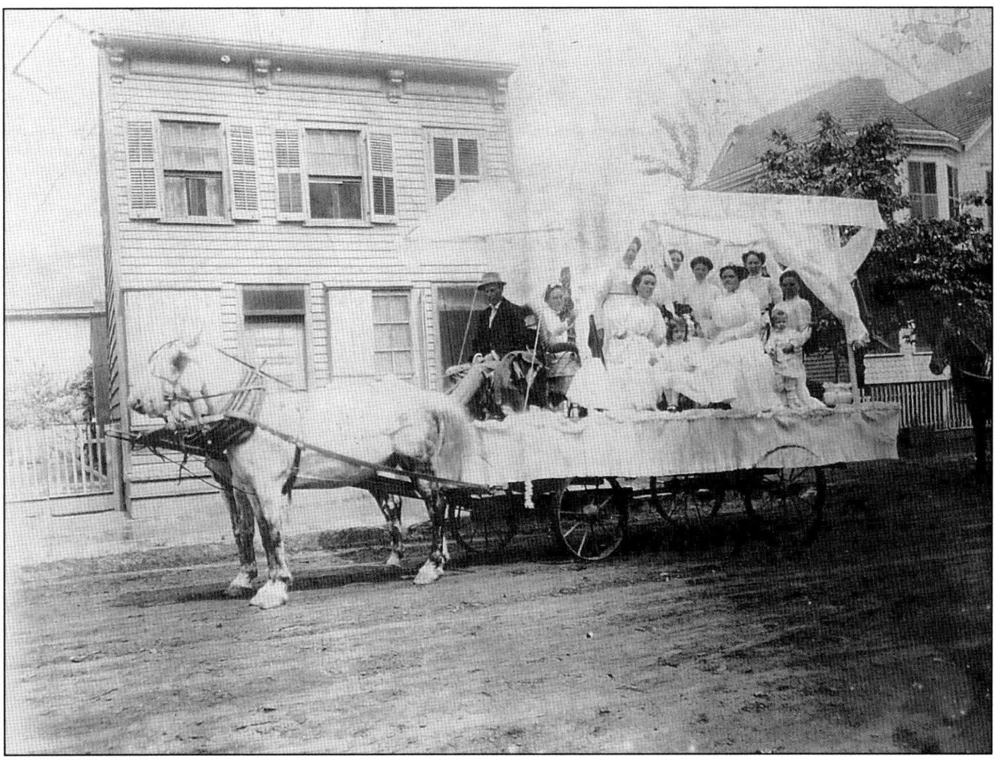

MAIN STREET, NEAR FRONT, 1900. As the new century was ushered in by Keyport, I doubt the folks on this float realized the impact that the next century would have on their daily life. Life was about to change on Main Streets all across America for better, or maybe for worse.

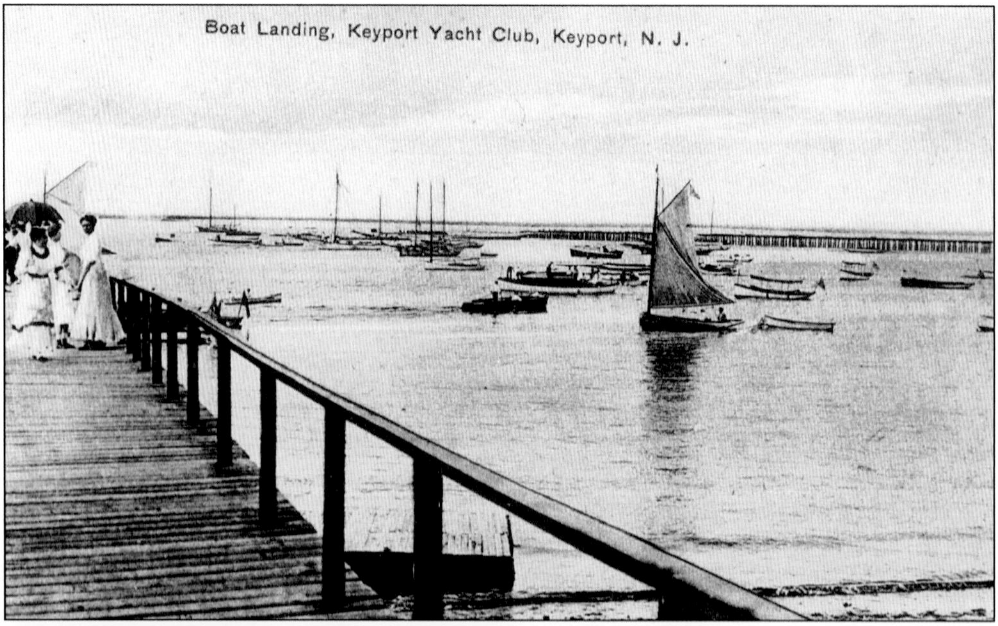

THE YACHT CLUB DOCK, C. 1908. All dressed up in their finery, these ladies are strolling along the first pier of the Keyport Yacht Club. The Keyport Yacht Club was begun in 1908 by English Yachtsman Henry Toft. Toft was so impressed with Keyport Harbor that he inspired four men, Harry Coons, William Gill, and Thomas and Richard Burrowes, to organize the club, which by 1936 had a membership of over 125.

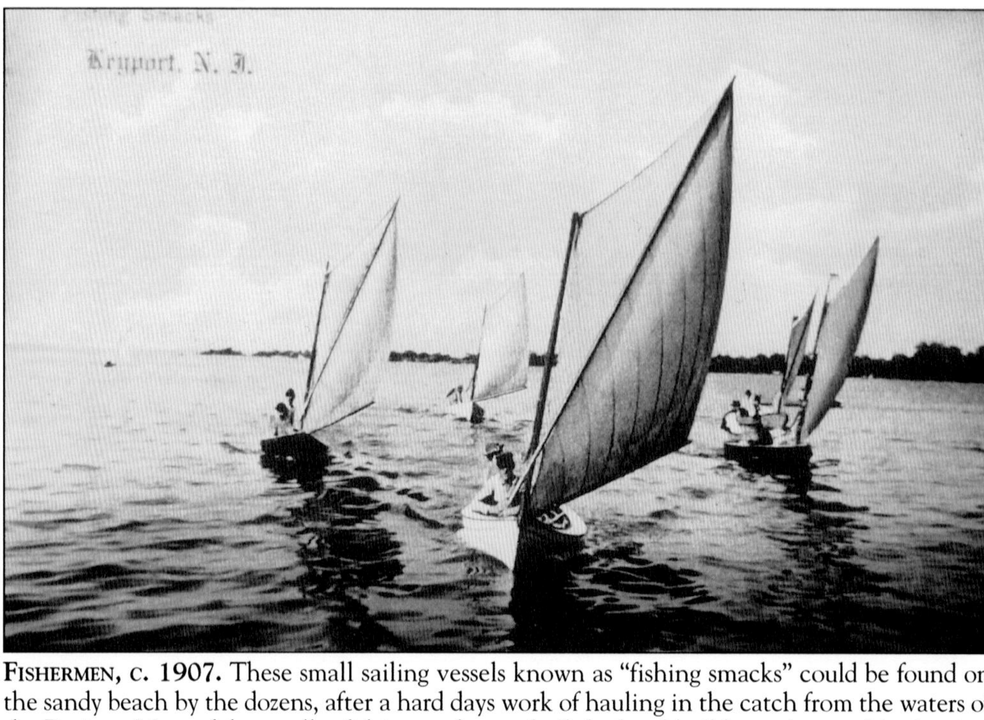

FISHERMEN, C. 1907. These small sailing vessels known as "fishing smacks" could be found on the sandy beach by the dozens, after a hard days work of hauling in the catch from the waters of the Raritan. Most of the smaller fishing craft were built by local builders, who would take time out from larger jobs to turn out these boats.

Mayor E. E. Conklin, 1909. Keyport ceased being operated as a town by an act of the state legislature on April 2, 1908. The first elections were held on November 3,1908, and on January 1, 1909, Edwin Emmet Conklin became the first mayor of the Borough of Keyport at 12:00 p.m. sharp. Mayor Conklin arrived in Keyport in the 1880s and soon went into partnership with Edwin Beers, becoming Conklin and Beers, a grocery business. Mayor Conklin served the borough until 1910. In 1926 Edwin Conklin died at his Broadway home from pneumonia, leaving behind his wife, Elizabeth, and two children.

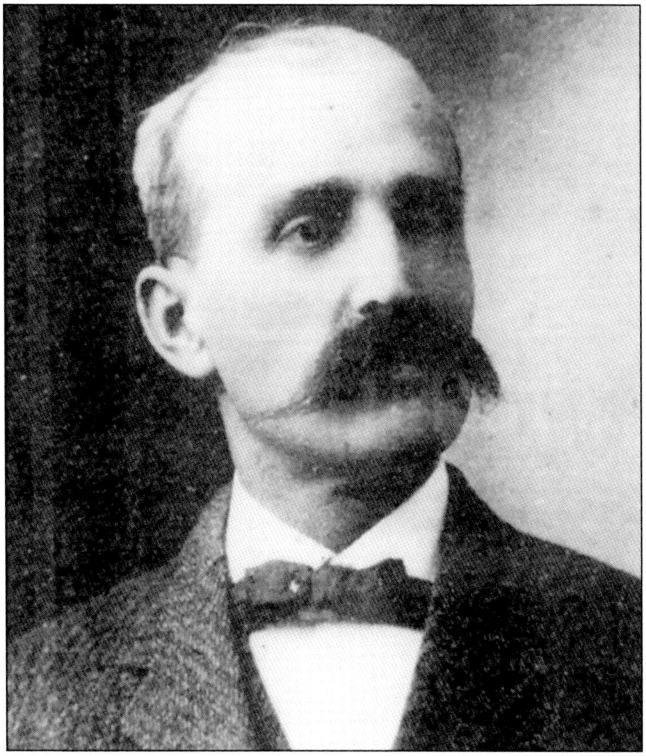

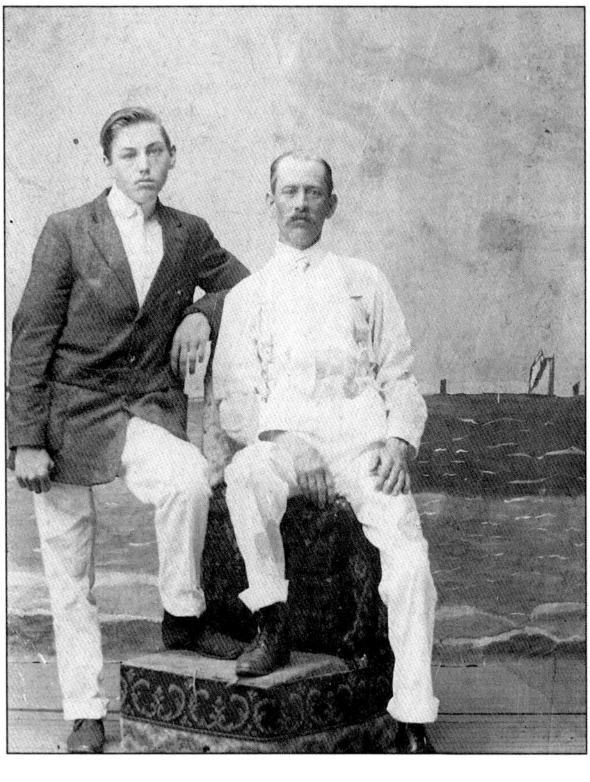

A Father and Son, c. 1902

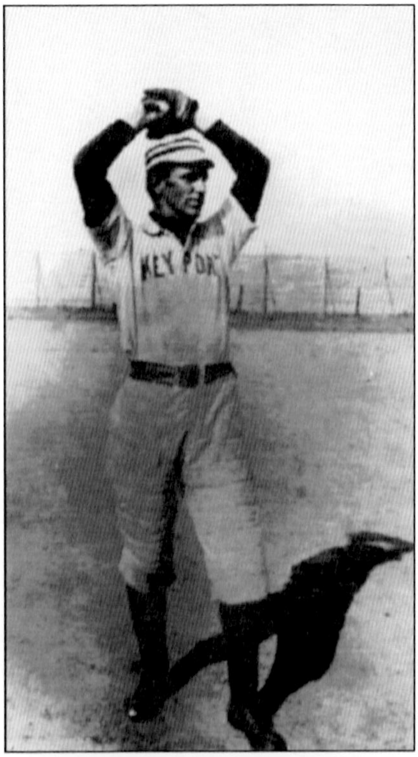

CHRISTI MATHEWSON, 1904. Local rivalry between Keyport and Matawan ball clubs reached an all-time high by 1900. It was common practice to secure the talents of "big leaguers" for important games. In September of 1904 the Keyport club hired Christi Mathewson of the New York Giants to pitch for them. By the time that game was over, no Matawan player had reached beyond second base and the hometown Keyport Club walked away with a 2-0 victory. Christi Mathewson was inducted into the Baseball Hall of Fame in 1936.

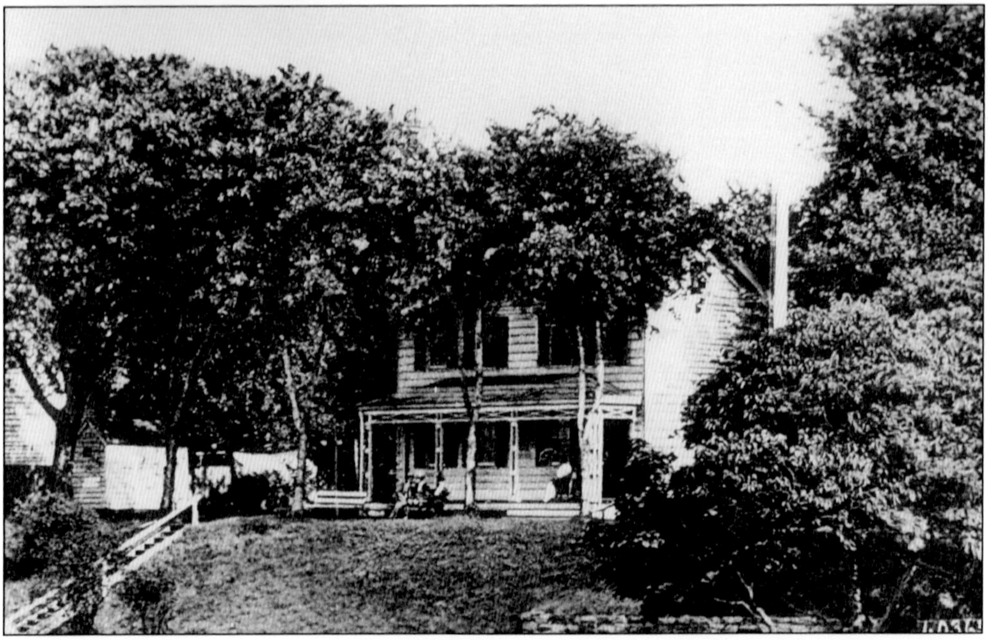

THE CLUBHOUSE OF THE KEYPORT YACHT CLUB, C. 1908. The members of the Keyport Yacht Club purchased the old Hoff property of First Street in 1908. The rambling house, which was built in the 1840s, was well suited for the summertime affairs of the yachtsmen and their guests. Throughout the years many additions changed the original structure. Sadly, on the morning of February 5, 1981, the structure was destroyed in a spectacular fire.

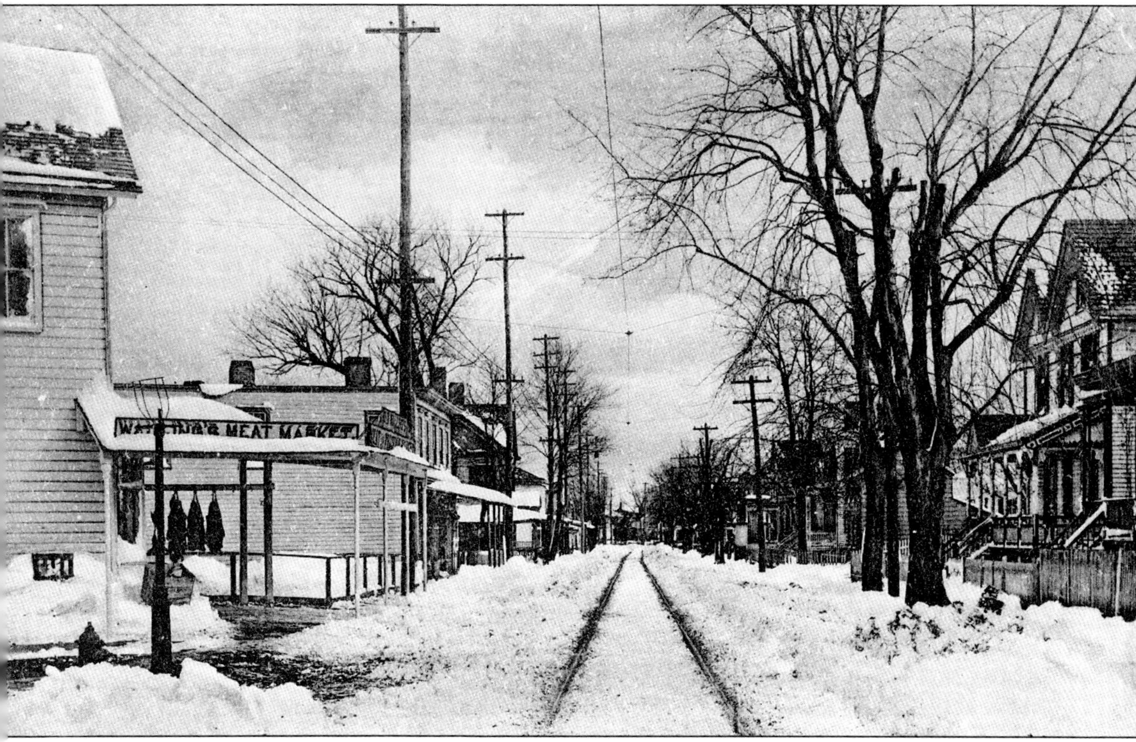

First Street, c. 1910. Standing in the center of First Street, the cameraman captured the butcher shop of Ormond D. Walling, on the northeast corner of First and Prospect Streets. Mr. Walling took full advantage of this deep freeze and hung some meats out on the porch in the days before supermarkets and walk-in freezers. Next in line is the store of J.E. Terry. Views of Lockport (Eastern Keyport) are extremely rare and are always a welcome addition to any collection.

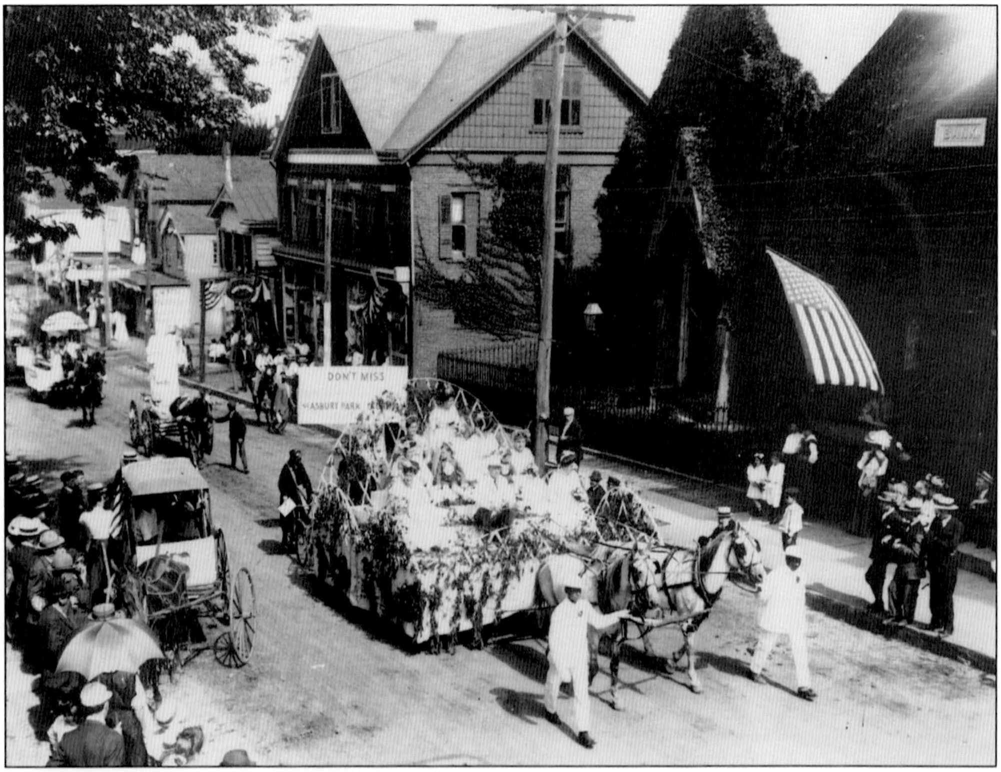

EAST FRONT STREET, C. 1906. This parade is seen making its way up East Front Street, passing St. Mary's and the People's National Bank. This photo was taken from the second-floor porch of the Mansion House Hotel. The brick store to the east of the church still stands, though remodeled, while the old post office and Bedle's Paint Store all disappeared by 1978.

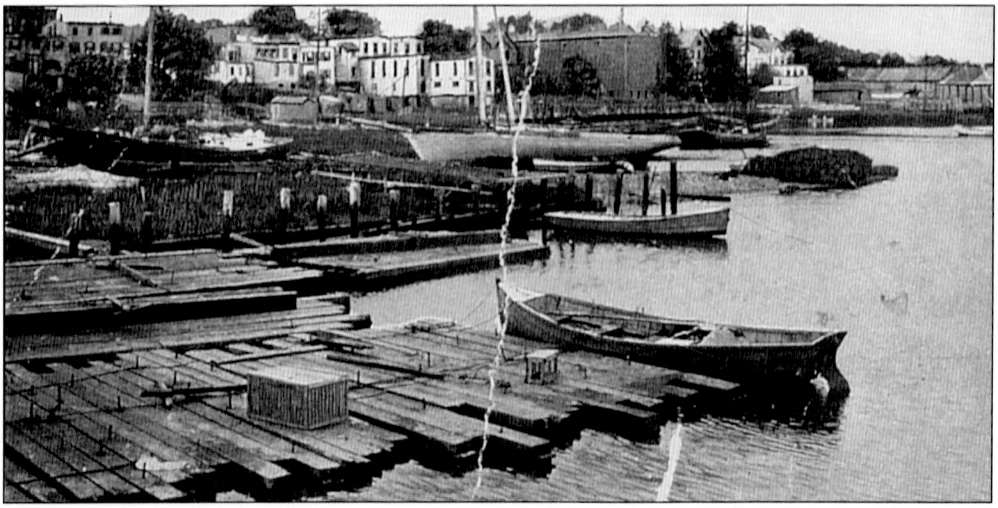

WEST OF THE STEAMBOAT WHARF, 1909. Keyport's fishing fleet included all types of boats and ships including sloops, sailboats, prams, rowboats, smacks, skiffs, and just about anything else that would afford the fisherman a reliable working craft. This quaint scene along the shore behind the business district shows a rare view of the area that in 1970 was bulkheaded and filled to become American Legion Drive.

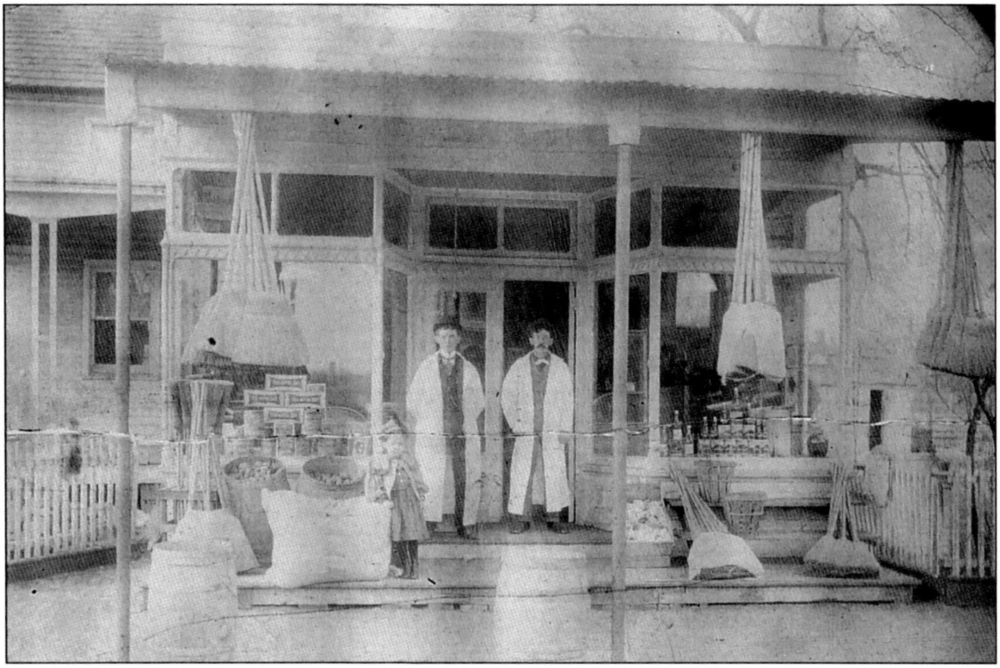

THE FULTON CASH MARKET, 1900. Located at the corner of First and Fulton Streets was this general mercantile store operated by C.J. Post. In 1905, Mr. Post advertised that he had fine turkeys, meats, celery, etc., for an "Xmas dinner." A second floor was added on to this structure in later years, and its fine storefront was enclosed in the late 1950s. The building was well known as "Buddy's" used furniture store until about 1990. Its fine turn-of-the-century storefront remains hidden, awaiting restoration.

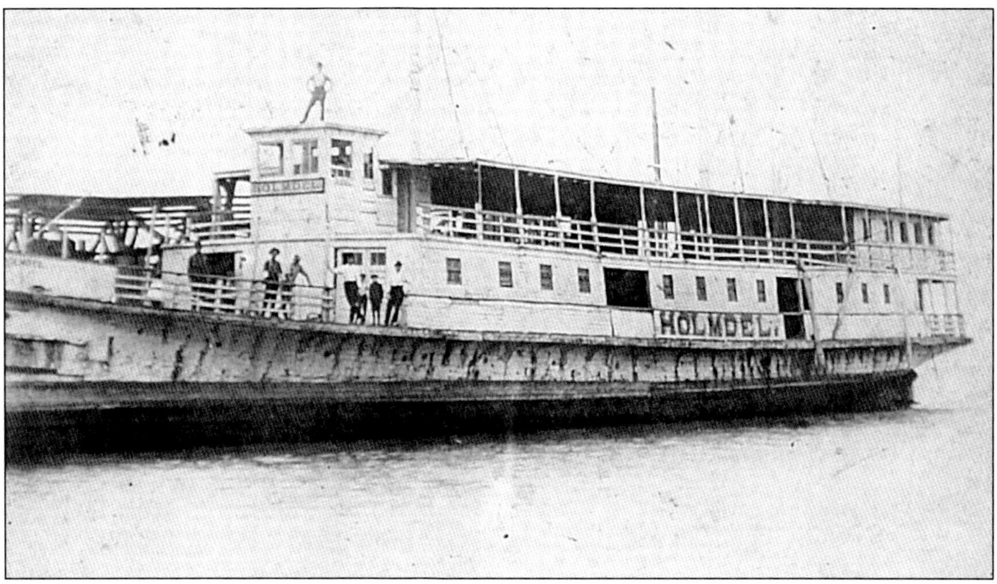

THE *HOLMDEL*, C. 1901. Capt. Conover would have been proud of his old steamboat, still hauling freight and produce between Keyport and New York City at the turn of the century. In this photograph, the *Holmdel* is near the end of her career, which was a proud one lasting from 1865 until 1905.

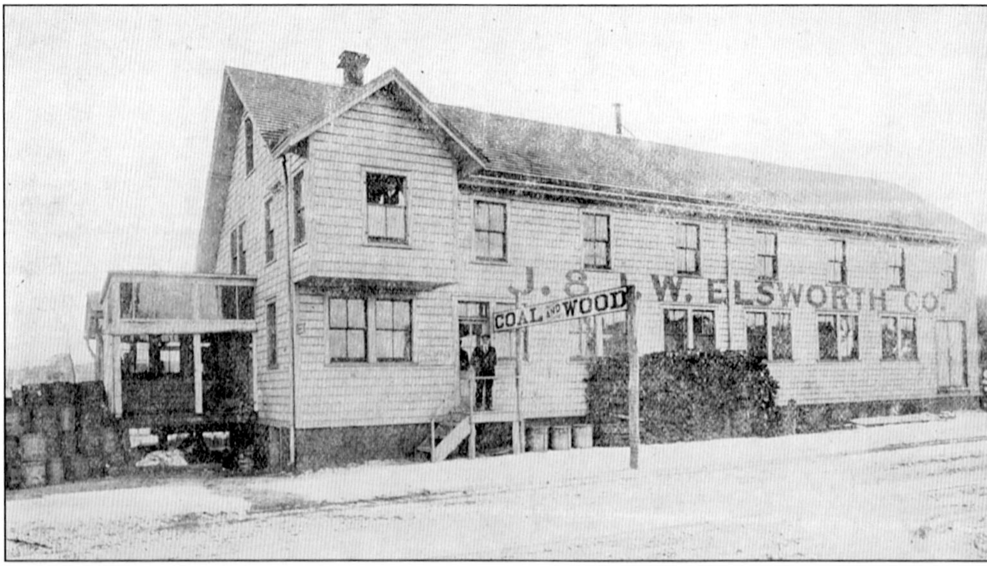

The Elsworth Oyster House. This photograph depicts the appearance of the oyster house as it was originally built in 1899. In later the years the overhang, which contained the offices of the foreman, was removed. For nearly 30 years, this property along Front Street was the oyster Mecca of the East Coast and was one of the most important industries ever to call Keyport home. Over 80 men were employed by the J. & J.W. Elsworth Company during its heyday. The oyster house itself was destroyed by fire in the late 1970s.

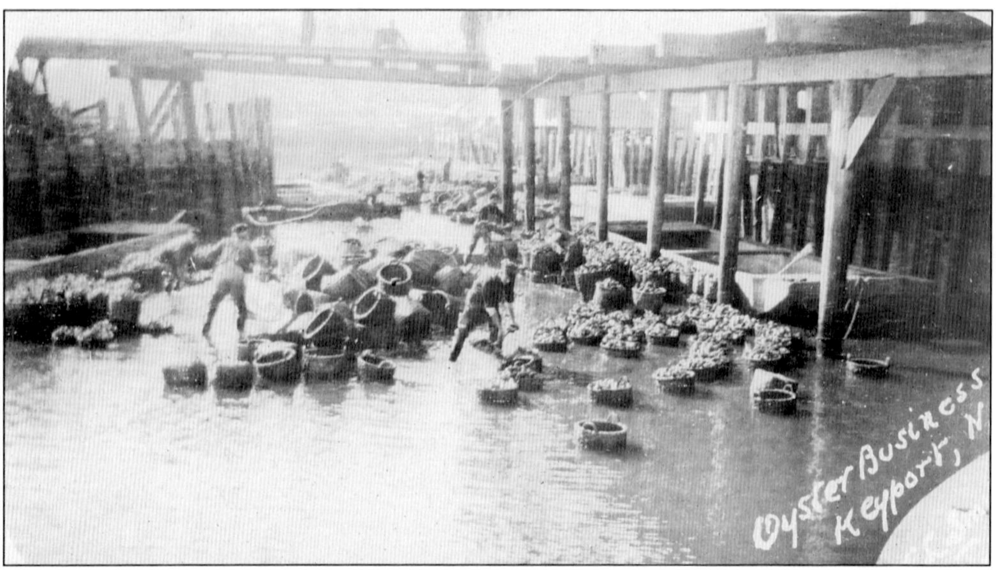

Oyster Creek. Oystermen are busy going about business down in the cold waters of the Luppattatong Creek. The bridge above was constructed to allow the empty shells to be taken across the creek and dumped into the shell pile, which in later years reached a height of nearly 40 feet. By 1998 the only remains of the once-flourishing oyster industry and that great pile is a small pile of shells about 4 feet tall. This photo was taken by Frank L. Smith on January 8, 1907.

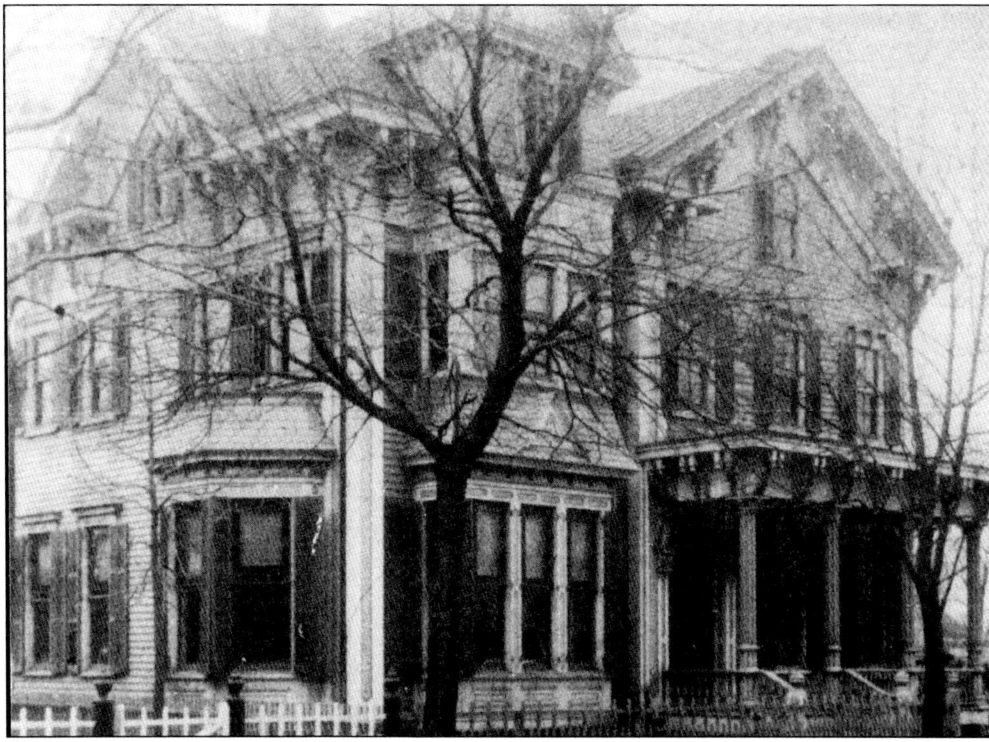

THE WILSON BROWN HOUSE, FIRST STREET. One of the most palatial residences in the village was constructed on the southeast corner of First and Atlantic Streets. Work began on the Wilson Brown house in May of 1853 and was completed in 1855 at a cost of over $22,000, making it the costliest home constructed in Keyport up to that time. The builder of the house was Richard W. Strong, who settled in Keyport shortly before construction began. The house, still standing in 1998, has been stripped of its gingerbread and fine woodwork, and to many appears as just another big apartment house by the water.

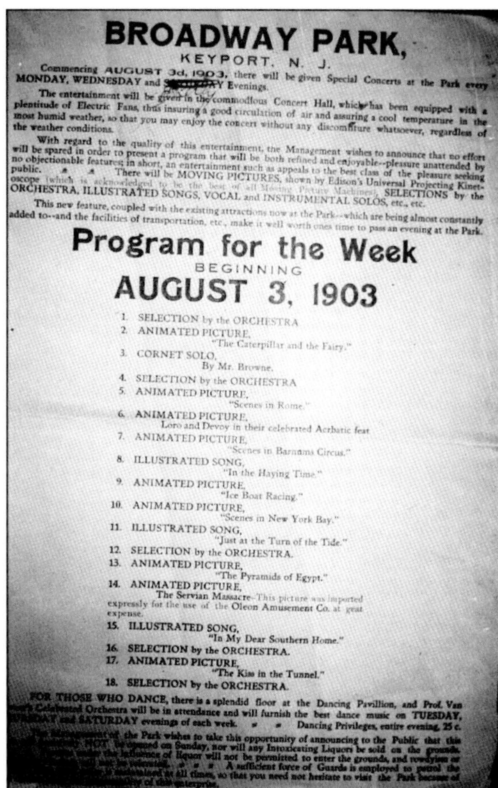

AN ADVERTISEMENT FOR BROADWAY PARK. Located in Browns Point, Broadway Park was in direct competition with Beach Park, located in the center of town adjacent to the wharf. No persons were allowed to consume alcohol at Broadway Park and, as stated in this advertisement, a sufficient number of guards were employed to keep the "hooligans" out and to ensure that good people could enjoy themselves.

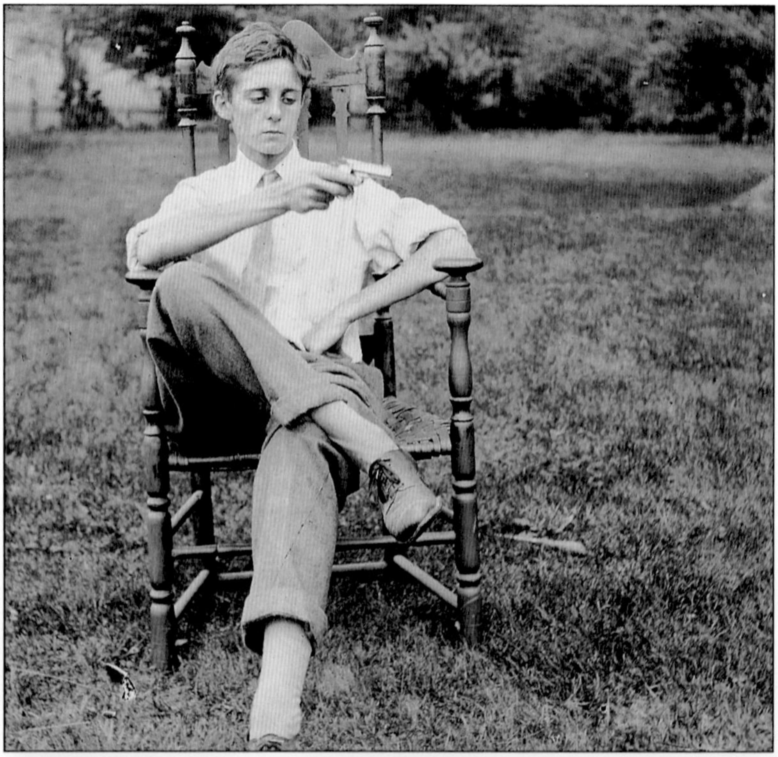

The Brandons, c. 1905. It appears that the dapper young Blake Brandon is showing off his stylish single-shot Derringer, while his wife, Erica L. Brandon, gazes at him with a look of pride. During the turn of the century, the couple resided in the Browns Point section of town.

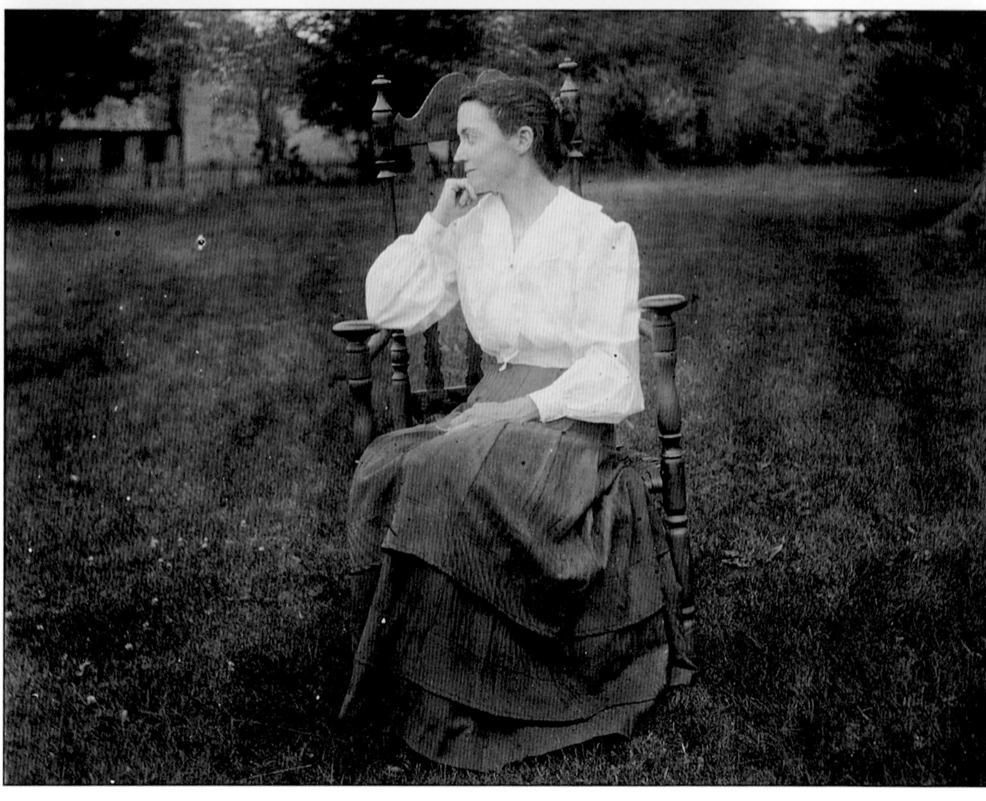

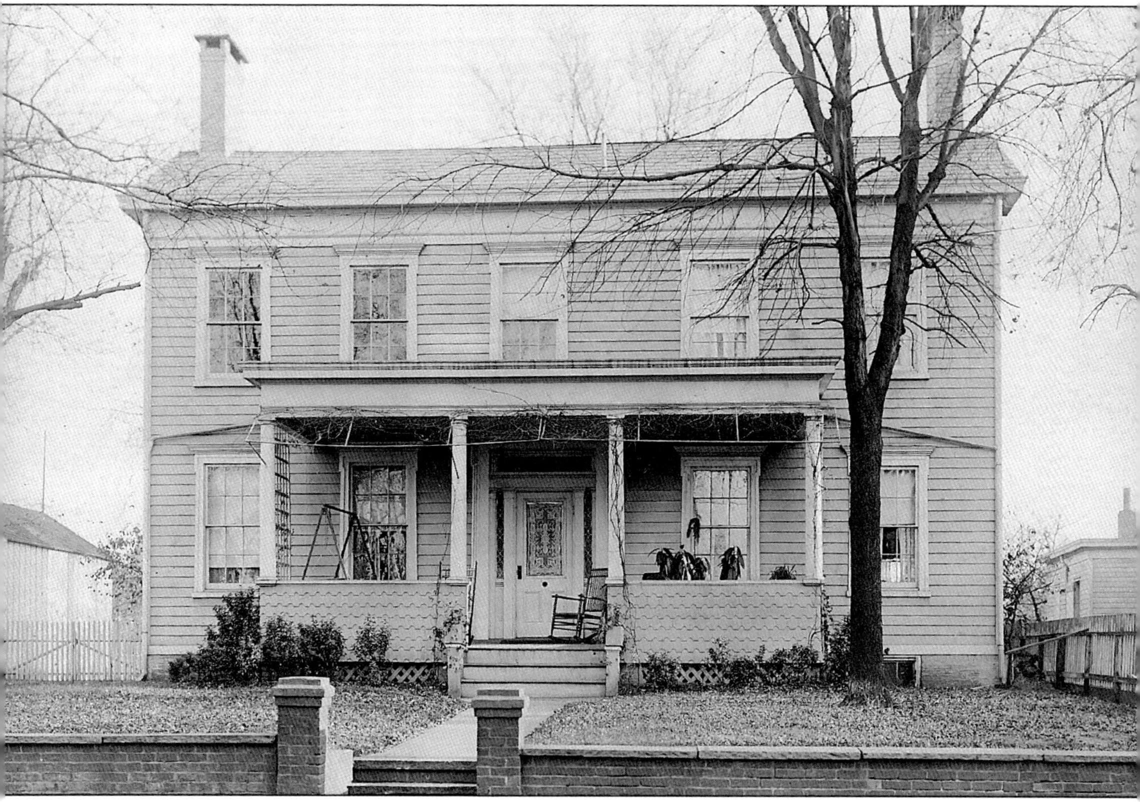

The Captain G.W. Johnson House. This fine clapboard Greek Revival home was built at 74 Front Street in the early 1850s. Already nearly 60 years old when this image was made, the house—minus the front porch—stands in 1998 as proudly as it did in the days of Keyport's infancy.

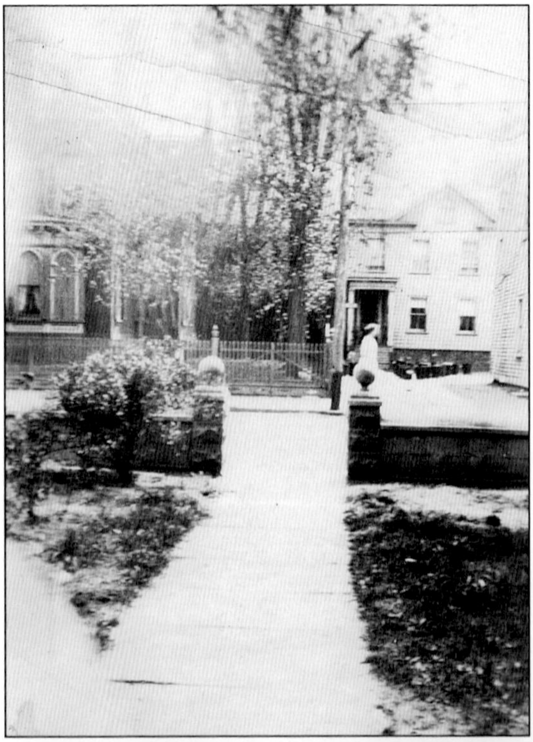

THE WALKWAY OF THE J. EVERETT SILCOX HOUSE. Here can be seen the large Victorian home of Samuel G. Fairchild (on the left) and the old Asher Collin's home (on the right), which was moved from Church Street to First Street during the turn of the century. This photo was taken from the porch of Dr. Silcox's house.

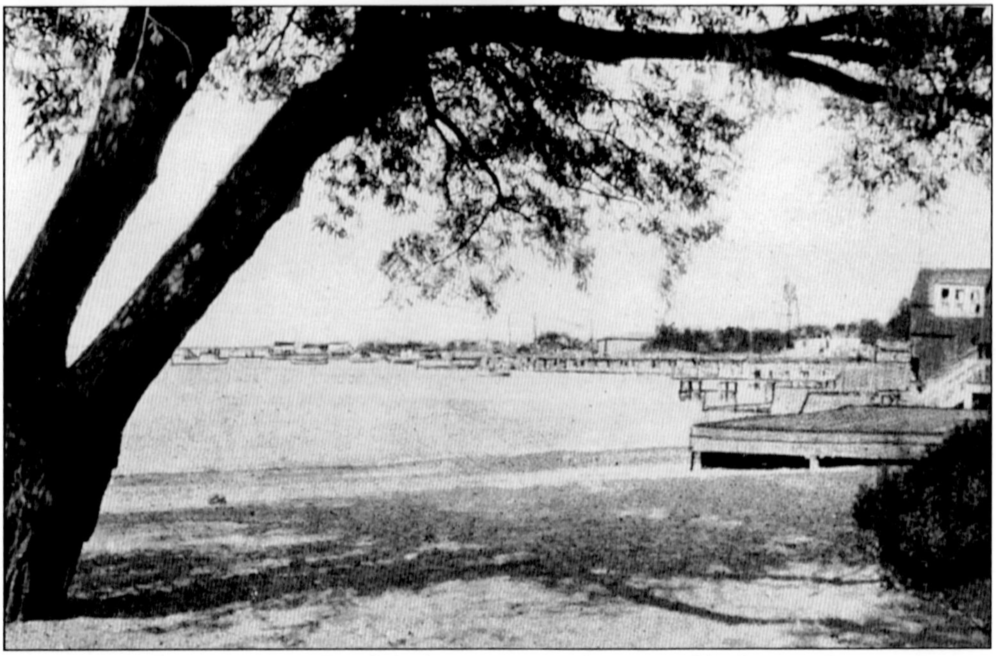

BEACH PARK. For many years, Beach Park was a privately operated bathing and entertainment spot. Around 1910 the spot was purchased by the borough and developed into a quiet bathing spot. In this view the park's old dancing platform can be seen to the right of the photo. In the 1940s a small wading pool was built on the park's eastern end, which was used by many in the summer heat well into the 1960s.

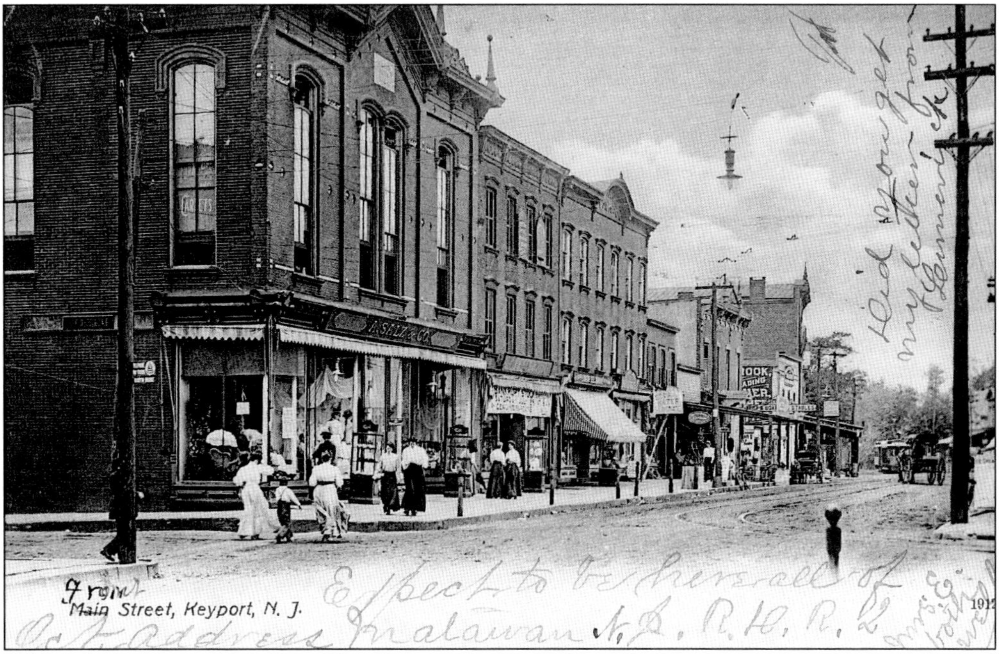

WEST FRONT STREET, C. 1907. Little had changed along the south side of Front Street since it had been rebuilt after the "Big Fire" of 1877. Walling Hall was completed in 1878, as were the two adjacent brick stores. Next in line were two small frame stores and the Sproul building, all built around 1879–1880. Sadly, the two large brick stores next to Walling Hall were removed in February of 1964 and the lot has remained vacant since that time. It is hoped that someday new stores will be constructed on this location.

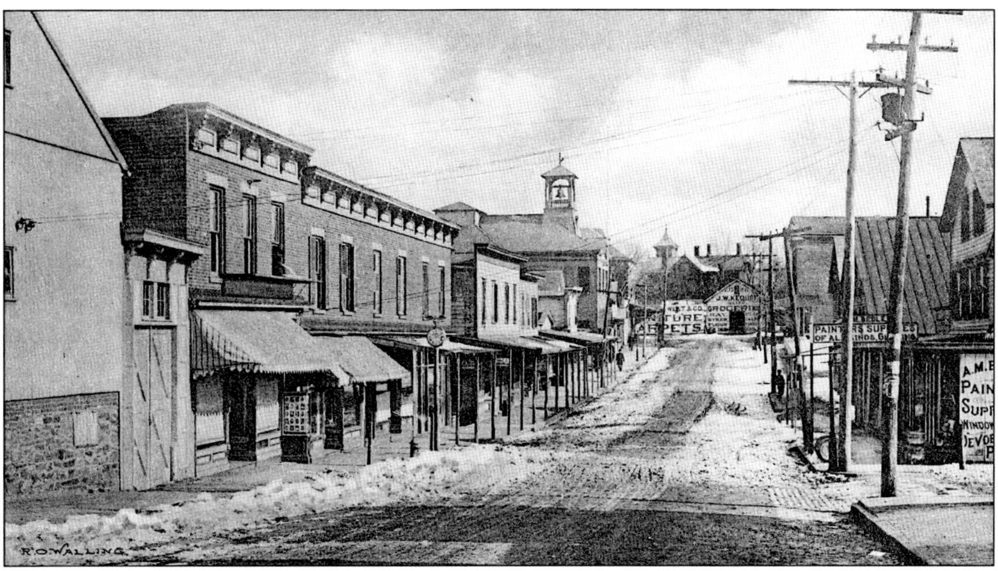

THE EAST FRONT STREET BUSINESS DISTRICT, C. 1903. It must have been a very cold day when this photo was taken, as only three brave souls can be found walking the streets. Every building in the foreground of this photo vanished by 1970. Poor real estate ventures and a failed luxury high-rise apartment building plan combined to rob Keyport of one of its oldest and most historic shopping districts.

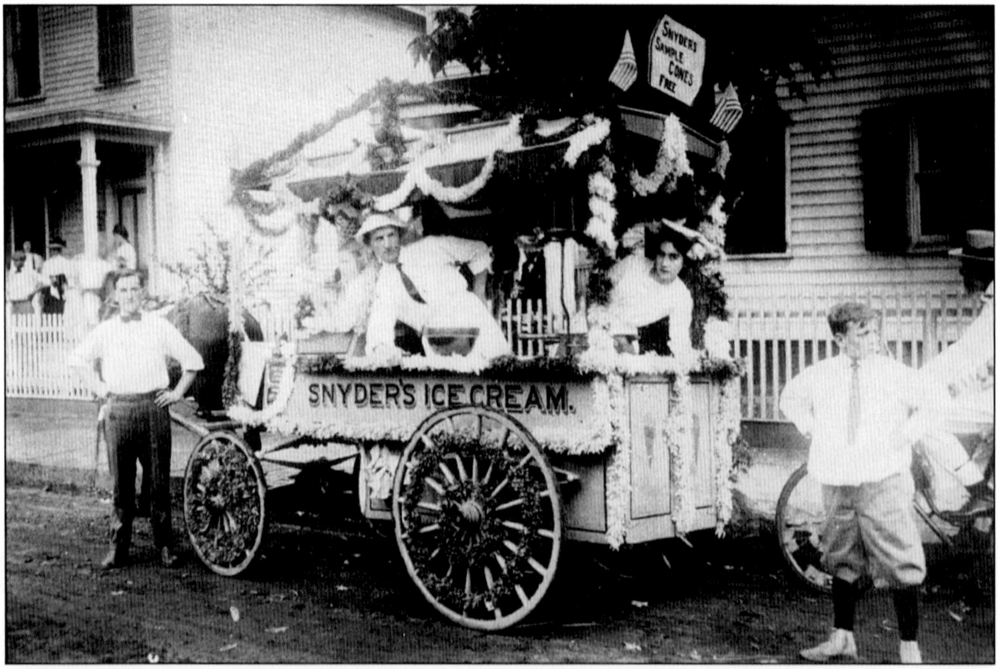

SNYDER'S ICE CREAM WAGON. Whenever parades came to town, people would be sure to see Snyder's Ice Cream wagon. Originally located on First Street, Snyders later moved to Front Street, near Broad.

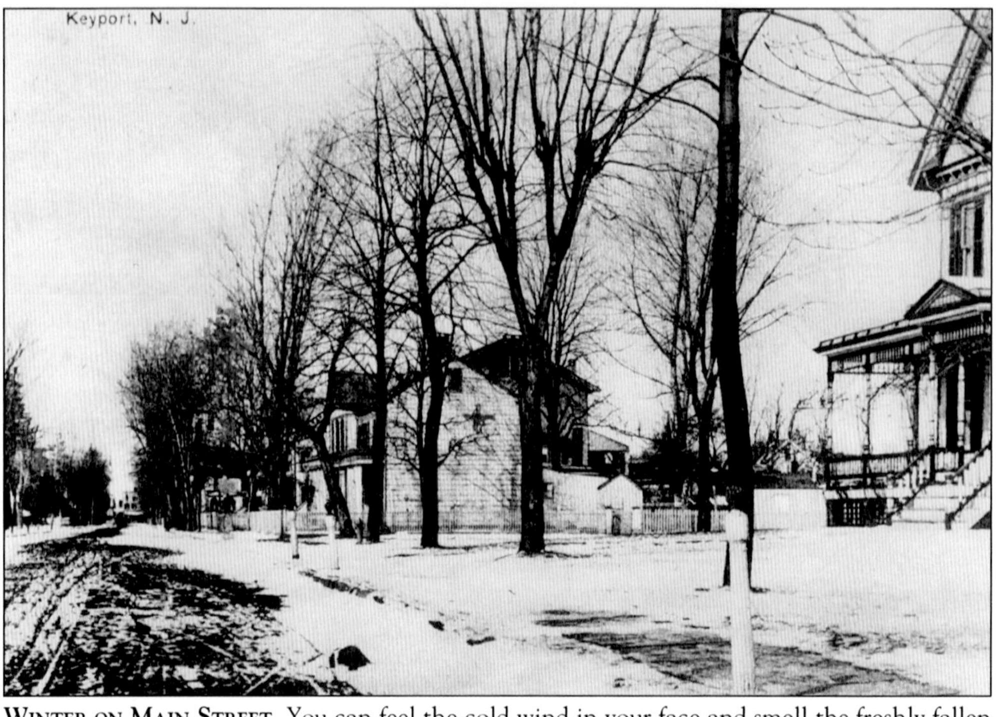

WINTER ON MAIN STREET. You can feel the cold wind in your face and smell the freshly fallen snow, as you walk toward "town" to pick up a few letters at the post office. You have to walk just like in the old days, for your new automobile is pitifully frozen in your garage.

Two

1911–1920

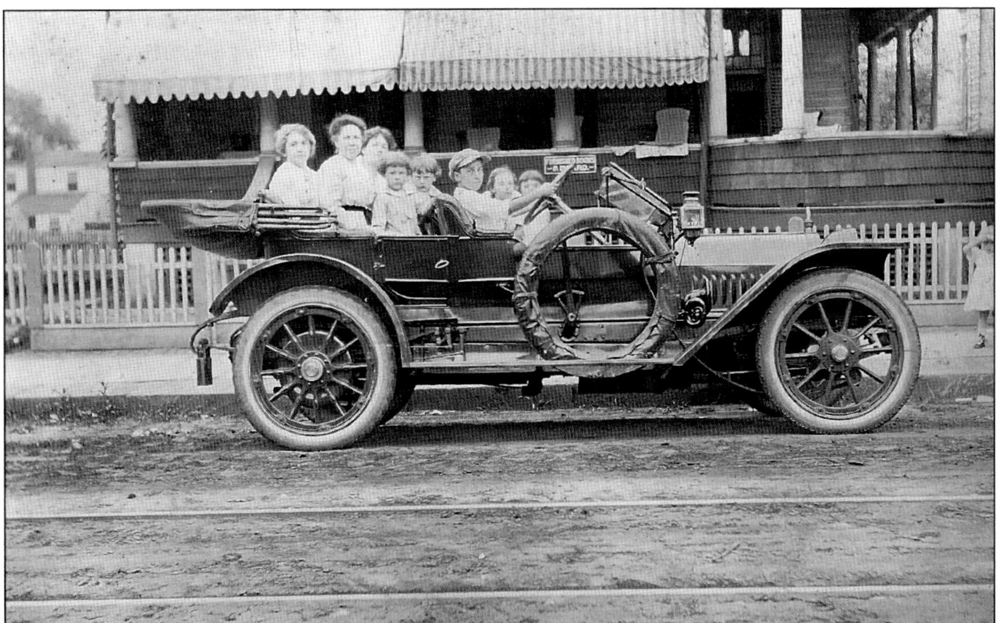

THE BIG RIDE, C. **1914.** You would be hard pressed to find a passenger car that could seat eight people today, but this large touring car did it easily in the early days of automobiles. The auto is sitting in front of 200 First Street, which at the time was a summer boarding home.

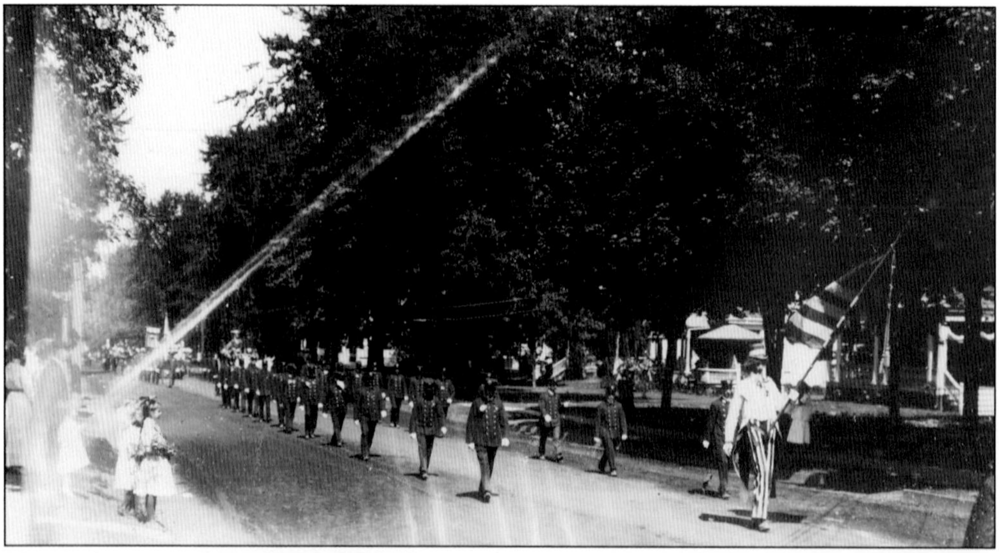

Harry Aumack, 1911. Harry Aumack was a lifelong resident of Keyport and member of the Keyport Hook & Ladder Company. He led the fire department in this Fourth of July parade dressed as Uncle Sam. Harry was known to be quite tall; however, he wore wooden stilts on this day, which raised him to an impressive height of 8 feet 2 inches.

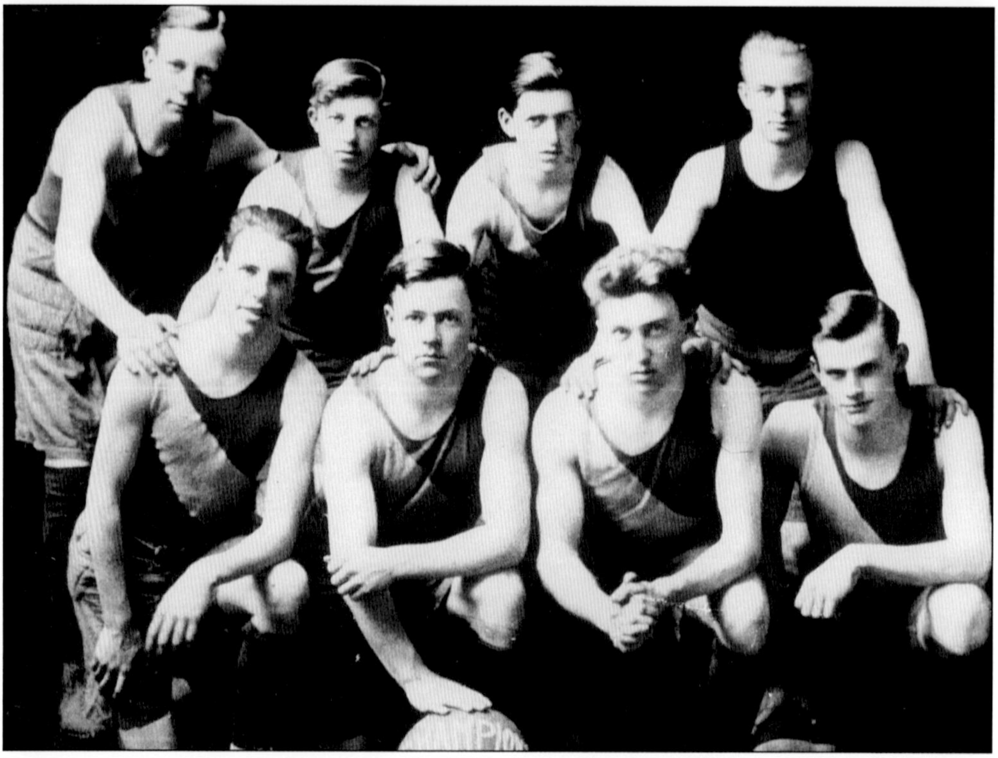

Basketball Champions, 1912–1913. By 1911, the rivalry among local high schools was great. In the days before big football showdowns, basketball and baseball contests dominated the sports pages of the *Keyport Weekly*. It was not uncommon for the Keyport boys to travel as far away as Phillipsburg or parts of Pennsylvania to take part in important championship games.

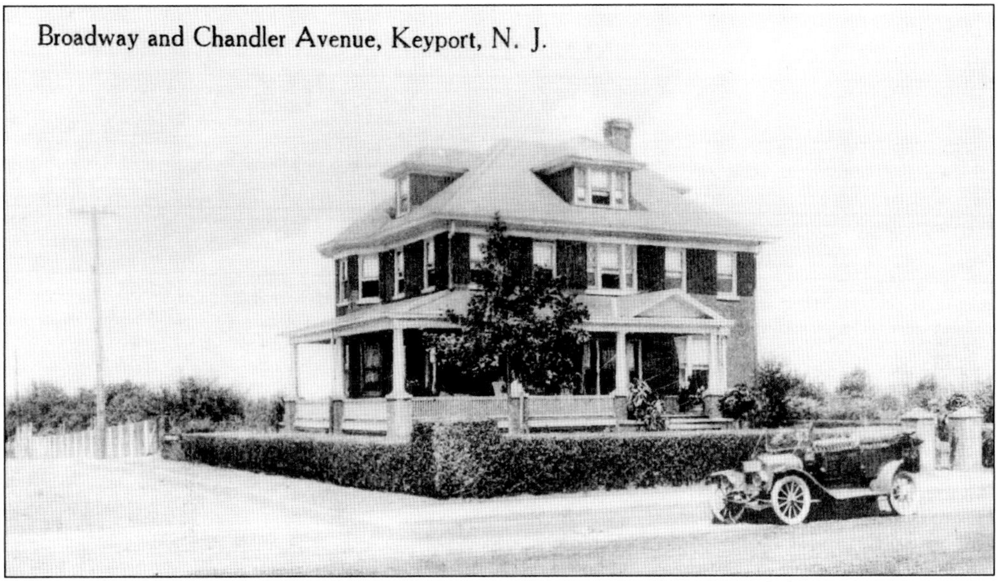

The House at Broadway and Chandler Avenue, c. 1915. One of the more interesting styles of American architecture was the Prairie style, which began in the Chicago suburbs and was originally developed by renowned architect Frank Lloyd Wright. Keyport has several homes in this style; however, this one stands out among the rest, both for its sheer size and its recent meticulous restoration. It stands on property that was once part of the Croes Estate.

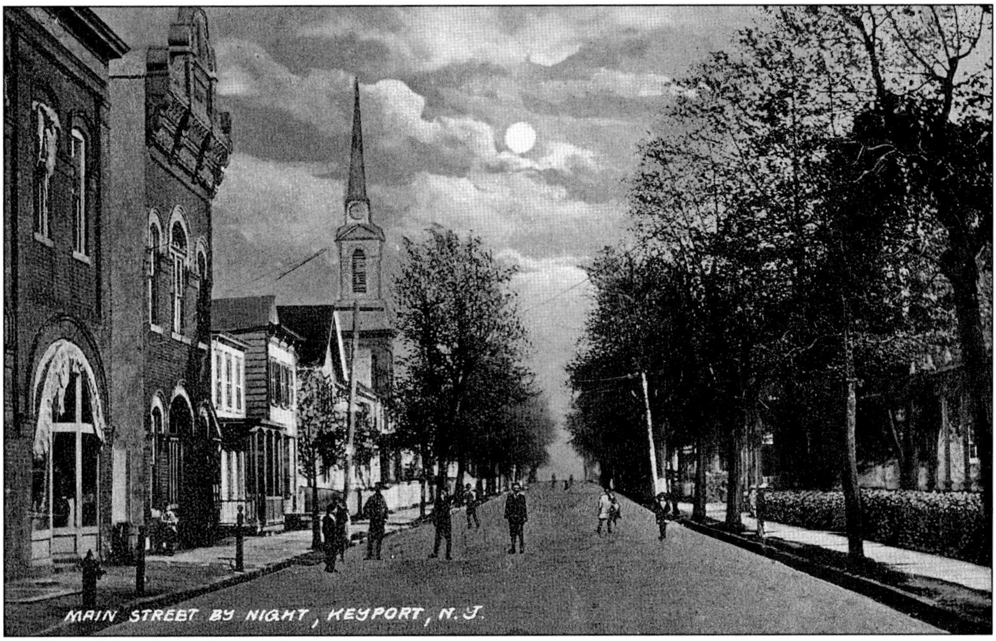

Main Street, Looking South, c. 1915. Just outside the business district, Main Street quickly became the location of Keyport's most prominent families. What 100 years before was just a rye field now played host to the fine home of the Chemical Engine Company (left), the Baptist church (left with spire), and many fine Greek Revival and Second Empire homes. Some of those who resided along this street were Peter P. Conover, Cornelious Ackerson, Nimrod Bedle, and William Conover and their families.

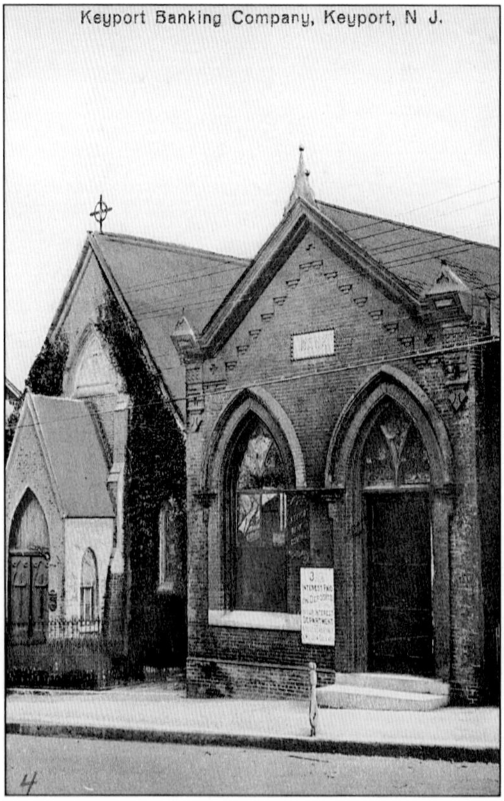

THE KEYPORT BANKING COMPANY, c. 1916. The Keyport Banking Company was organized on March 24, 1884. Prior to this date all banking for Keyport citizens was done in nearby Matawan. The fine bank building was completed in September of 1884 on East Front Street, on property which had been the north churchyard of St. Mary's. The bank continued transactions at this location until 1928, when a larger bank was built at the corner of Front and Broad Streets. By the mid-1930s this bank had resources totaling over $3 million.

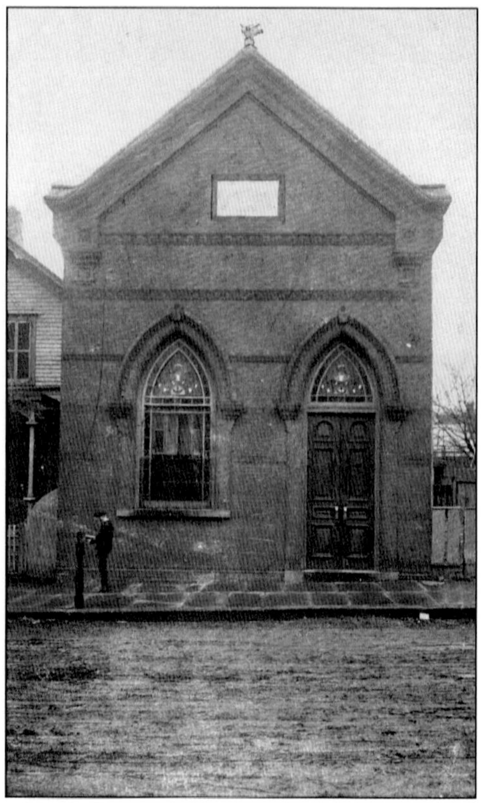

PEOPLES NATIONAL BANK, c. 1912. This building looks awfully familiar! The People's National Bank of Keyport was chartered on September 30, 1889, and moved into their new home in 1890. Located just around the corner from the Keyport Banking Company, the bank must have really envied the other structure, for the building nearly duplicated the Keyport Banking Company's edifice. By 1930 Horace Burrowes served as cashier and the bank president was the Honorable Henry Ackerson, who also served on the New Jersey Supreme Court.

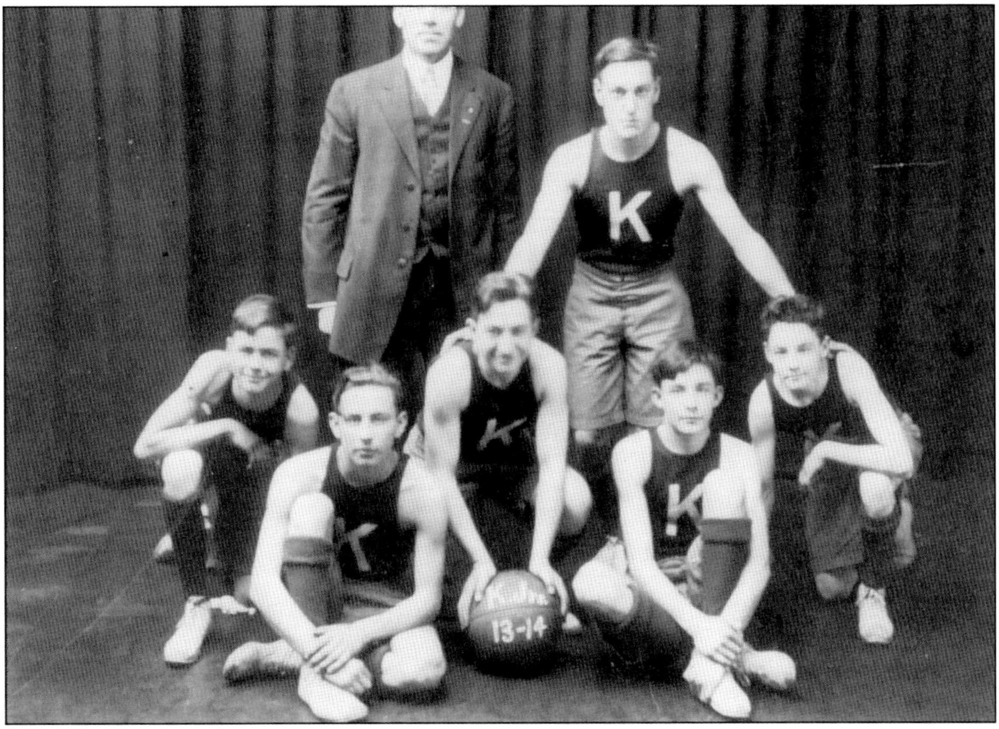

A BASKETBALL TEAM, THE KEYPORT JUNIORS, 1913–1914.

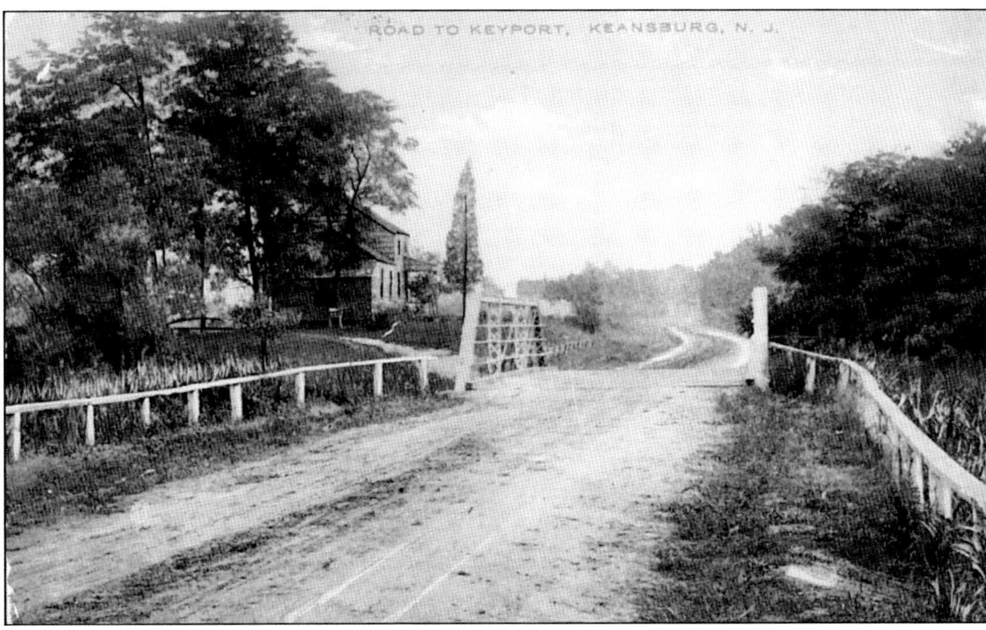

THE "MIDDLE ROAD," C. 1913. As late as the 1940s, if you left the borough limits and headed southeast, you encountered an area of roadside stands, old truss bridges, and ancient houses. This view looks down Middle Road toward Keyport in Raritan (Hazlet) Township. This same area had changed considerably by the 1960s (see *Images of America: Hazlet*, by Bill Longo) with vast housing developments and highway strip malls.

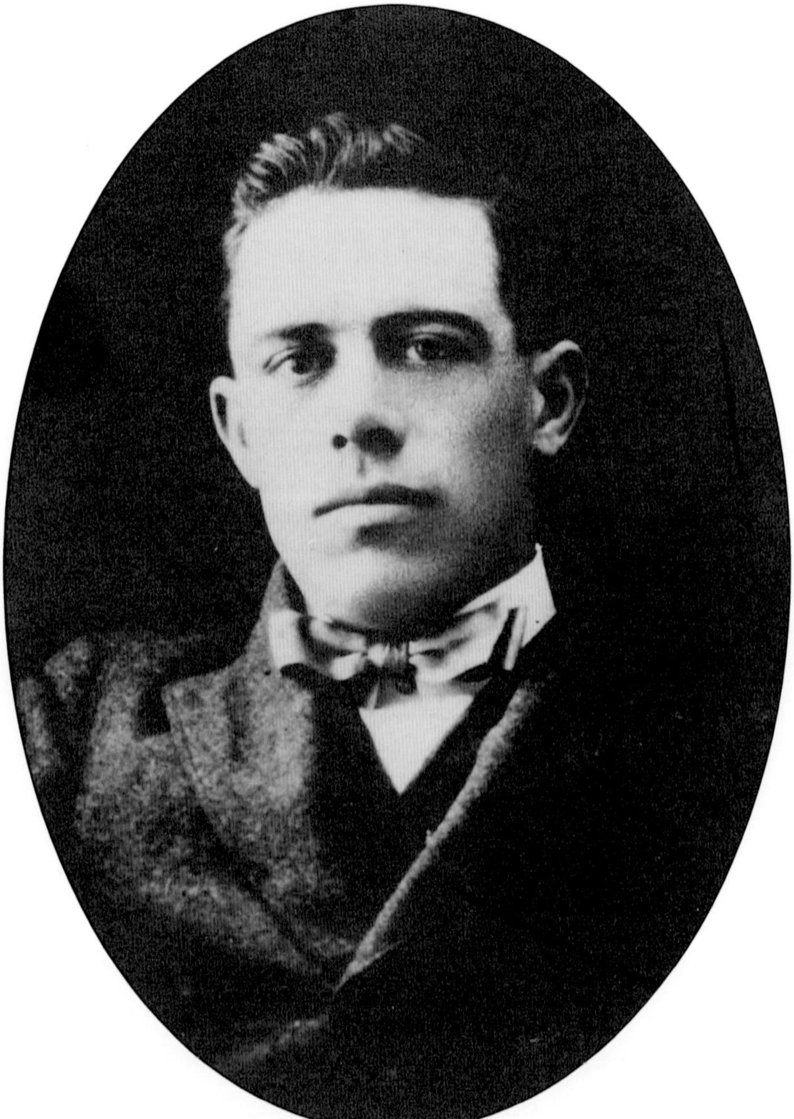

PRIVATE FIRST CLASS LUKE M. SLOVER. Luke M. Slover was born in Keyport around 1888. Growing up meant eventually joining the volunteer fire company and Luke went with the Eagles around 1910. Eight years later, Luke Slover was drafted into the Army to fight in World War I. Sadly, Private Slover never returned to Keyport. A telegram was received by his parents in the fall of 1918 stating that he had been killed in action in the Battle of Vieville-En-Hay in France. Several years later PFC Slover's body was finally returned to Keyport, and he was laid to rest with honors in Green Grove Cemetery. Luke M. Slover Jr. received the Distinguished Service Cross, second only to the Medal of Honor, for his heroic actions.

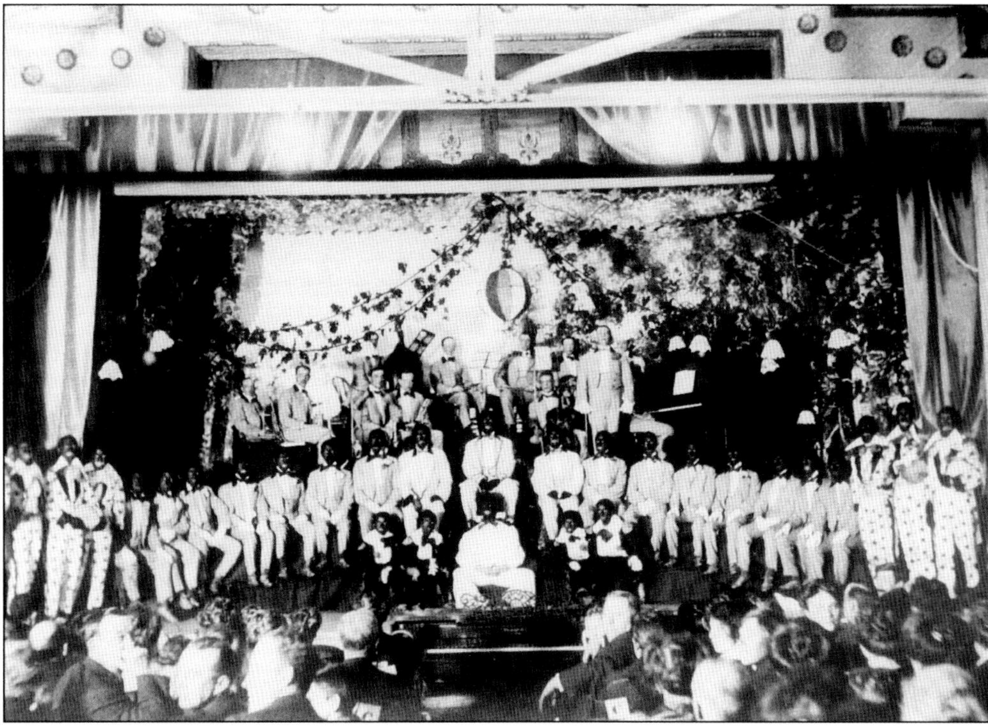

A c. 1912 Minstrel Show at the Armory Theatre.

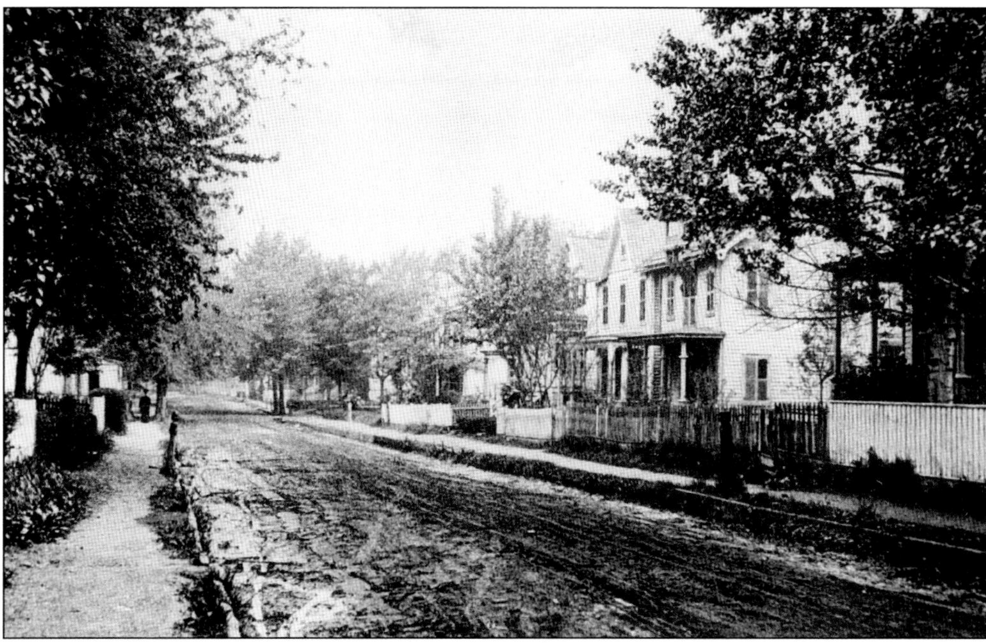

Church Street, Looking South. Most of the residences along Church Street were completed between 1840 and 1890. Church Street itself was laid out between 1831 and 1836, as a direct result of the well-worn old path to the "Little Red Schoolhouse," which stood at Church and John Streets. It is told that for many years afterward tree stumps remained in the roadway and had to be avoided as they were not removed during the street's original grading.

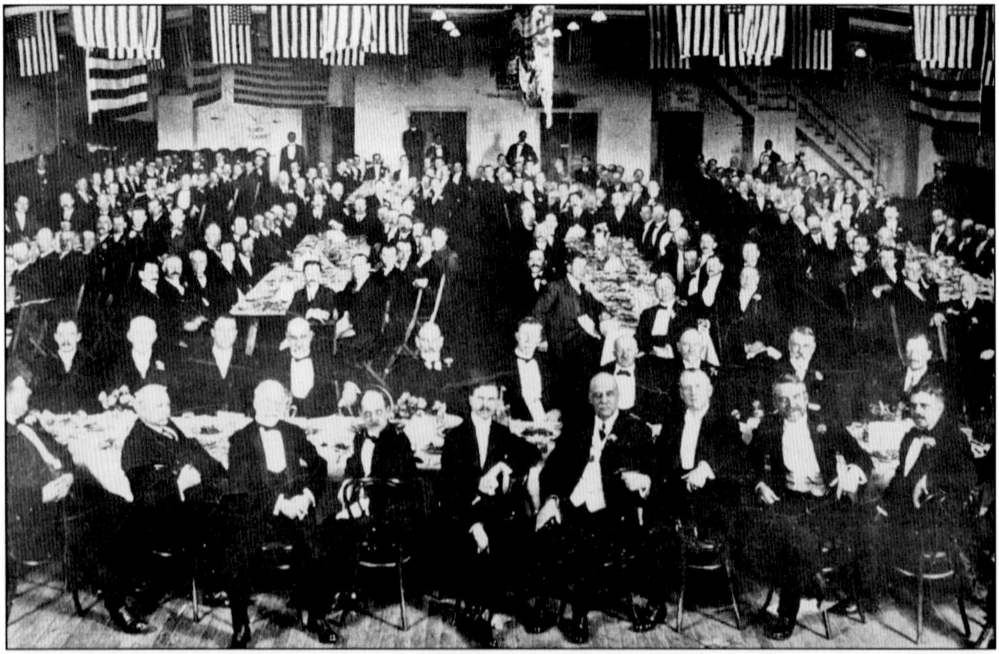

A Publicity Dinner, February 29, 1912. This large group of prominent business people gathered at the Armory Theatre for good food and smooth drinks, which when combined made for some very interesting financial transactions. The photograph was made by the Keyport Photographic firm of Maag and Stewart.

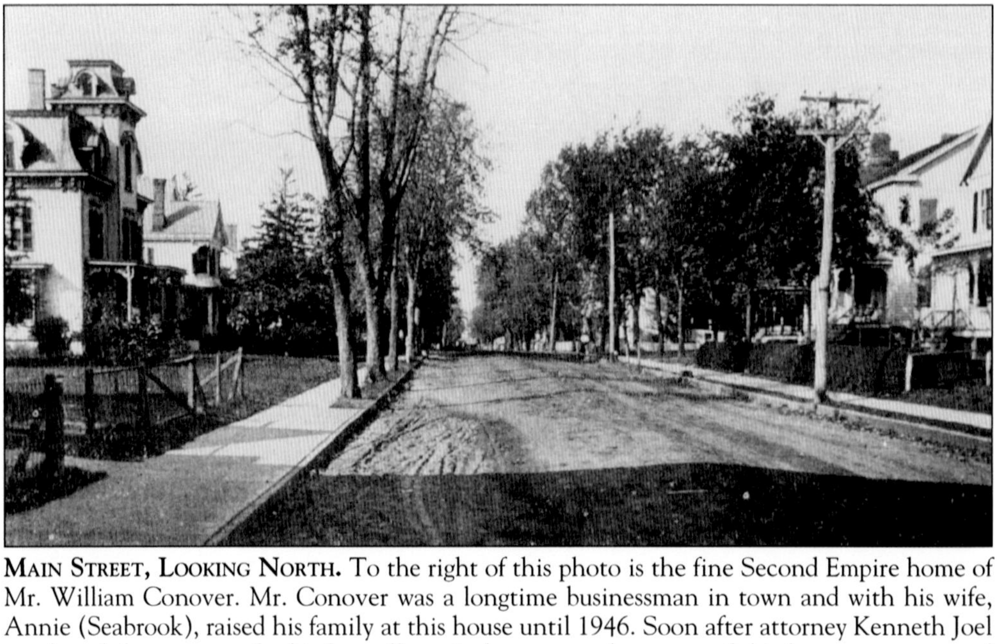

Main Street, Looking North. To the right of this photo is the fine Second Empire home of Mr. William Conover. Mr. Conover was a longtime businessman in town and with his wife, Annie (Seabrook), raised his family at this house until 1946. Soon after attorney Kenneth Joel purchased the property for his law offices. In later years the tower of this house was removed and the entire home was shingled. It is one of only two surviving houses of this architectural style in town.

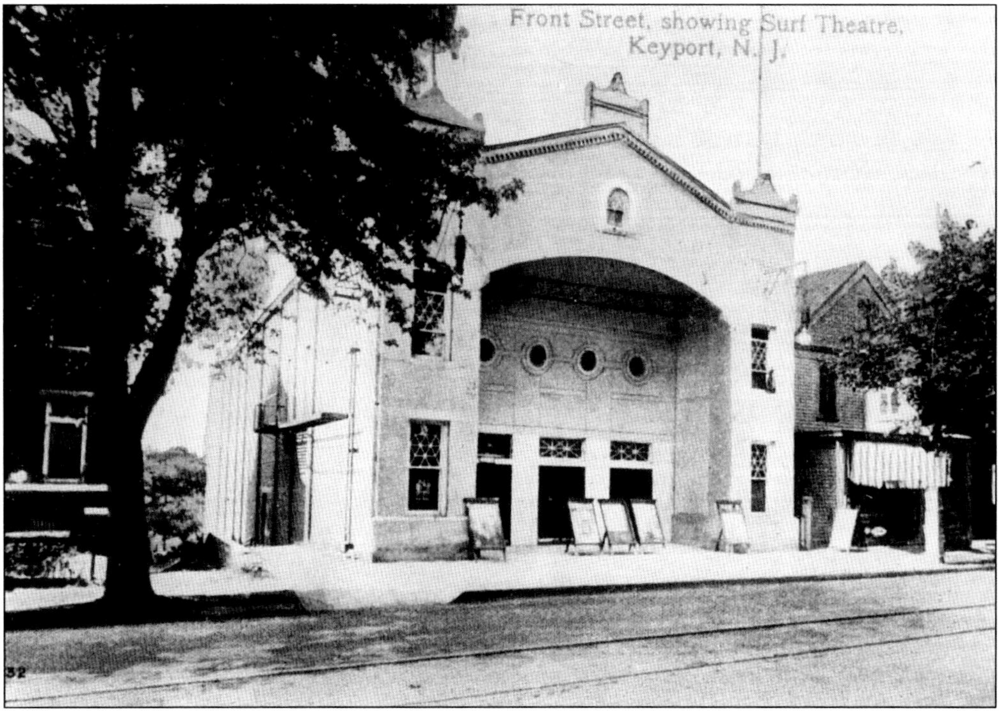

THE SURF THEATRE. Keyport's most well-known theatre was constructed on Front Street overlooking the bay, *c.* 1908. The theatre, with its bold facade, was heralded as a fine addition to the business district. Originally playing the great silent movies, the theatre adapted easily with the advent of talking pictures during the 1920s. During the early years competition for the attention of moviegoers was great. Even in a small town, on a Friday night where would we go to see the show—The Surf, The Palace, The Armory, The Broadway, or Beach Park? Decisions, decisions.

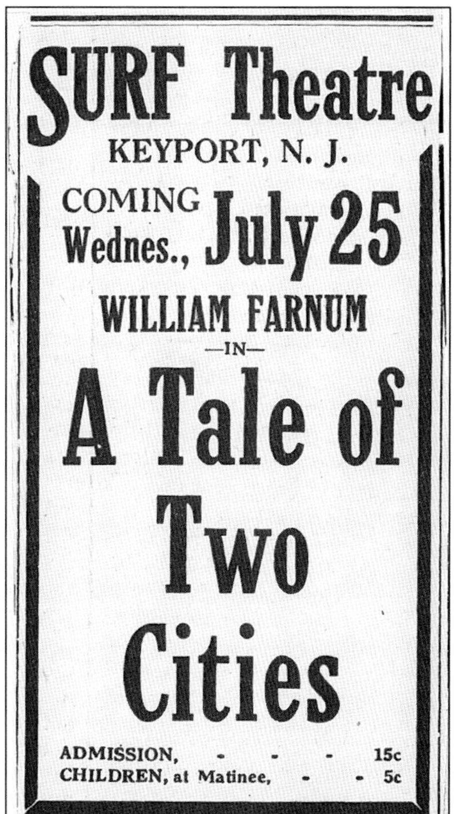

A 1911 ADVERTISEMENT FOR THE SURF, FROM THE *KEYPORT WEEKLY*.

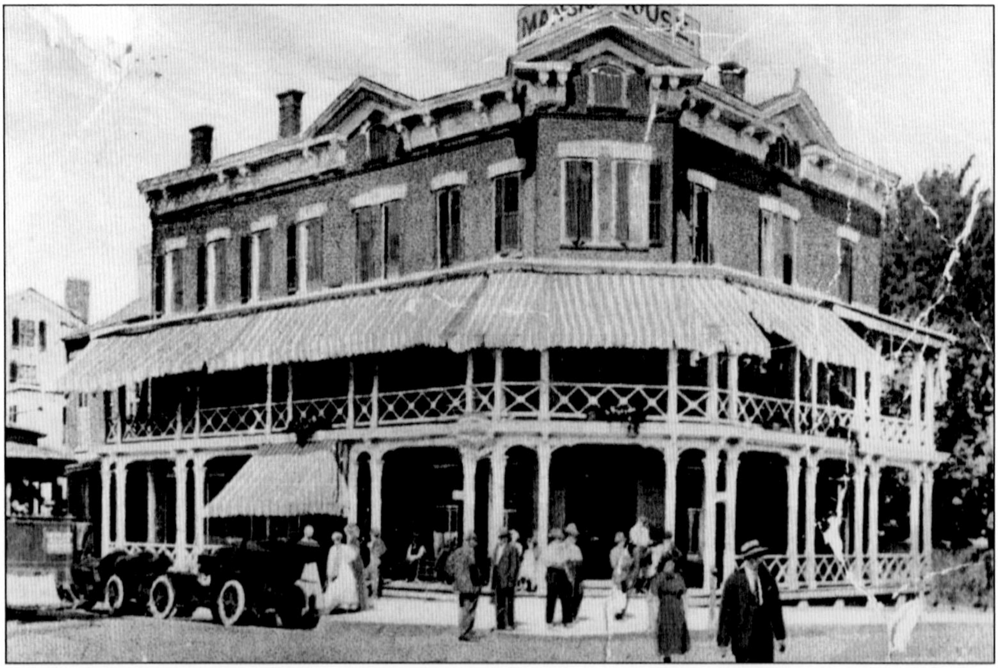

THE MANSION HOUSE HOTEL, 1915. The town's two largest hotels—the Pavilion and the Mansion House—competed for business less than 50 feet apart. The Mansion House was built in 1878 to replace the former building, which had been destroyed in the 1877 fire. The new structure, which was finished in red brick, was graced with two stories of delicate porches and a large livery stable located in the rear of the hotel. In later years the hotel was closed and remodeled into apartments. Unfortunately, its fine porches and awnings have gone the way of the streetcar.

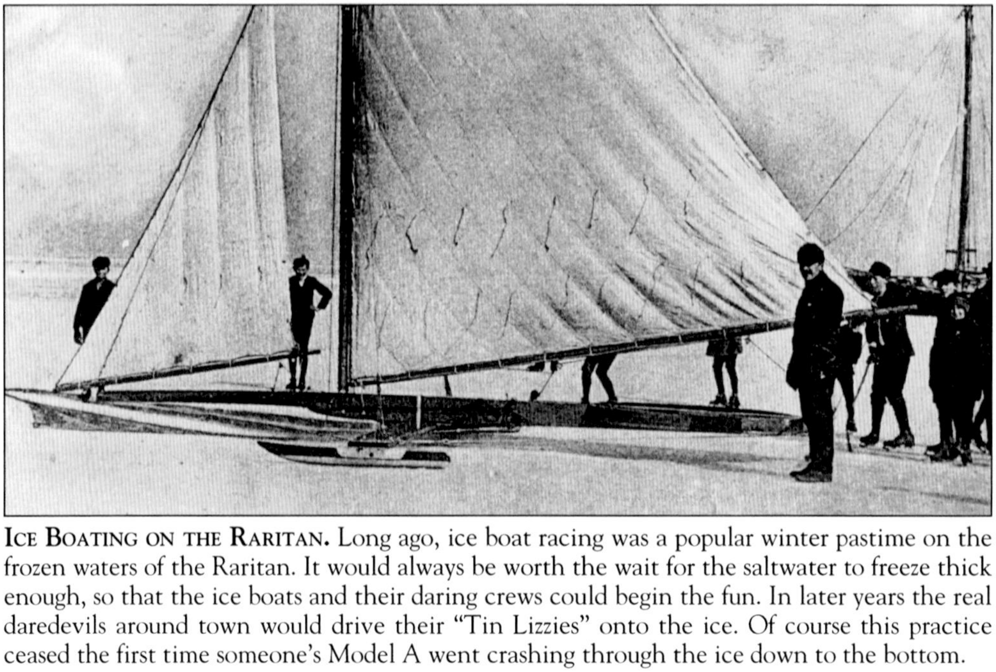

ICE BOATING ON THE RARITAN. Long ago, ice boat racing was a popular winter pastime on the frozen waters of the Raritan. It would always be worth the wait for the saltwater to freeze thick enough, so that the ice boats and their daring crews could begin the fun. In later years the real daredevils around town would drive their "Tin Lizzies" onto the ice. Of course this practice ceased the first time someone's Model A went crashing through the ice down to the bottom.

THOMAS REGAN, c. 1916. Tom Regan was born in Cliffwood Beach. He married his wife, Olive, in 1936 and moved to Keyport with her soon after. Mr. Regan operated the Sunoco station at the corner of Route 35 and Cliffwood Avenue for many years.

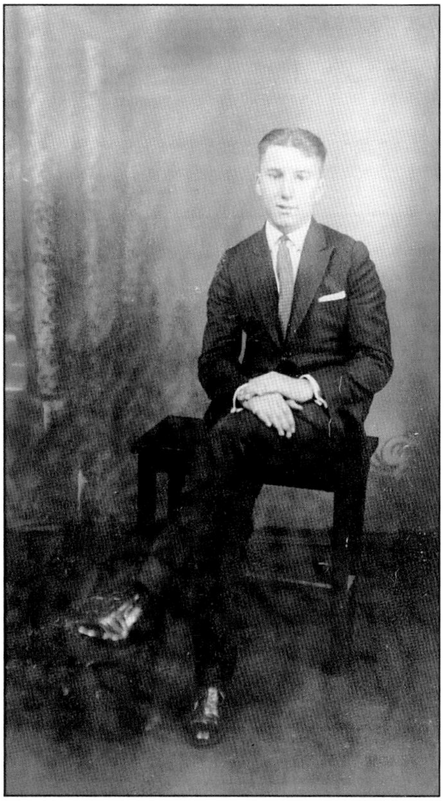

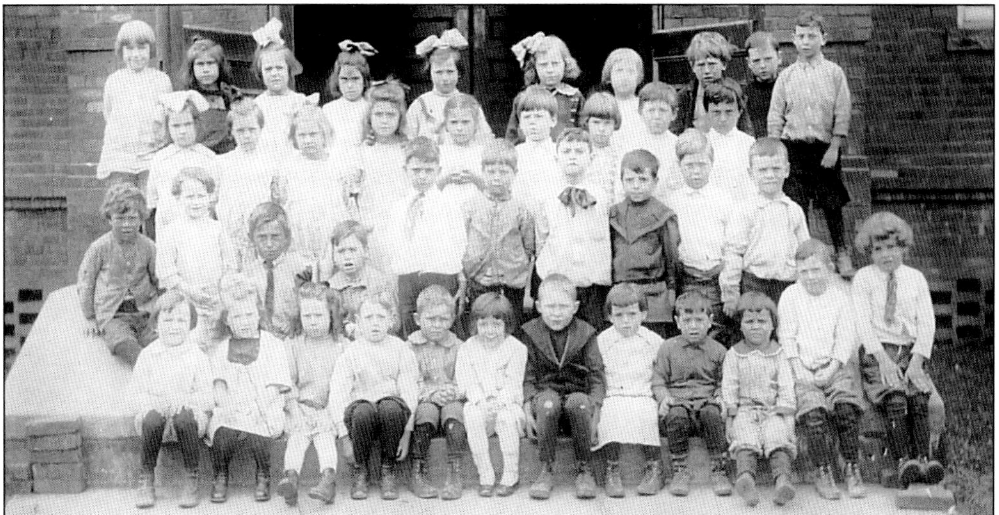

THE EAST KEYPORT SCHOOL, c. 1909. The Lockport school district was first chartered in the mid-19th century, due to the growing population in the eastern end of town. By the 1900, the district had been dissolved and all children were attending the Graded School. In 1904 it was decided to rent a building and begin classes once again in Lockport. In 1909 the East Keyport School was erected on Second Street, east of Harrison Street. The schoolchildren all lived in Lockport and belonged to such families as the Lees, Applegates, VanPelts, Posts, Nagles, and many others.

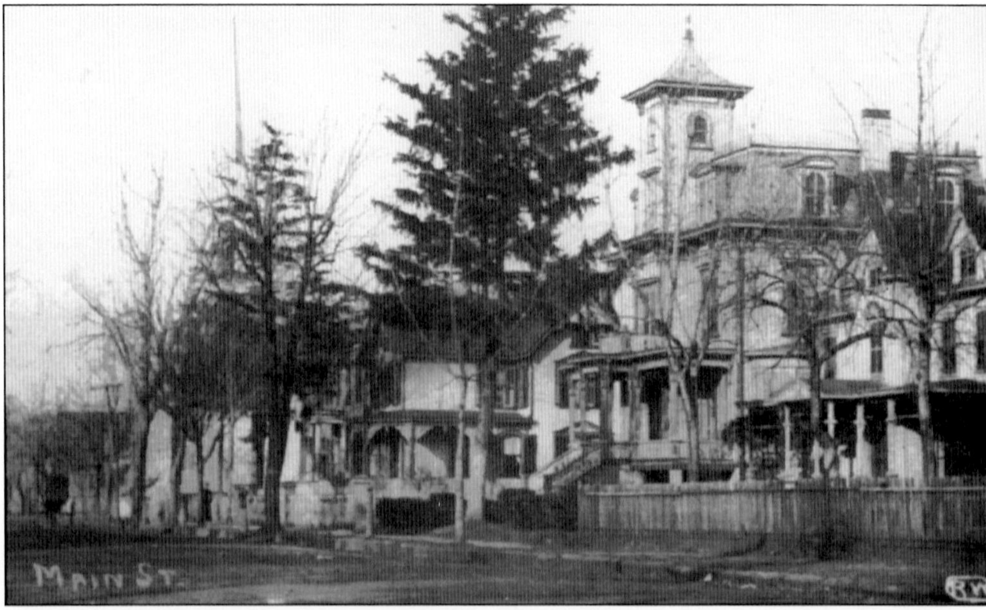

MAIN STREET, NORTH FROM WARREN STREET. The old home of Nimrod and Mary Bedle, seen in the far right of this photo, was built in 1830–1831. The majestic Second Empire home next door was constructed in the mid-1870s by Capt. H.E. Bishop. By the early 1970s not only had the tower been removed, but the entire mansard roof had been taken off and replaced with a simple gable roof. The new look was practical, and in keeping with the "if it's old tear down" mentality that reigned throughout America up until the late 1970s.

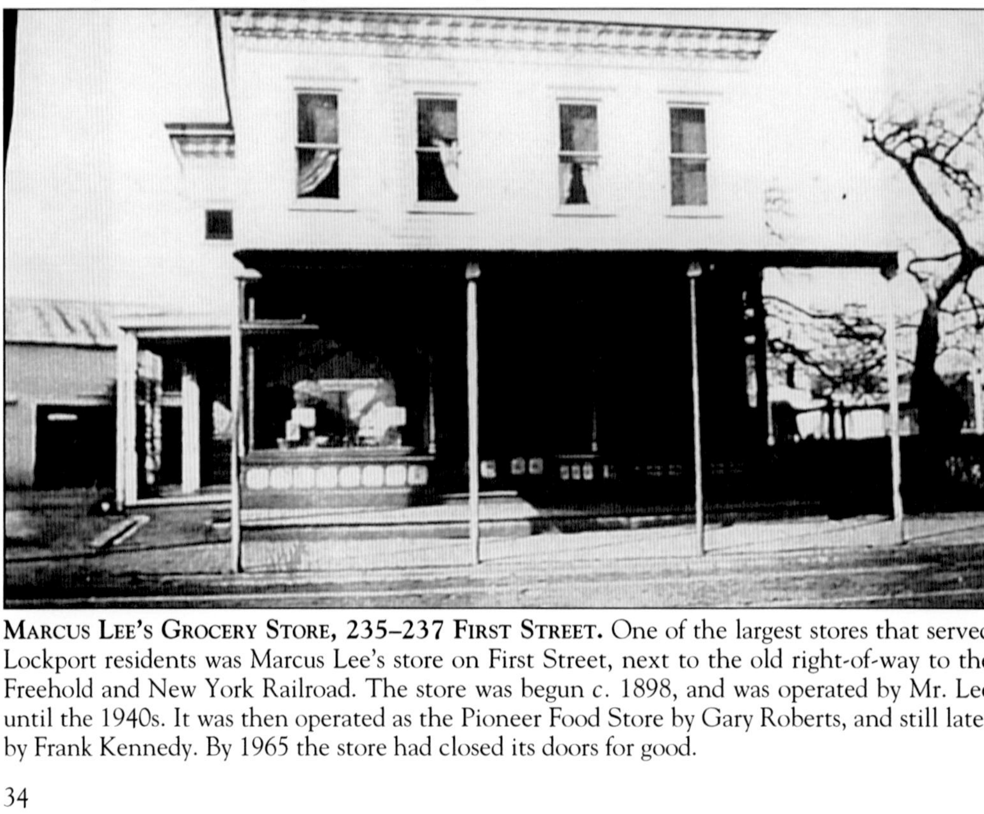

MARCUS LEE'S GROCERY STORE, 235–237 FIRST STREET. One of the largest stores that served Lockport residents was Marcus Lee's store on First Street, next to the old right-of-way to the Freehold and New York Railroad. The store was begun *c.* 1898, and was operated by Mr. Lee until the 1940s. It was then operated as the Pioneer Food Store by Gary Roberts, and still later by Frank Kennedy. By 1965 the store had closed its doors for good.

Three

1921–1930

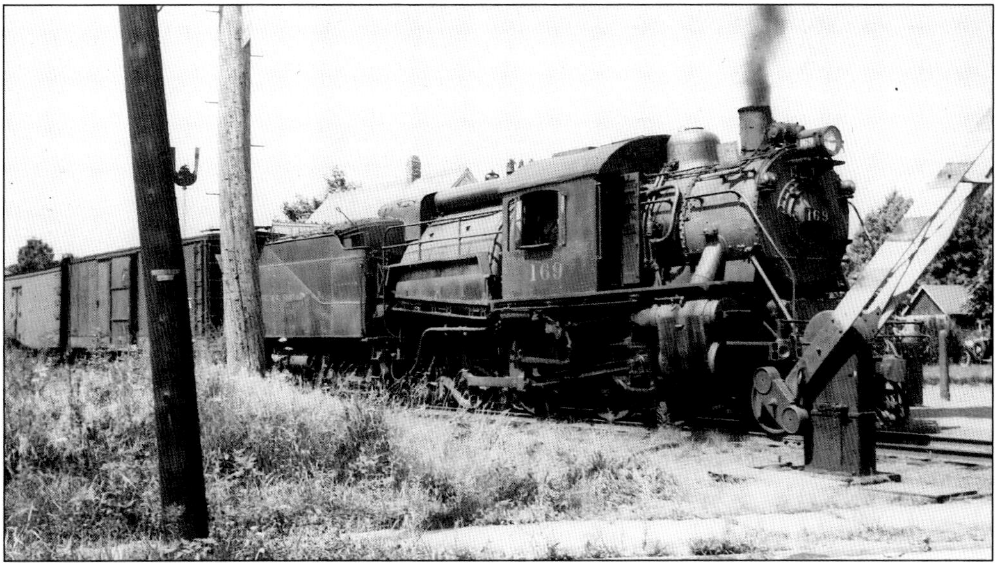

The Broad Street Crossing, c. 1923. Here a big "Camelback"-style engine is sitting idle at the old Broad Street Station. This Central Railroad of New Jersey engine has a full load of freight cars in tow, bound for points east such as Keansburg and Atlantic Highlands.

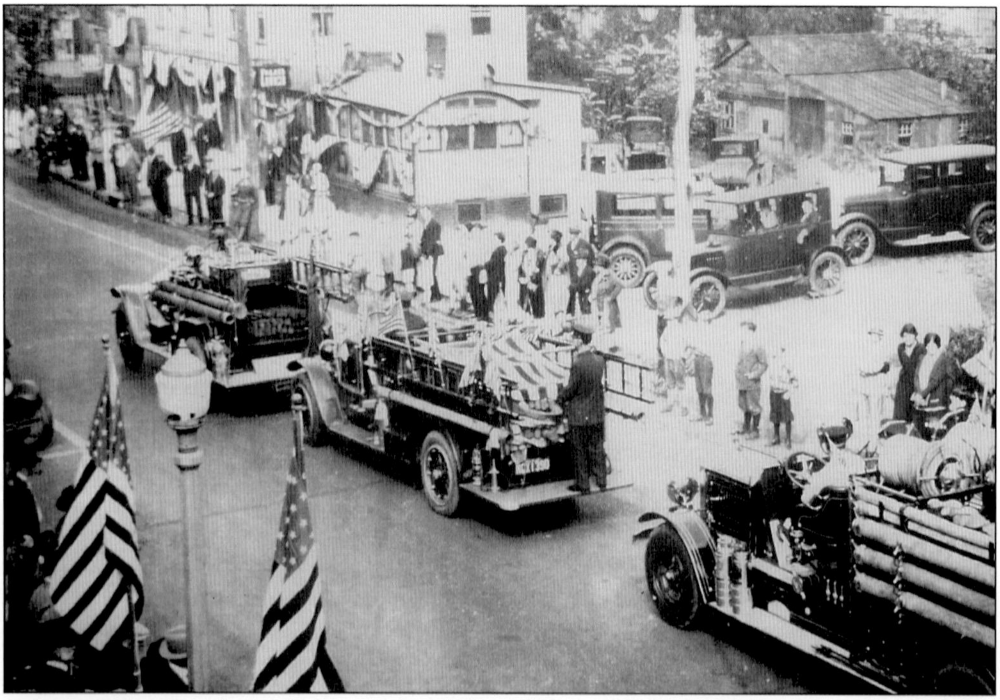

JULY 4, 1928. People have come from all over town and the local farms to watch the big Decoration Day parade. These visiting fire companies are heading north on Broad Street toward the Pavilion Hotel, where bands would entertain all well into the evening. Patriotism was at a all time high in the 1920s, and when the Fourth of July came it was always cause for quite a celebration.

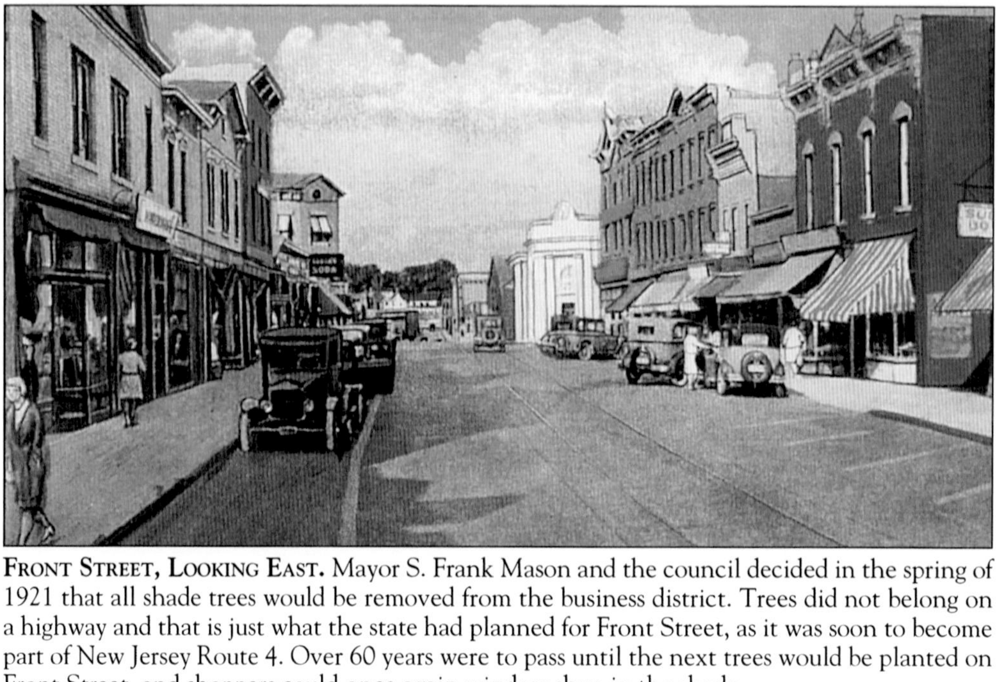

FRONT STREET, LOOKING EAST. Mayor S. Frank Mason and the council decided in the spring of 1921 that all shade trees would be removed from the business district. Trees did not belong on a highway and that is just what the state had planned for Front Street, as it was soon to become part of New Jersey Route 4. Over 60 years were to pass until the next trees would be planted on Front Street, and shoppers could once again window shop in the shade.

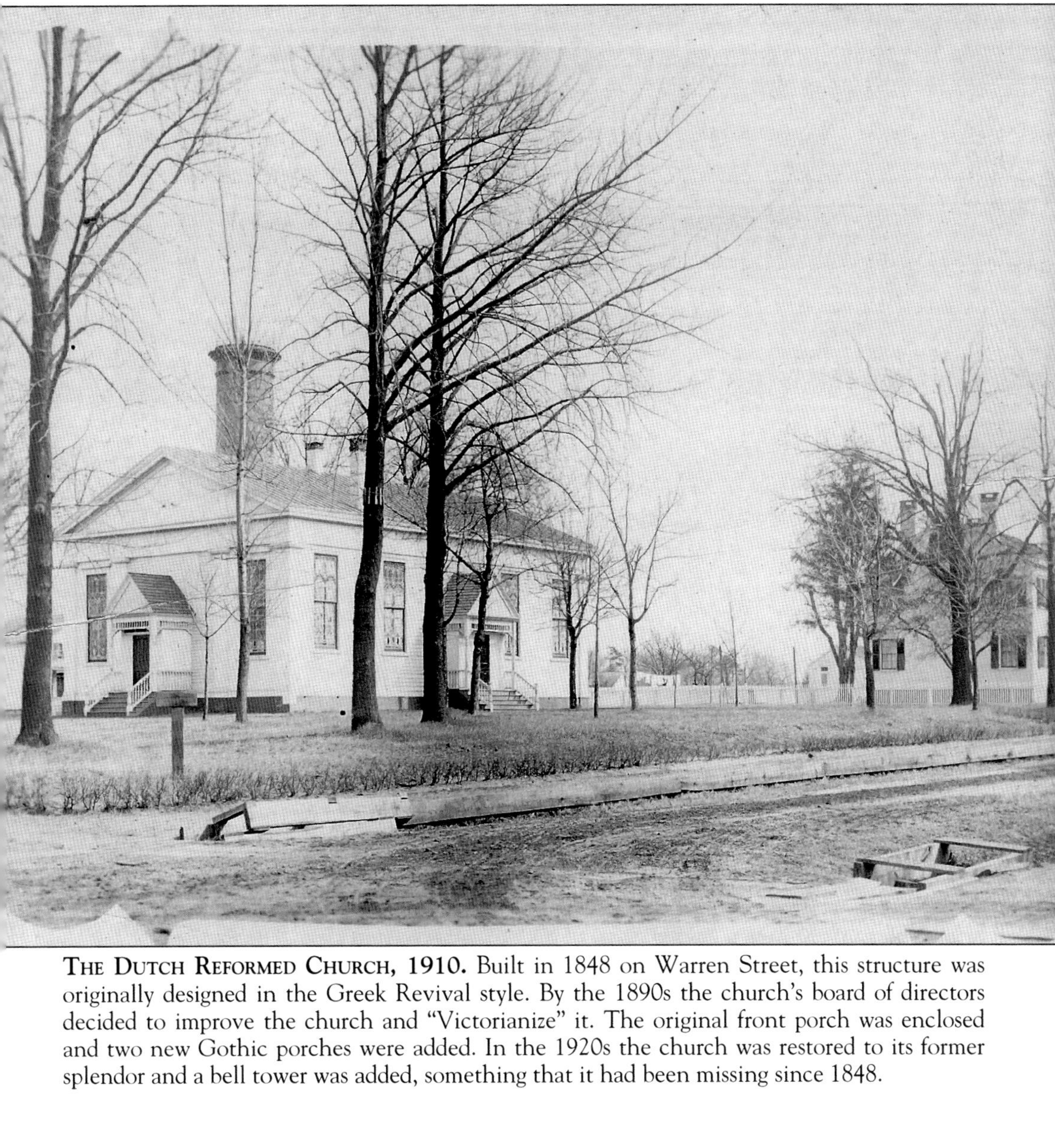

THE DUTCH REFORMED CHURCH, 1910. Built in 1848 on Warren Street, this structure was originally designed in the Greek Revival style. By the 1890s the church's board of directors decided to improve the church and "Victorianize" it. The original front porch was enclosed and two new Gothic porches were added. In the 1920s the church was restored to its former splendor and a bell tower was added, something that it had been missing since 1848.

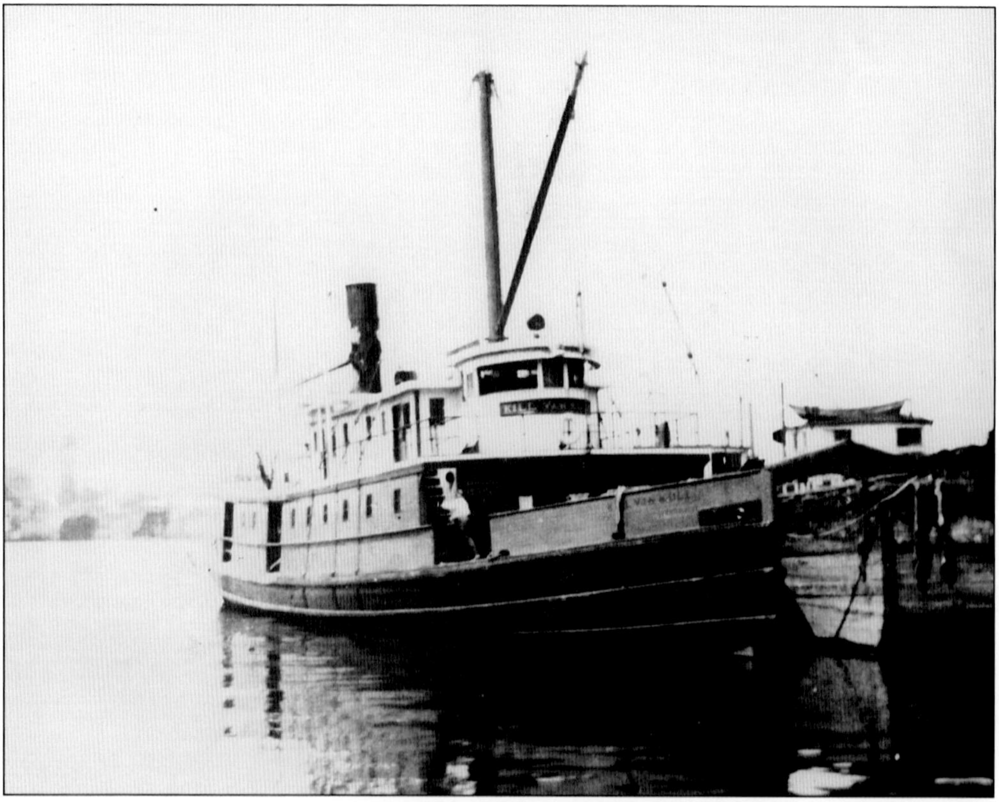

THE *KILL VAN KULL.* Named after a local body of water, the *Kill Van Kull* started freight service between Keyport and Perth Amboy in 1915. The bright orange and white colors of this colorful vessel were a common site on the bay until 1935, when Keyport's last remaining link to the active steamship trade bid farewell to the wharf, ending over 100 years of steamship trade.

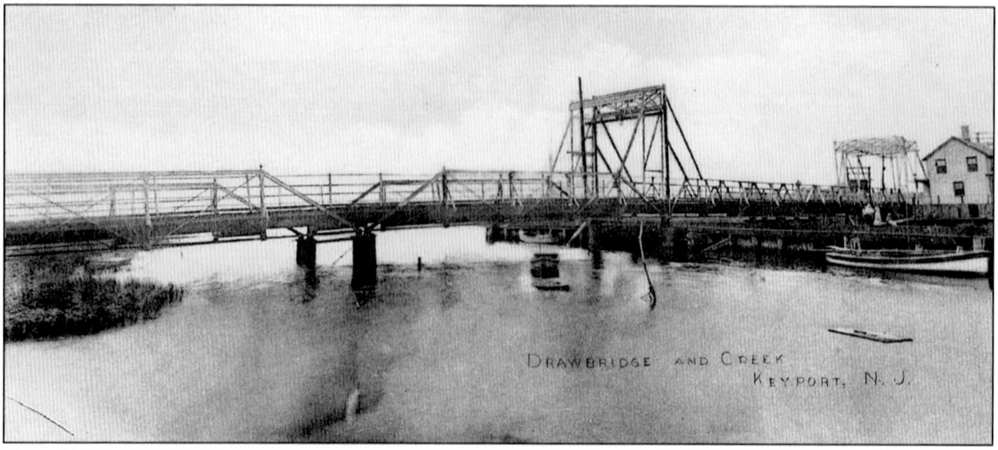

THE MATAWAN CREEK DRAWBRIDGE. By 1888 it was decided to erect a new bridge to span Matawan Creek. This steel truss drawbridge was completed in that year and was in use until 1915. The building to the right of the photo is thought to be the house of the bridge tender, whose responsibilities included closing the gates, stopping traffic, and raising the draw, a job that later went the way of the lighthouse keeper.

John Regan (1903–1973). Born and raised in Cliffwood, John Regan married Gladys Evans of Keyport in 1927. They resided at 2 Spring Street and raised their two sons in that home. John and Gladys operated the well-known Regan's Tavern in Cliffwood for nearly 40 years. John is shown here in what appears to be his 1927 Chevrolet sedan.

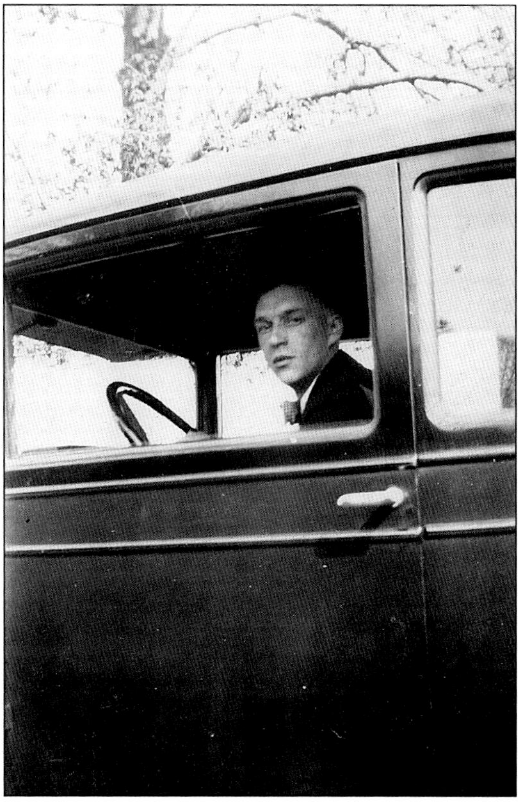

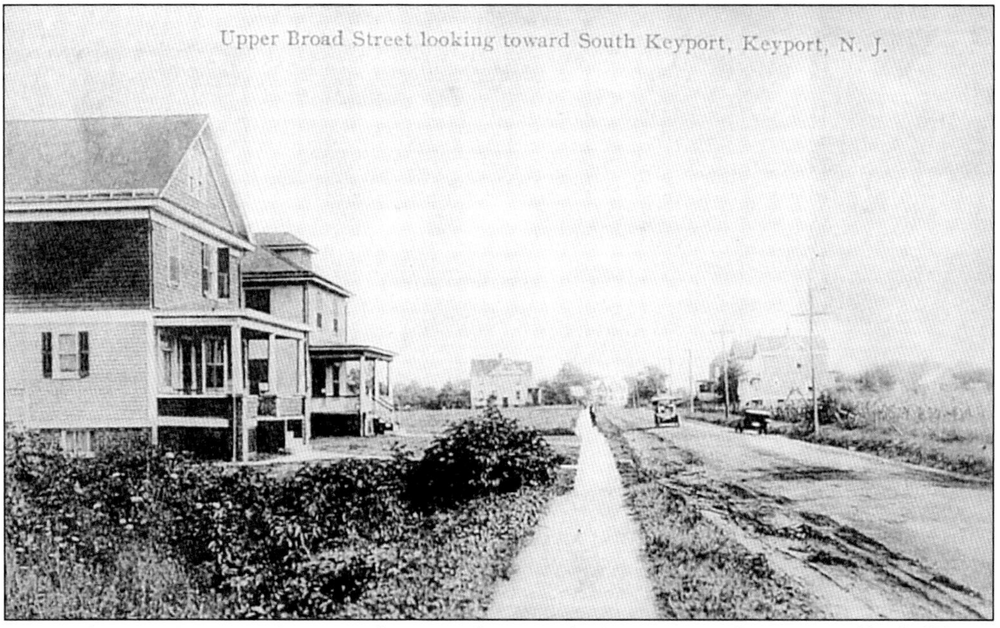

Broad Street, Looking South. The seven houses which appear in this postcard had all been recently completed along Broad Street. This property was originally part of the Asher Holmes tract and was not built upon until about 1919. The area was nearing total development by 1950, and by 1990 no open building lots remained along "Upper Broad Street."

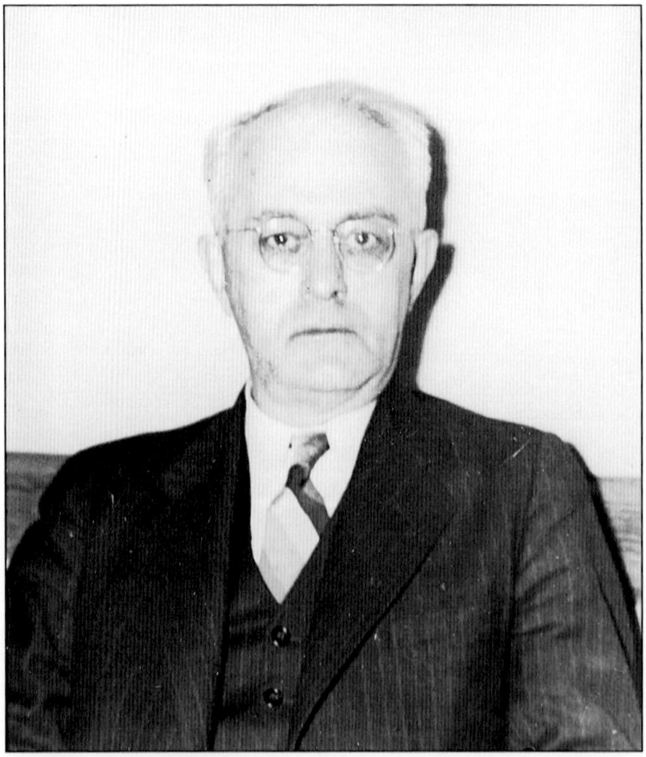

WILLIS BILDERBACK. Mr. Bilderback served as supervising principal of the Keyport Schools from *c.* 1929 until his death in 1940. He was succeeded by John O. Hartzler in that same year.

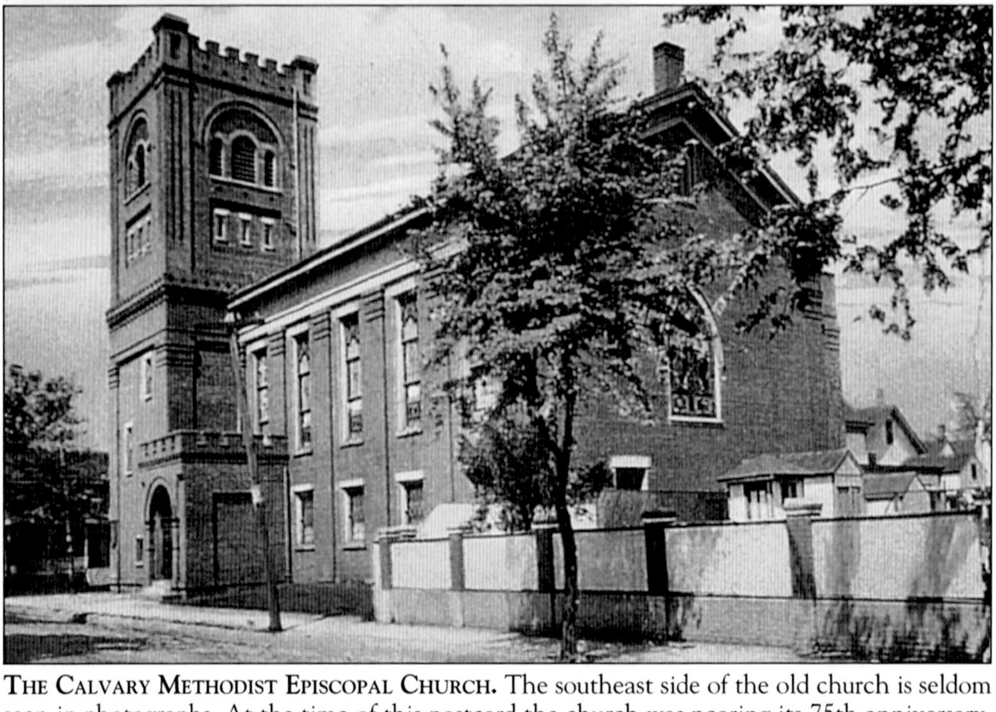

THE CALVARY METHODIST EPISCOPAL CHURCH. The southeast side of the old church is seldom seen in photographs. At the time of this postcard the church was nearing its 75th anniversary. Although remodeled several times, this fine house of worship remains much as it did when built in 1856, at the corner of Third and Osborn Streets.

CHARLES "BULL" HOWARD, c. 1926

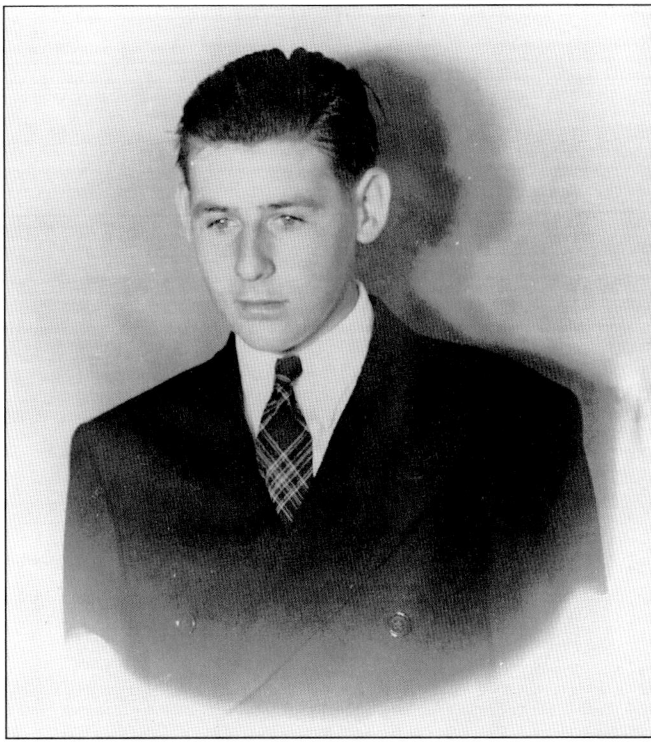

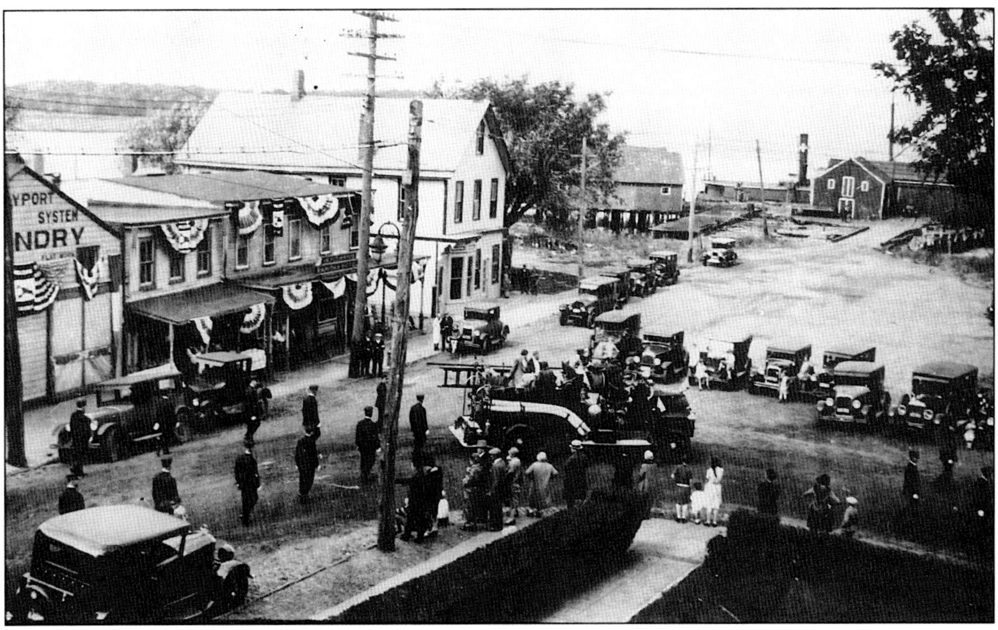

THE 50TH ANNIVERSARY OF THE FIRE DEPARTMENT. The foot of Broad Street and the steamboat wharf were seldom photographed. This shot captures the old wharf (built 1830–1865), the Bayside Hotel (built *c.* 1879), the Raritan Hotel (built *c.* 1890), and the Single System Laundry (built *c.* 1919). The photo itself was taken from the third floor of the long-vanished Raritan Inn, which went up in flames in 1962. Shown rounding the corner is the "Big Mack" of the Lincoln Hose Company.

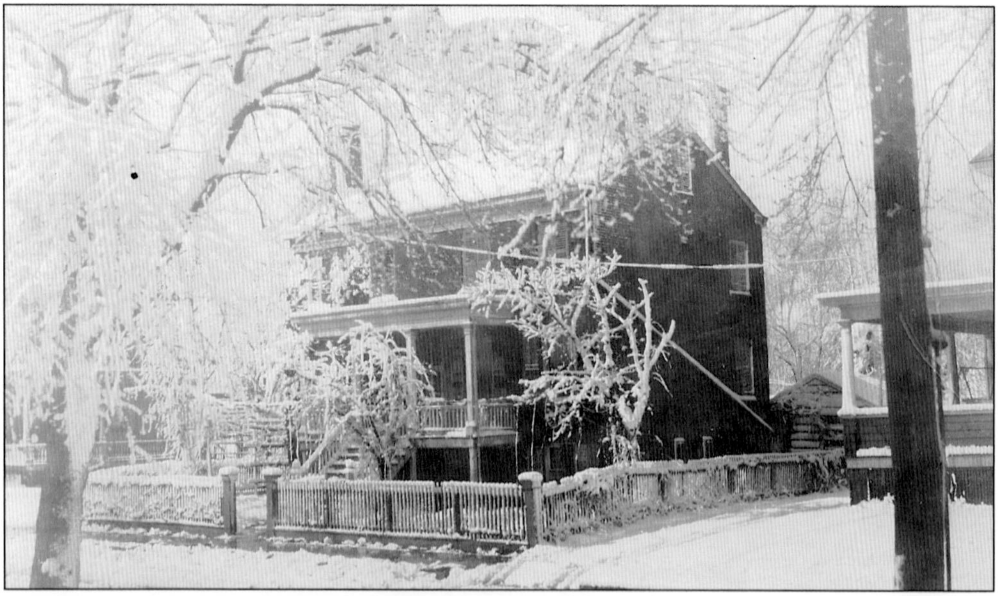

The Strange Storm of April 1, 1924. It all started at 1:45 p.m. on April Fool's Day, when the dark clouds rolled in from the west. By 2:15 p.m. the storm had turned for the worse with heavy rain and thunder and lightning. At 2:30 p.m. the rain turned into a blinding snowstorm with thunder and lightning which lasted for over six hours. This series of four photos were all taken by Phelps Cherry. The top and bottom photos show the Cornielous H. Brown house, built in 1855.

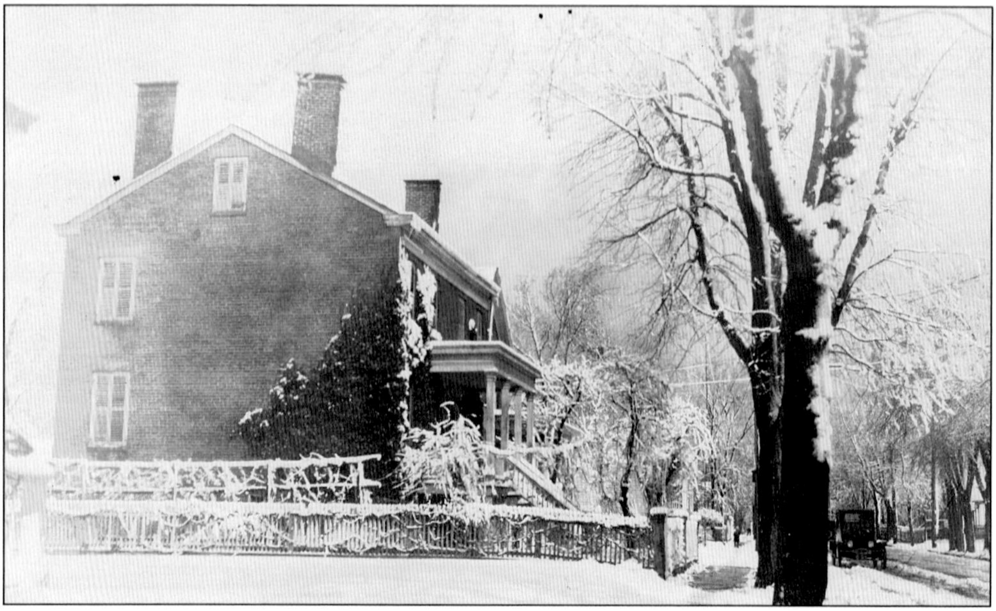

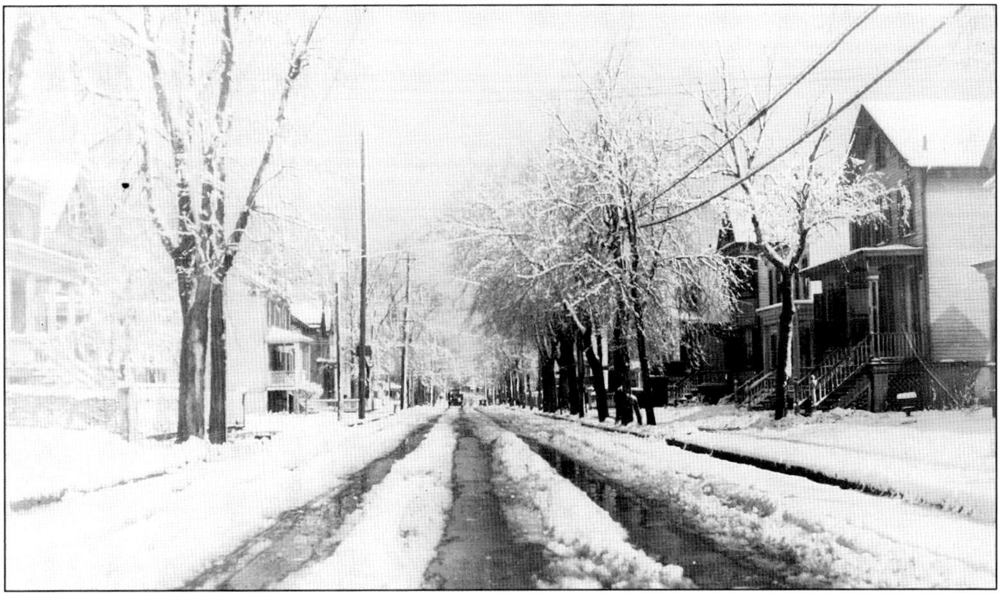

Broad Street in the 1924 storm. Shown in the top photograph is 161 Broad Street, the J. VanPelt House, built in 1870; north of that at 159 Broad (in the bottom photograph) is Henry Cherry's house, which is said to have been the first house completed on Broad Street in 1854.

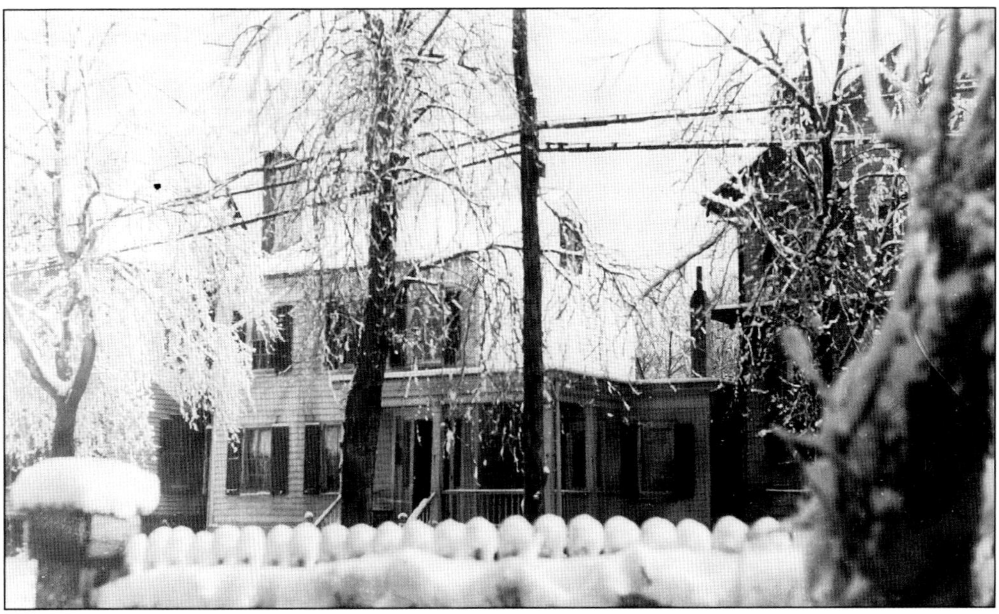

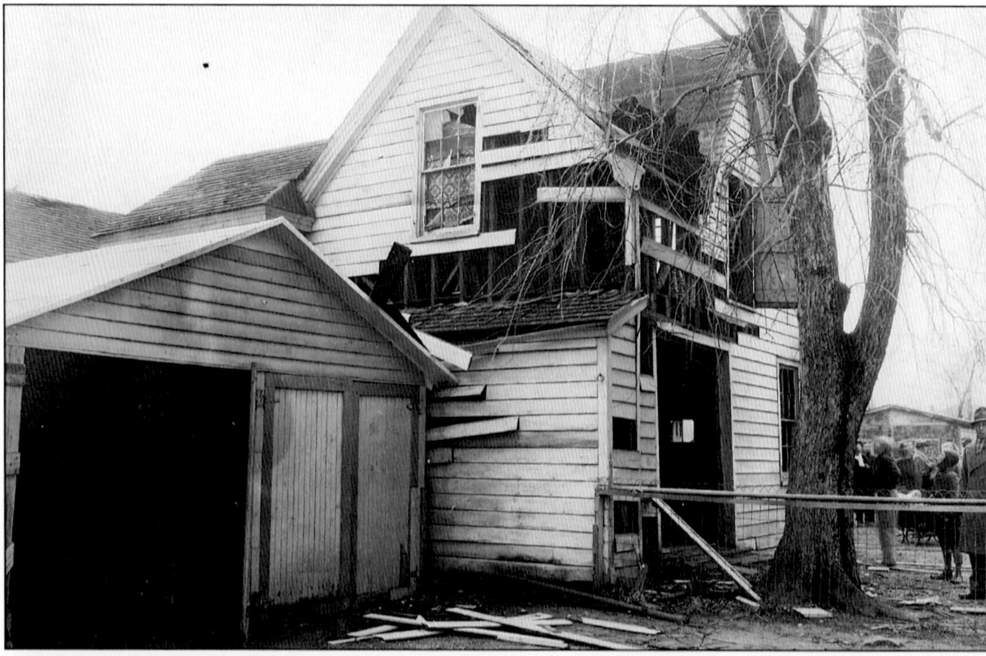

LIGHTNING STRIKE, C. 1929. Lightning is well known to travel the path of least resistance, even if that means going through the roof and siding of a local carriage house. This structure, which once stood along First Street, was nearly destroyed in this dangerous strike.

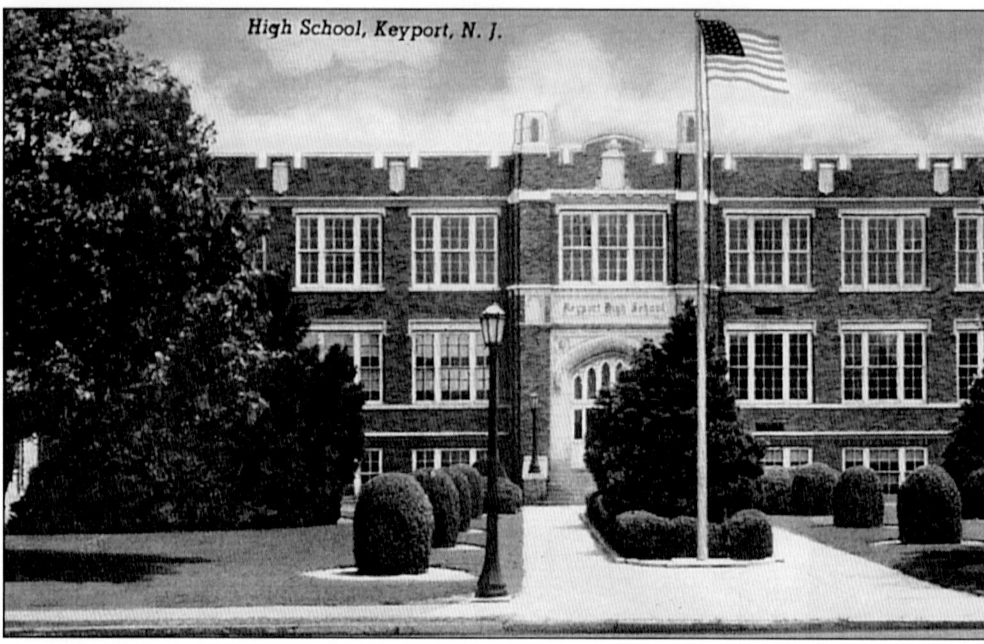

THE HIGH SCHOOL, 1929. Keyport's "new" high school was completed on South Broad Street, on property which was part of the large Asher Holmes tract. Keyport's high school was built in a time when sculptures and fanciful brickwork were thought to enhance learning. Whether it did or not is open to debate, but the building remains one of only two operating classic high schools in Monmouth County.

Four

1931–1940

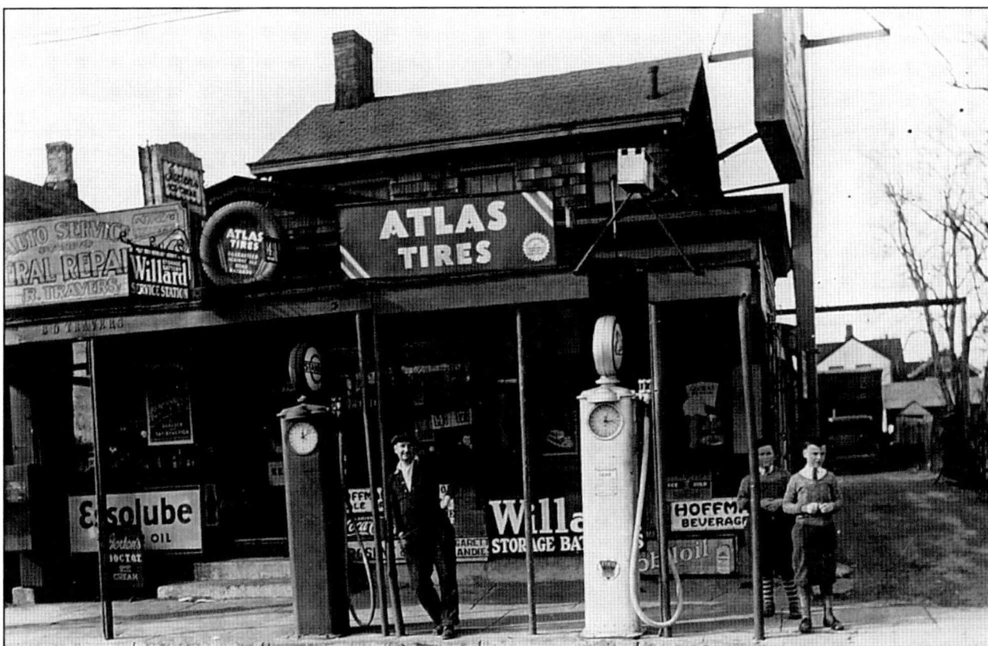

B.D. TRAVERS' ESSO FILLING STATION. Just down the street from the old freight station was Ben Travers' gas station. Typical of small-town curbside filling stations, it wouldn't be long before oil companies began erecting super service stations on highways all over the country, quickly replacing this bit of Americana.

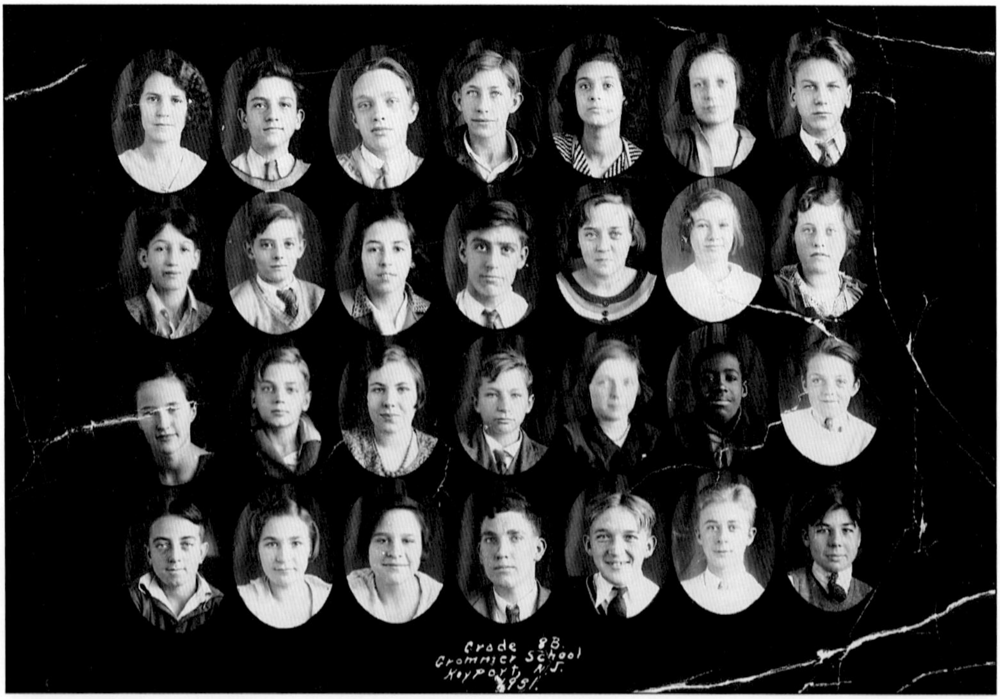

Grade 8B of the Keyport Grammar School. This 1931 class picture belongs to Mrs. Dot Poling, who appears in the top left of this photo. Also appearing in this photo is Benjamin Kelly (second from the top, second in from the left), who was killed in action while serving as a second lieutenant in the United States Army during World War II.

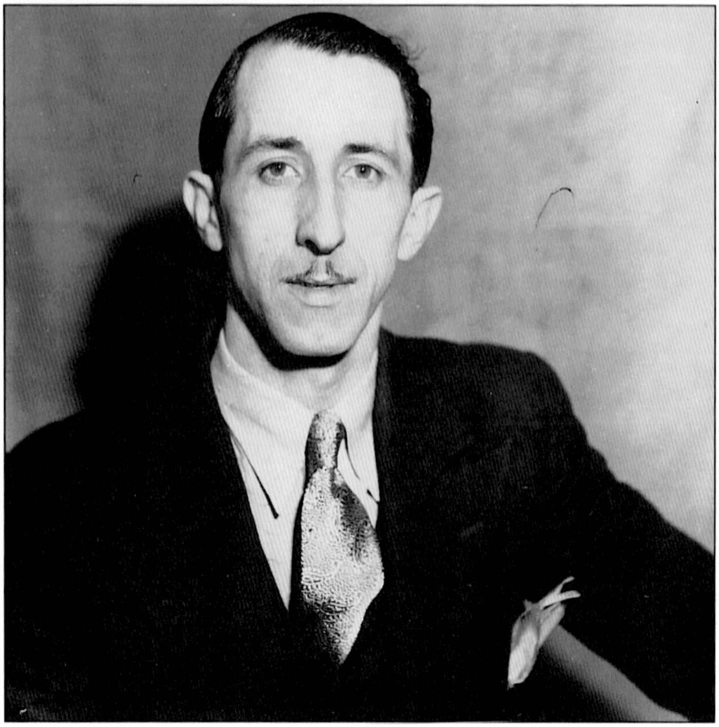

Joe Lanzaro. The *Keyport Weekly* ran a story on June 3, 1937, about Mr. Joe Lanzaro, who had recently been fired by his company in Matawan. It seems that Mr. Lanzaro was soliciting for union membership when he was fired by the Hanson-Van Winkle Munning Company in Matawan. The *Weekly* followed the story for several weeks but it was soon replaced with new headlines about trouble overseas with a man named Adolf Hitler.

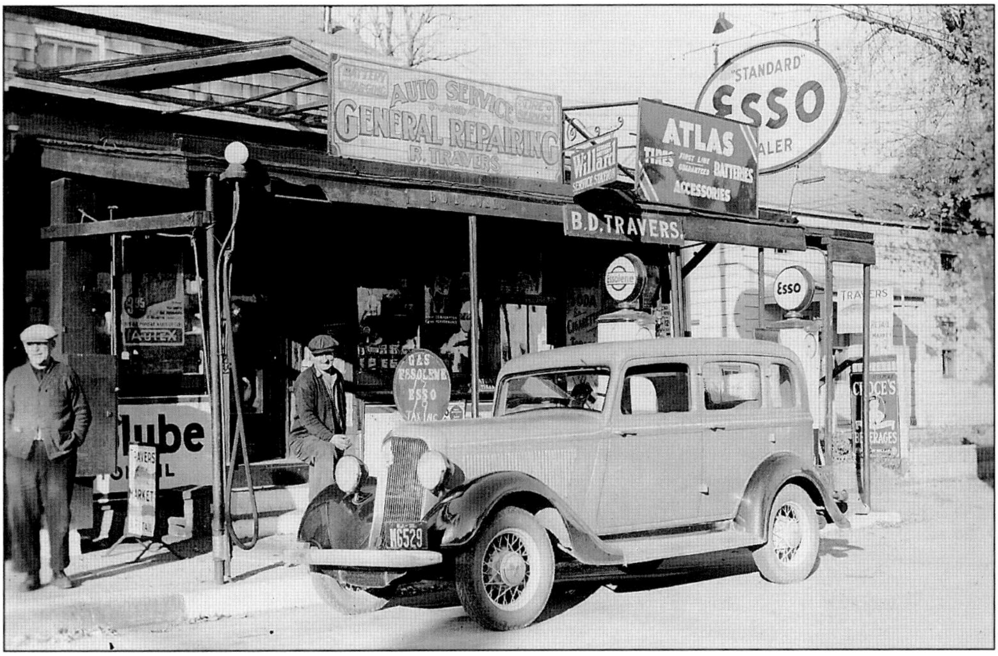

B.D. Travers' Filling Station. Standing to the left in this image is Benjamin D. Travers, owner of the Esso filling station at 177 Second Street. Mr. Travers moved to Keyport in 1890 and purchased the family service station in 1923. He resided there with his wife, Etta, and his children, Russell (in the center of this photo), Alfred, and Eva. In November of 1940 Mr. Travers fell at the station, breaking his hip. Sadly, only two weeks later he passed away at the age of 74. Mr. Travers was an Exempt Fireman, a longtime member of the Independent Odd Fellows, and a well-respected citizen.

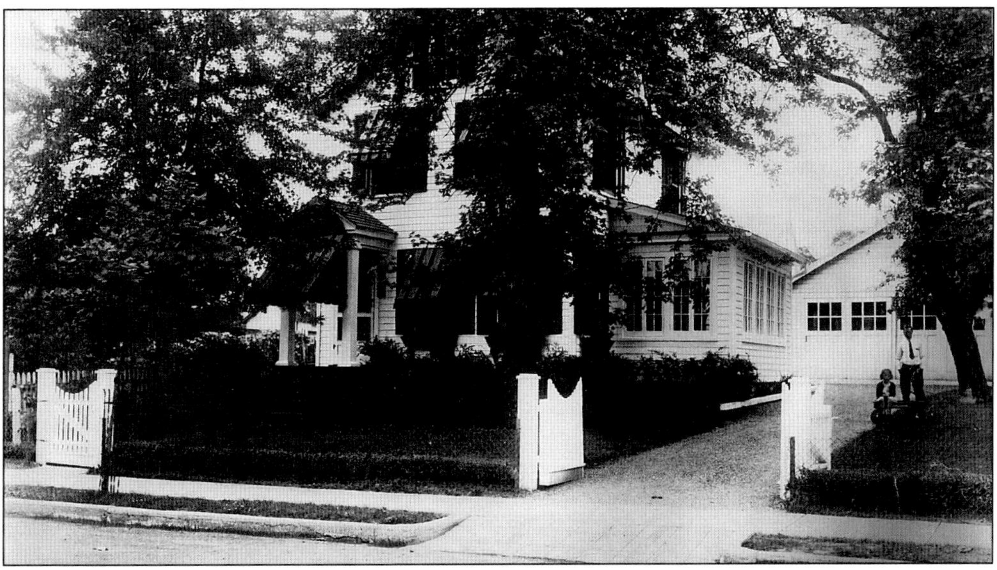

The Jack Haley House, c. 1906. This fine Washington Street home was owned by Mr. Haley during much of the 20th century. In later years the well-maintained home was purchased by Mr. Robert Wilson, owner of the Keyport Fishery, who raised his family at this location and continues to reside there as a new century approaches.

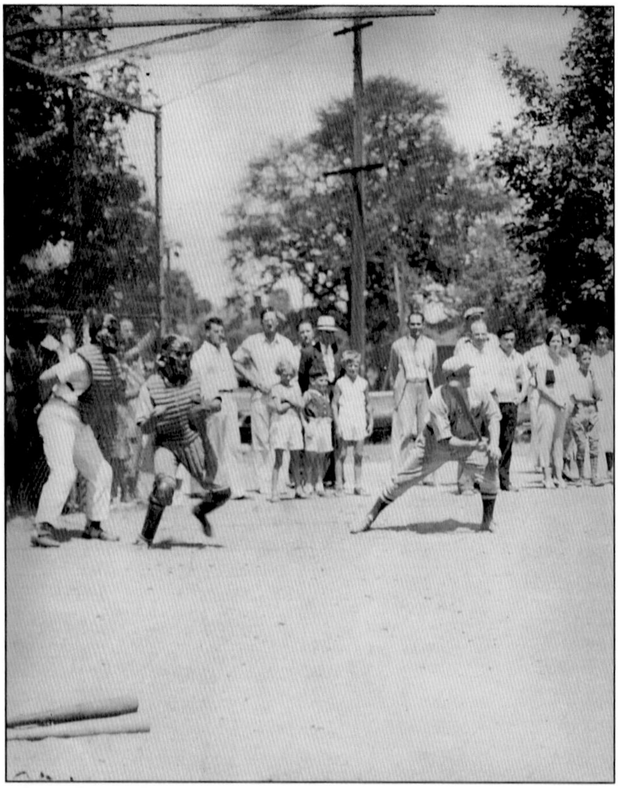

A Baseball Game, c. 1932. It looks as if Keyport's up to bat, but *swshhhh* it's a strike, thrown by the Matawan pitcher. Not to worry, the Keyport team is well prepared and soon the boys from Matawan will hang their heads in defeat. Throughout the years Keyport has had such teams as the Lockport Aces, the Keyport Athletics, and many others. Today, Keyport is home to no less than nine ball fields, all of which see lots of action each season.

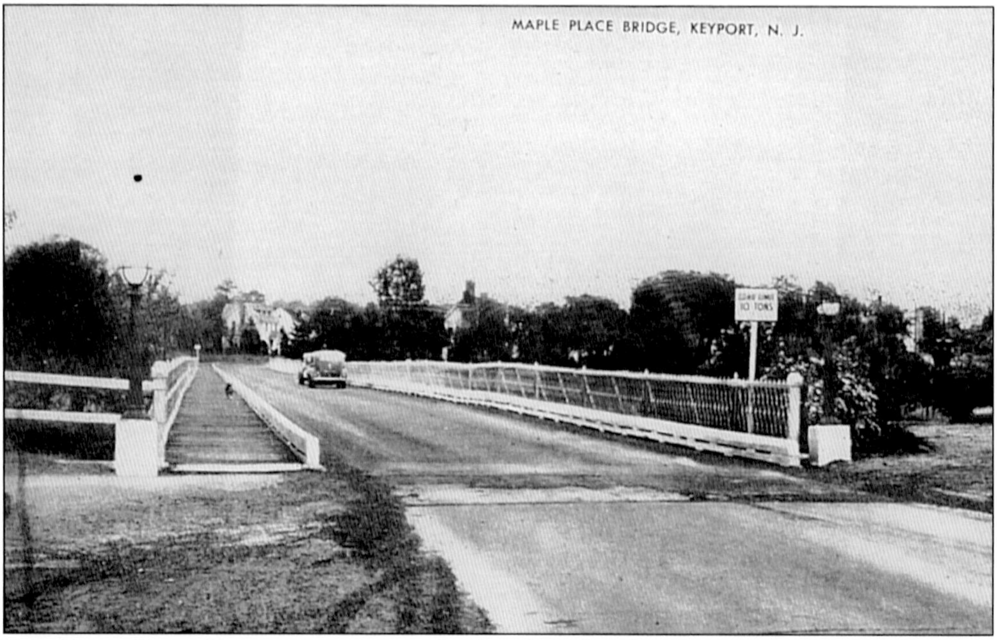

The Maple Place Bridge. This postcard referred to the old 1899 bridge as the Maple Place bridge, a name which it never officially held. Although Mott Street is no more and the bridge was removed in the 1960s, this section of Maple Place is still referred to as "The Mott Street Bridge."

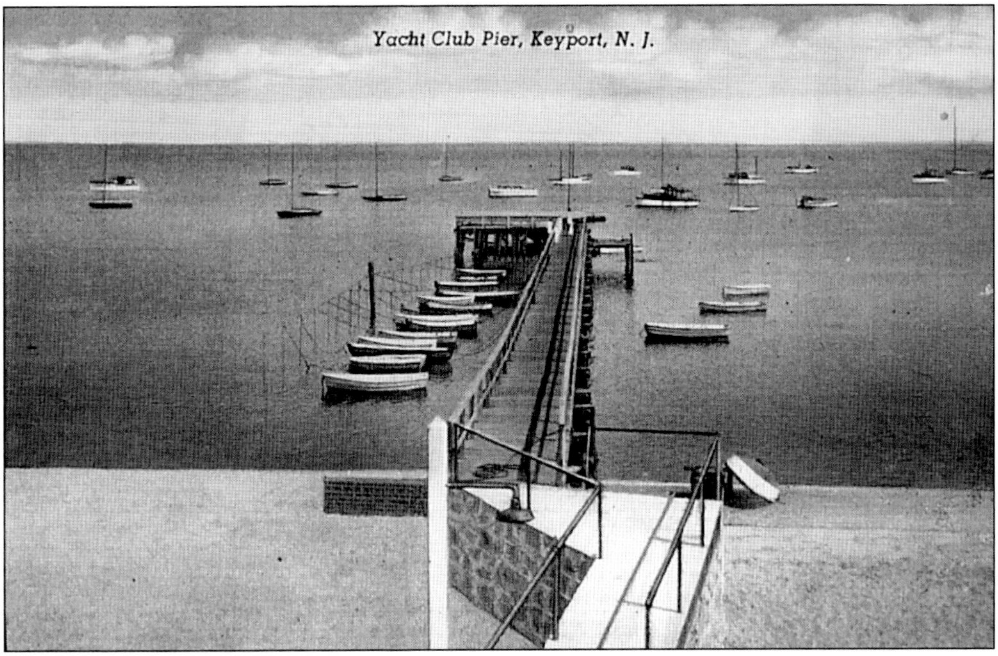

THE YACHT CLUB DOCK, C. 1936. Throughout the years, several piers have been used by yacht club members as a place to catch the launch to their sailboats. In this view only a fraction of the sailboats that would be moored by the 1970s are present. The dock was later destroyed by a 1960s hurricane.

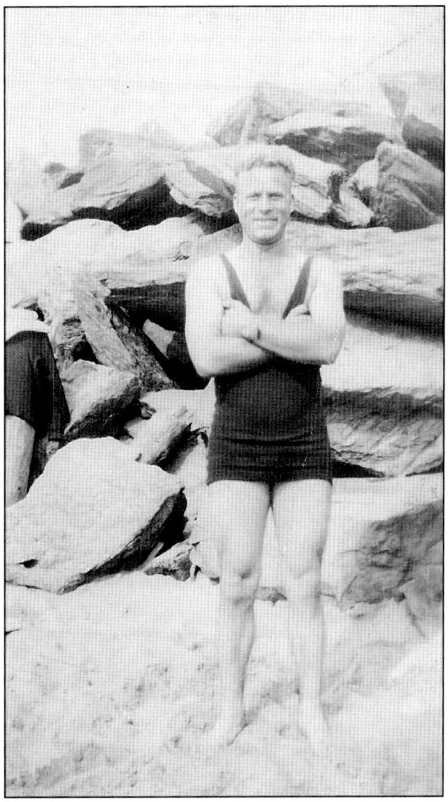

AN UNKNOWN LIFE GUARD, CLIFFWOOD, C. 1933.

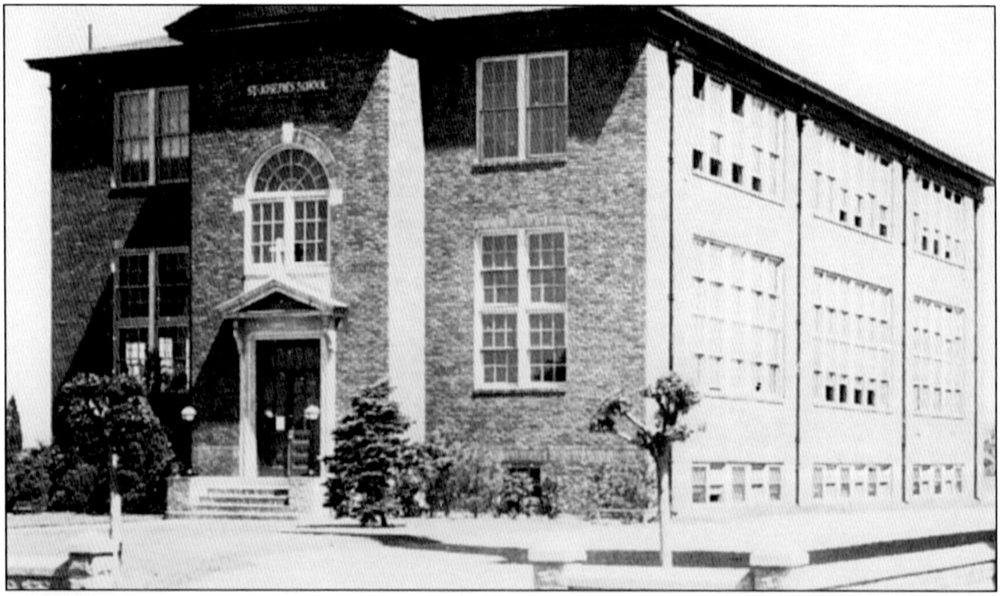

ST. JOSEPH'S SCHOOL. June of 1923 saw the arrival of Reverend Joseph A. Linnane, who was transferred from Tom River, New Jersey. Father Linnane immediately secured permission from the Trenton Diocese to construct a new school building to replace the old one, which was severely overcrowded. The new school was completed at a cost of $75,000 and contained six classrooms and a large auditorium. In 1952 the school was doubled in size and when finished became the largest parochial school in the Trenton Diocese.

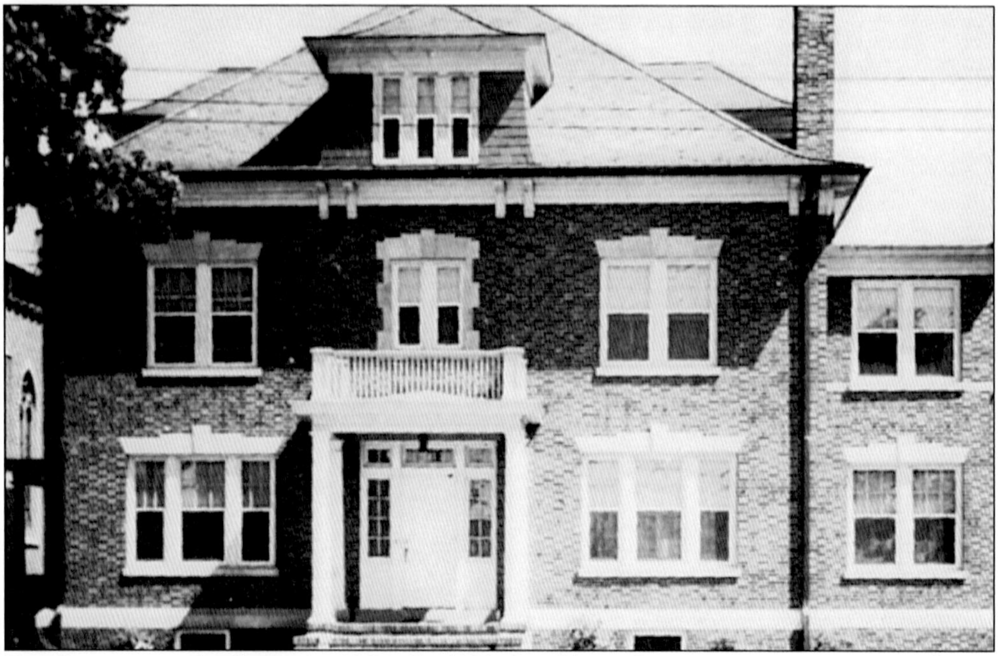

THE RECTORY OF ST. JOSEPH'S, 1931. By 1931 the old wooden rectory was in poor condition. Under the guiding hand of Father John P. Burke a new brick rectory was built. This structure was designed by Frederick. J. Schwarz of New York, and the builder was John Wester of Metuchen, New Jersey. On November 8, 1931, the $40,000 rectory was officially dedicated.

MONSIGNOR JOHN P. BURKE. Father Burke served as assistant pastor at St. Joseph's in 1913–1914. In 1929 Father Burke returned and within a few years had paid the entire debt off on the convent, had all the church paintings and sculptures cleaned, and had a new lighting system installed in the sanctuary. Prior to being ordained in 1908, Reverend John P. Burke was New York Giants pitcher John P. Burke, who in 1902 batted .159 during his 13-game streak with that team. In 1946 John P. Burke was promoted to Monsignor Burke. He passed away just four years later in Jersey City.

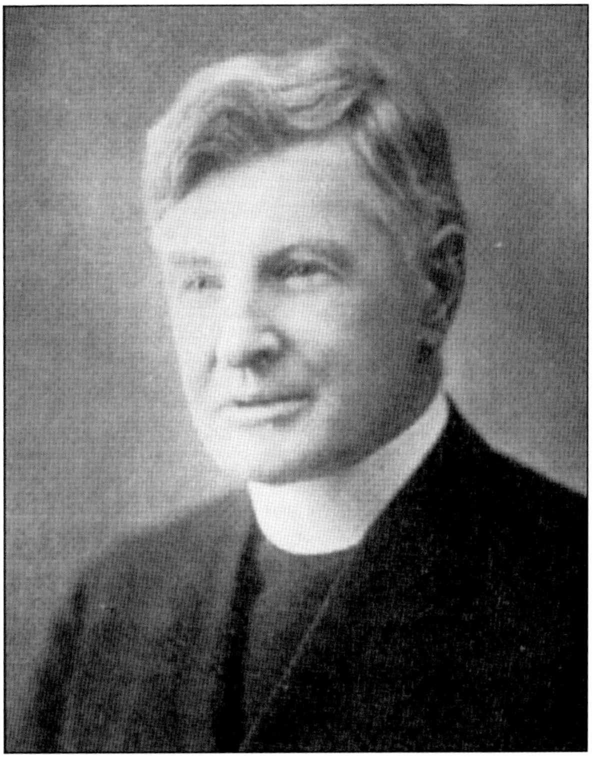

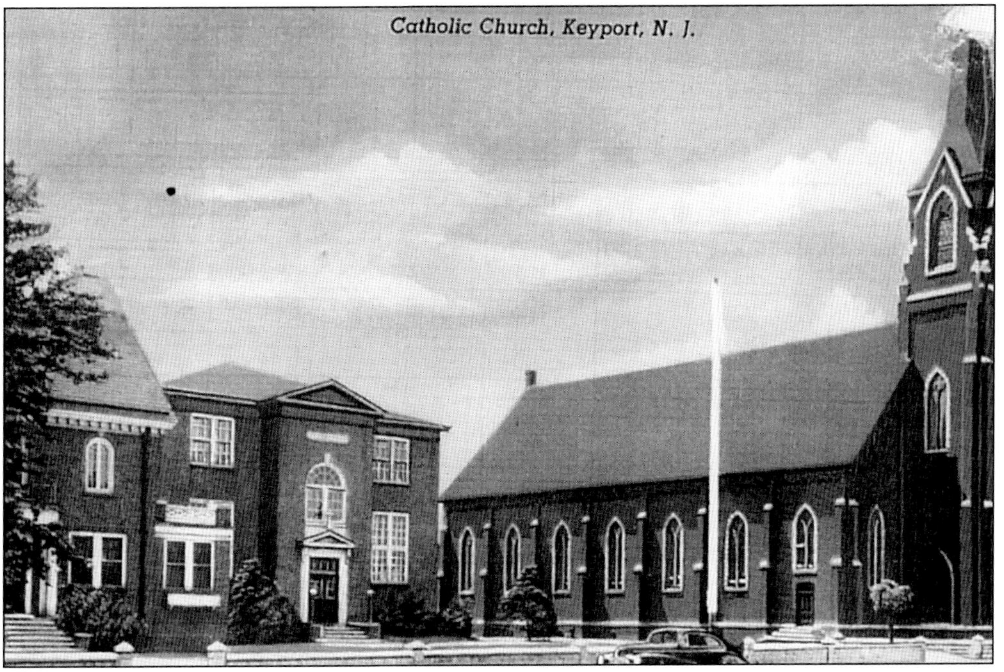

ST. JOSEPH'S RECTORY, SCHOOL, AND CHURCH. Even in this postcard view, the church and its surroundings appear beautifully maintained. In 1972 the 1879 Gothic church was declared "structurally unsafe" and was demolished soon after. This church was once one of the most impressive houses of worship in Monmouth County.

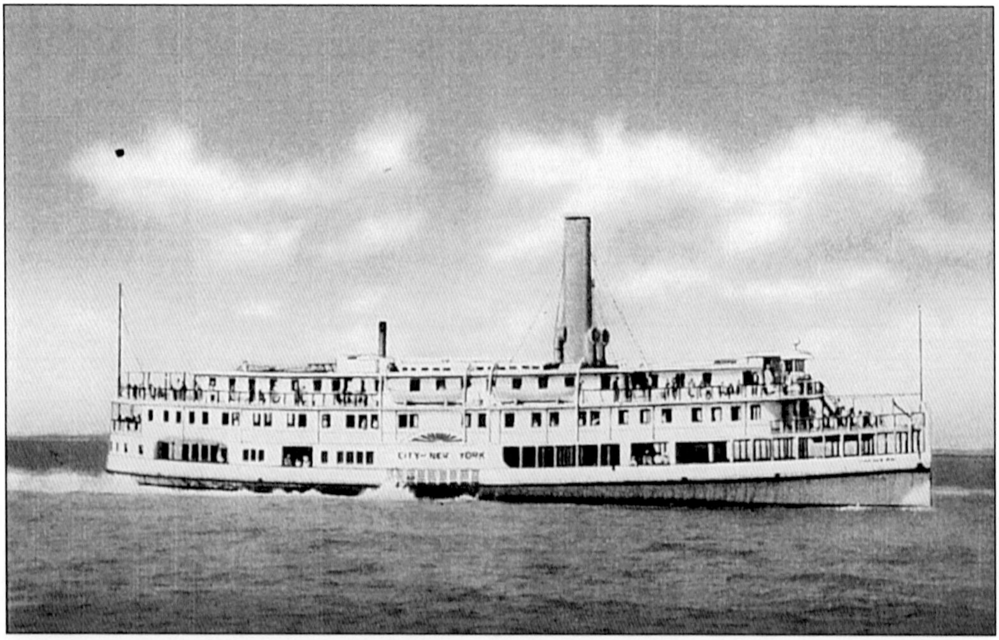

THE STEAMER CITY OF NEW YORK. Built as the *Talbot* sometime before 1920, this boat was purchased by Henry Gehlaus in 1937 and renamed the *City of New York*. The 75¢ ride was cheap enough; however, the old boat was a little top heavy and made for some stomach-turning trips on rough days. In 1950 the ship, along with several others, was torn from her mooring at the wharf and grounded at the foot of Broadway. She was scrapped soon after, ending her long and proud career.

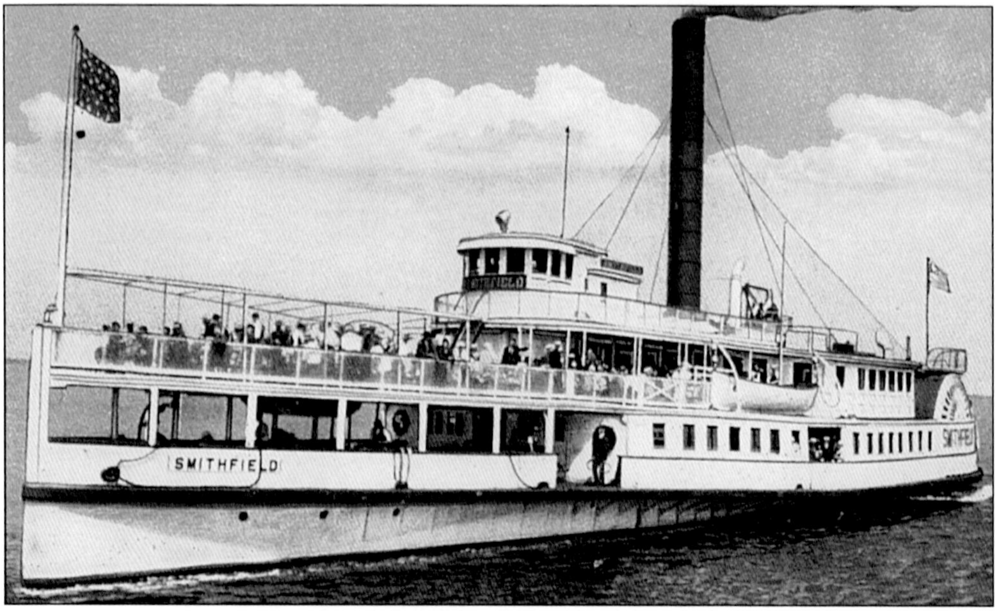

THE STEAMER SMITHFIELD. The *Smithfield* was built in 1901 and was originally named the *Hampton*. Although she did not see service in Keyport, she moored at the steamboat wharf during winters. This fine old ship was grounded after the 1947–1948 hurricane and was subsequently sold for scrap to Charlie Patterson of Keyport.

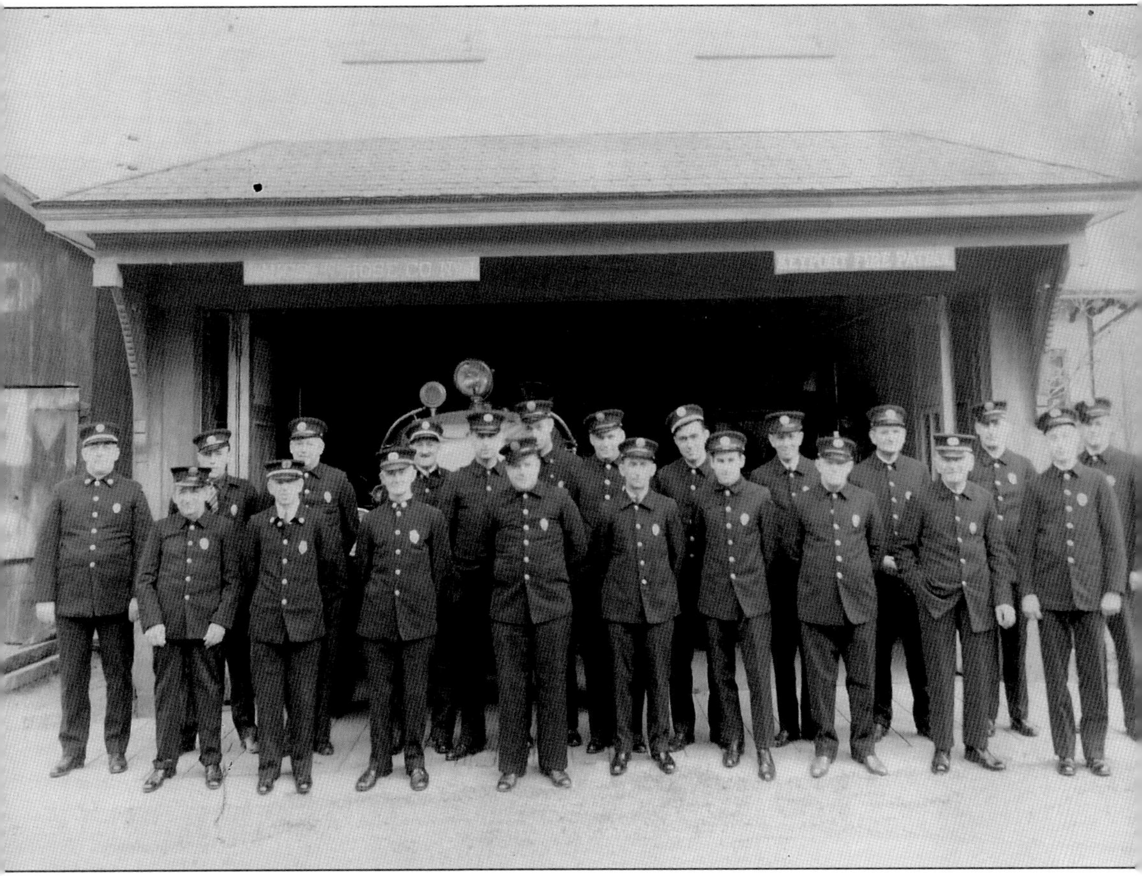

The Lincoln Hose Co., c. 1940. Proudly posing in front of the Waverly Street Hose House are the members of this unit prior to World War II. In the background is the 1920 Bulldog Mack of the Linc's and the old Chevy patrol wagon of the Fire Patrol. The two companies shared quarters until 1952, when the Hose Co. moved around the corner into the former Smith Lumber Co. showrooms.

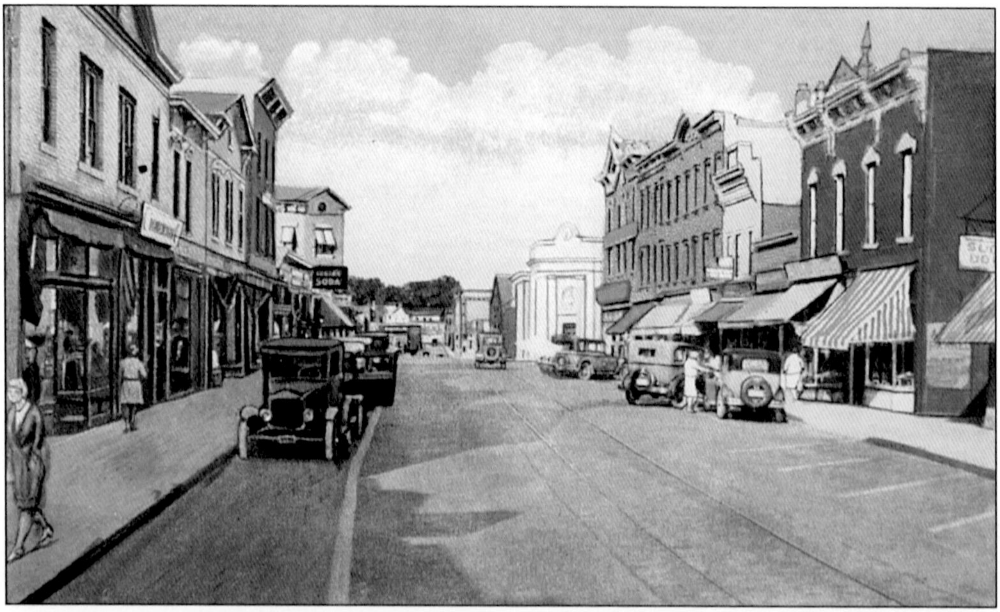

FRONT STREET, C. 1935. This postcard has almost cartoon-like characteristics about it. Although the artist took the time to paint over the telephone poles and utility wires, the old trolley tracks remain in the center of Front Street. To the left is the Bogardus Building, which had yet to be occupied by J.J. Newberrys, its longtime tenant. Newberrys five and dime remained here from 1939 to 1996 and was a staple of Keyport's business district.

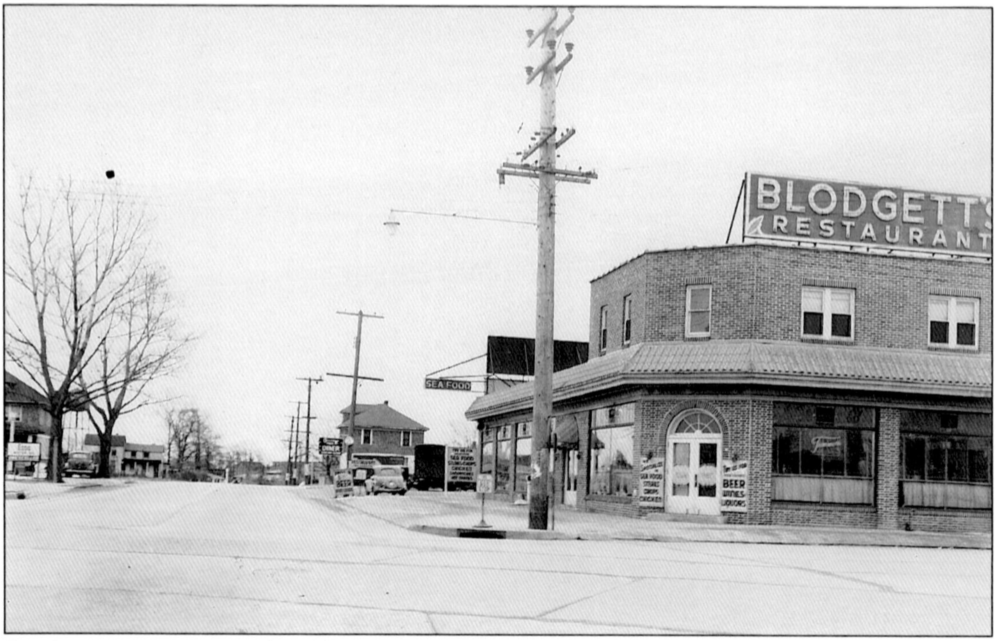

SIX CORNERS, C. 1937. The old Shore Highway was deserted this day, but soon summer "shore" seekers would pack Route 35 for miles and miles waiting to get their towels on the sand. In the days before the majestic Garden State Parkway this was the way to go .To the right is Blodgett's Restaurant, which was located in the Rollo Bus Terminal Building during the 1930s. In 1987 the structure was razed and a large automotive service center was built in its place.

FATHER HENRY FELL, ST. MARY'S EPISCOPAL CHURCH.

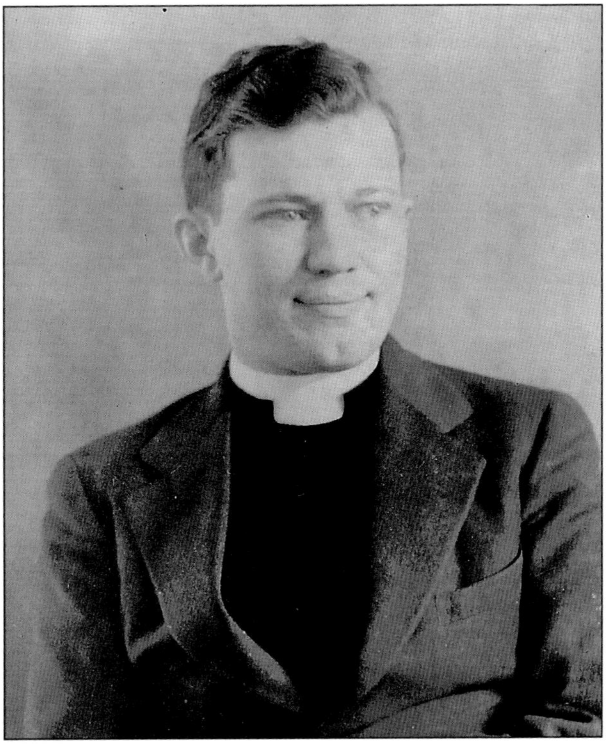

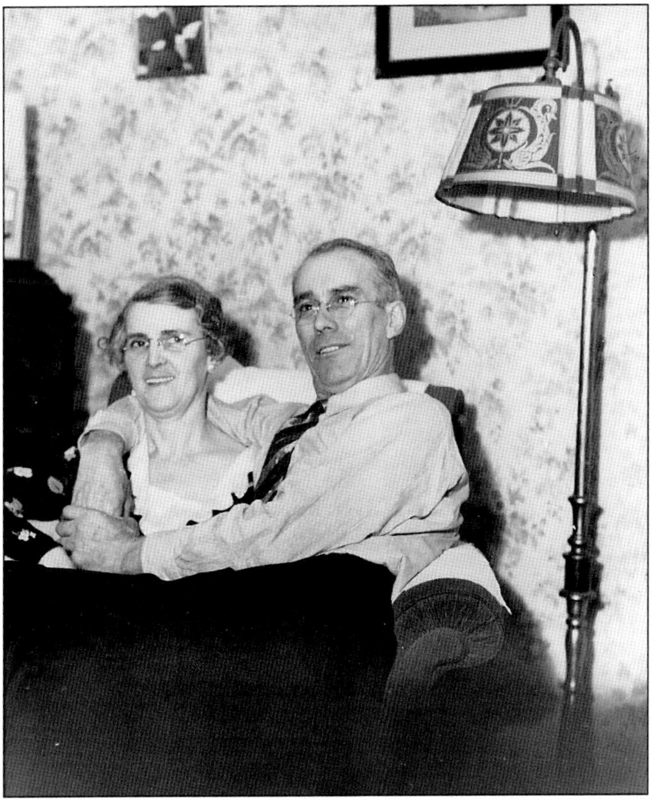

MR. AND MRS. J. LEWIS. James Lewis was an avid Keyport photographer and many of the images in this book were taken by him. He resided on Third Street, near the Methodist church. It is due in part to people like Mr. Lewis that history books may be written.

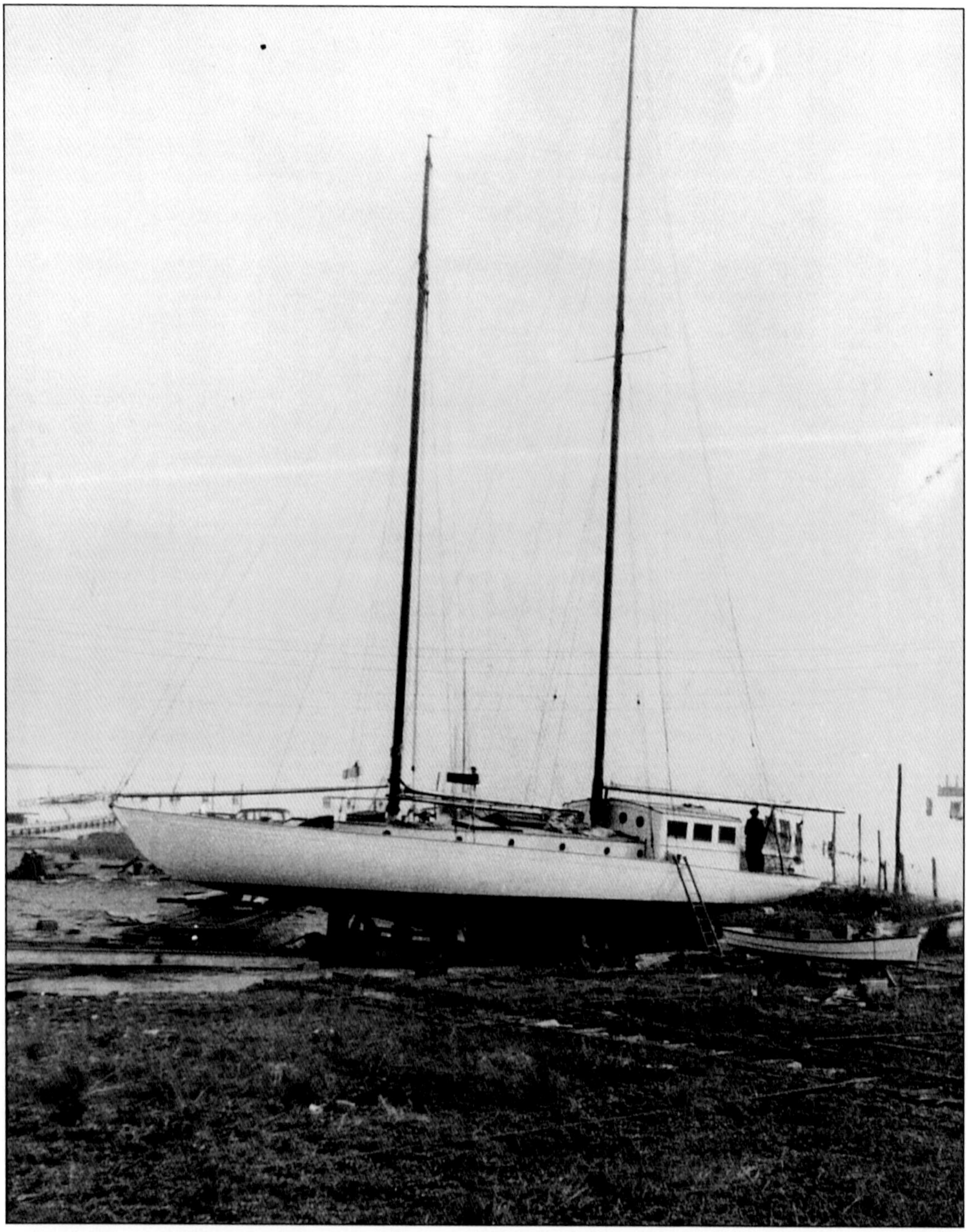

A SAILBOAT AT THE MARINE RAILWAY. Beginning in the 1860s, the first boat builders came to the foot of Myrtle Avenue and began constructing sea-worthy vessels. Benjamin Terry's yard began during the Civil War, and was later taken over by his sons. By the 20th century, Humphrey's Boat Works was established, turning out expensive yachts like the one pictured, none of which were less than 45 feet in length. Humphrey's yard was closed during the Depression, and in 1937 a former Humphrey's worker named Hans Pedersen returned to Prospect Street to begin the fine art of boat building once again.

Five

1941–1950

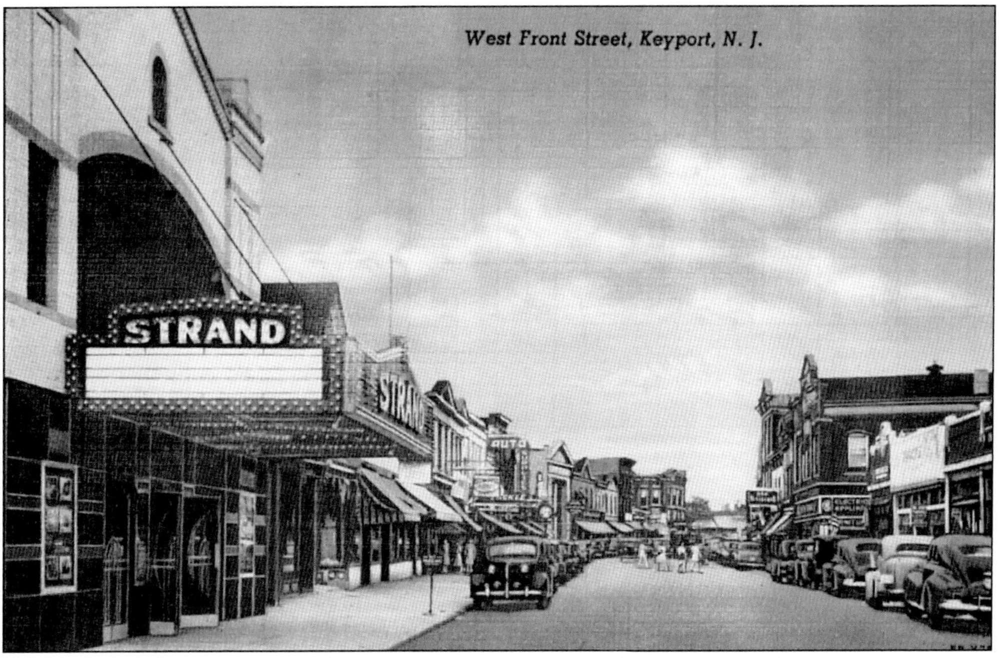

WEST FRONT STREET, C. 1943. It's been a busy day of shopping along Front Street. First it was off to the *Weekly* to renew your subscription, then to Newberrys for a hot dog and some odds and ends. From there it was time to stop into Pragers for that new watch for your wife's Christmas gift. Finally, you realize that it's time to hurry down to the Strand as that new movie with Ingrid Bergman and Humphrey Bogart is out, some love story called *Casablanca.* All this within a few hundred yards. Those were the days before shopping malls!

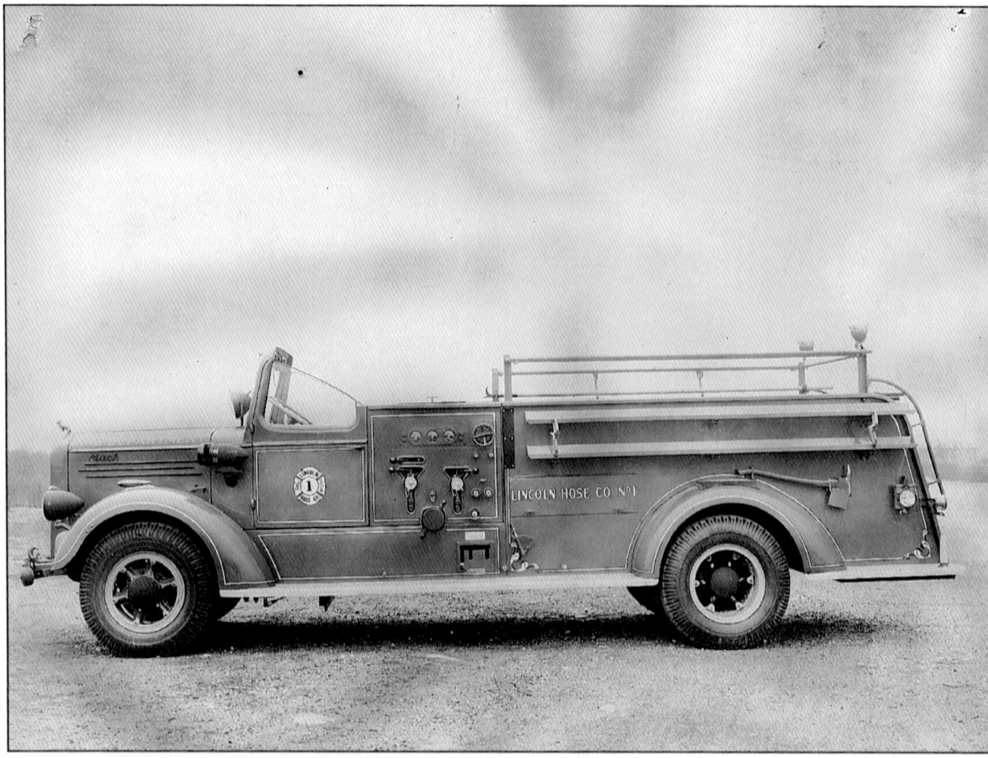

THE NEW LINCOLN HOSE ENGINE. The new engine of East Keyport's Lincoln Hose Co. had just rolled off the floor of the Mack Truck plant in Allentown, PA, when this picture was taken. The semi-open cab pumper was a model 80 and was capable of pumping over 750 gallons of water a minute. The engine was in service until 1968, when it was replaced with a new Mack engine.

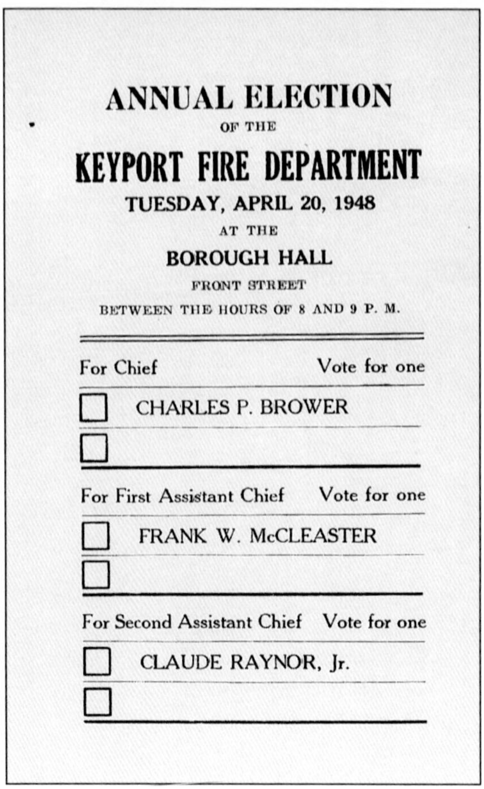

ANNUAL ELECTION
OF THE
KEYPORT FIRE DEPARTMENT
TUESDAY, APRIL 20, 1948
AT THE
BOROUGH HALL
FRONT STREET
BETWEEN THE HOURS OF 8 AND 9 P. M.

For Chief — Vote for one
☐ CHARLES P. BROWER
☐

For First Assistant Chief — Vote for one
☐ FRANK W. McCLEASTER
☐

For Second Assistant Chief — Vote for one
☐ CLAUDE RAYNOR, Jr.
☐

A FIRE DEPARTMENT BALLOT. The big election night was here. Who would win and would there be any write-in votes to shake up the night? Not this year, as Chief Brower won, as had Frank McCleaster in 1949 and Claude Raynor Jr. in 1950. In 1970 the position of third assistant chief was added to better supervise the department's growing activities.

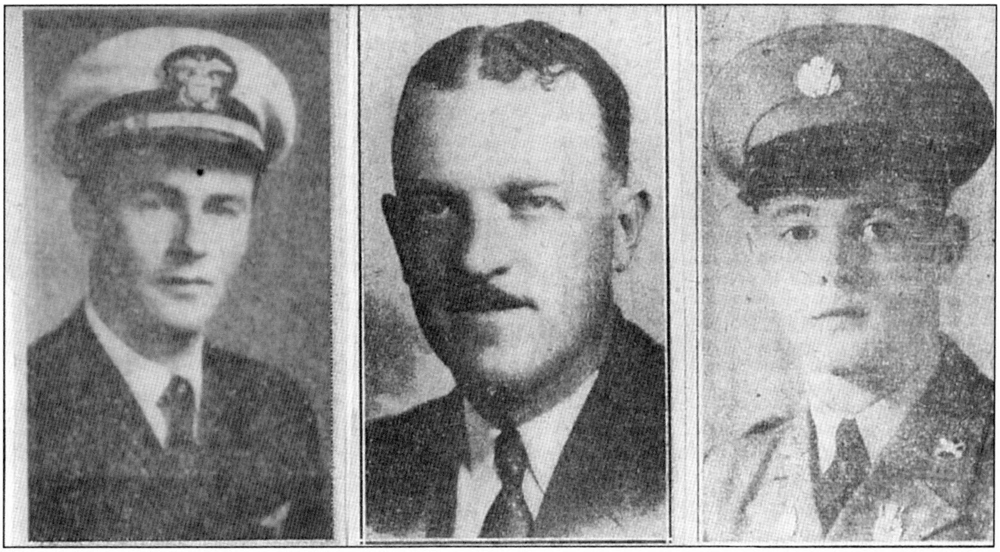

KEYPORT HEROES. Nearly 600 men and women from Keyport served in the United States Armed forces between 1941 and 1945. Of those 600, 15 brave men gave their lives in defense of our country. From left to right are as follows: (above) Lt. James R. Costello, First Lieut. Kenneth C. Demlin, and Second Lieut. Benjamin D. Kelly; (below) David Leroy Schanck, Joseph J. Morley, and SSGT John P. VanRixoort. Also killed in action were Jerome Carney, Harold Donald, Samuel Halsey, Paul P. Konish, J. Archibald MacEwan Jr., Jack A. Post, Edward O. Russel, Reynhold Nicholson, and Alvin H. Stoney.

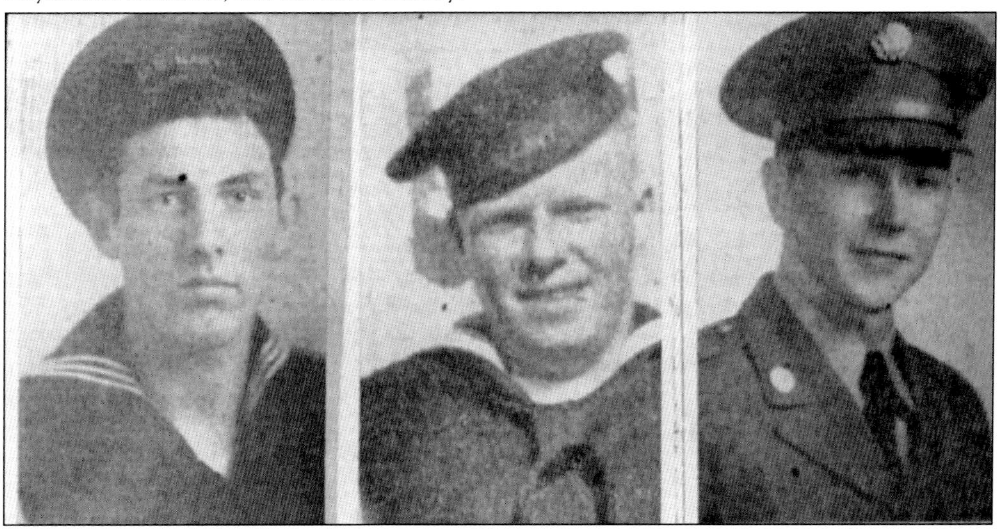

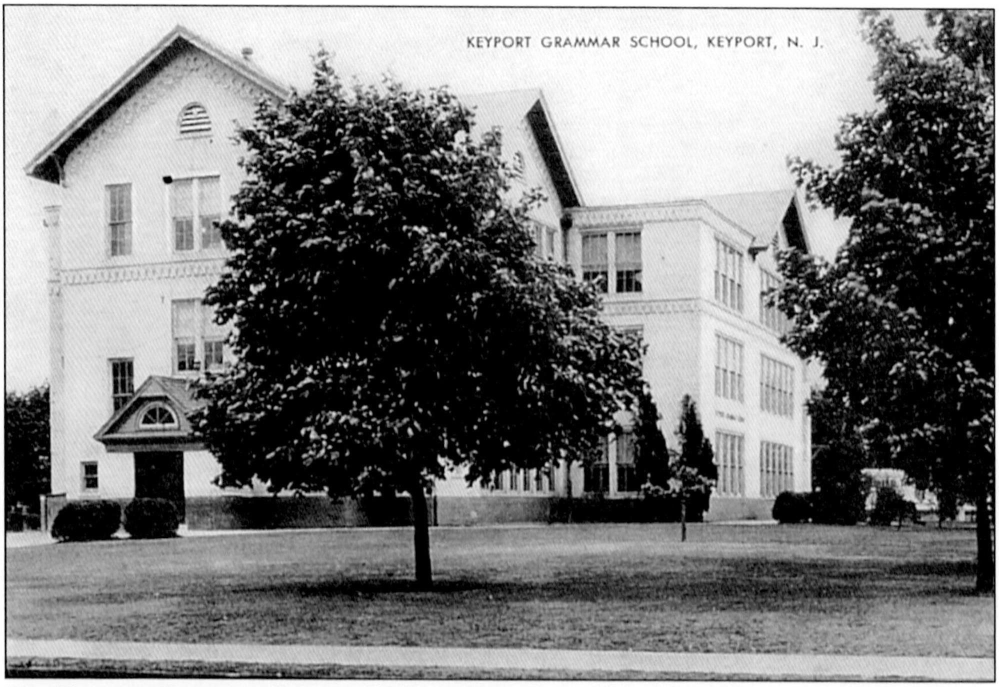

THE KEYPORT GRAMMAR SCHOOL. Still standing as proudly as the day it was built, the ancient grammar school was still holding its own when this photograph was taken. Stripped of its towers and remodeled at least three times, the old school was still recognizable from photographs dating to the 1880s. It stood from 1871 until 1967, when it was closed and soon leveled by the local wrecking ball.

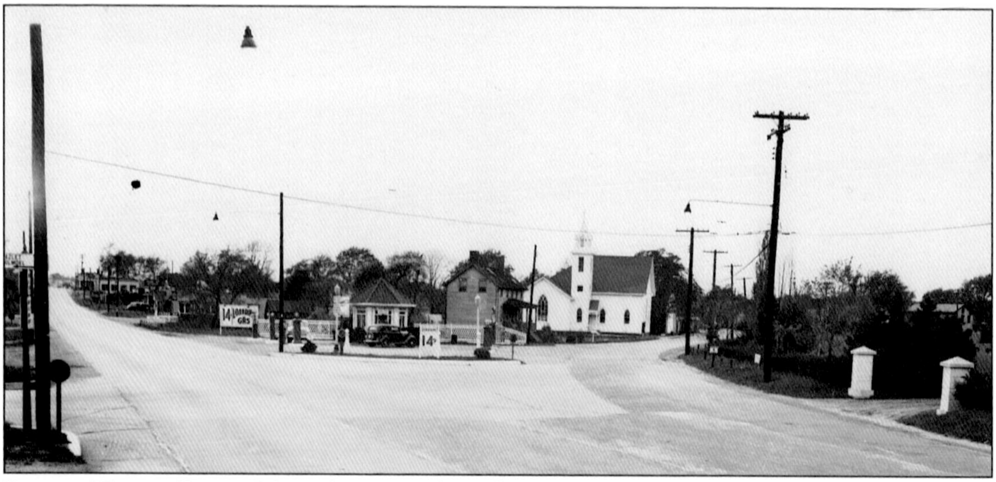

ROUTE 35 AND SOUTH MAIN STREET. The village of Mechanicsville actually lies in an area that extends into Hazlet Township. The remnants of this once-bustling village may be seen here in this image from the 1930s. The classic octagonal service station of the Lorraine Gas Co. was selling fuel for 14¢ a gallon, while a 19th-century home sits biding its time next to St. John's Methodist Church. By 1970, the gas station (and its predecessor) and the house had been removed for the construction of the Holmdel Road jughandle, while the church had burned in the mid-1960s. The site is now part of the Remsen Dodge car dealership. The concrete gates to the right led into Rosemont Cemetery.

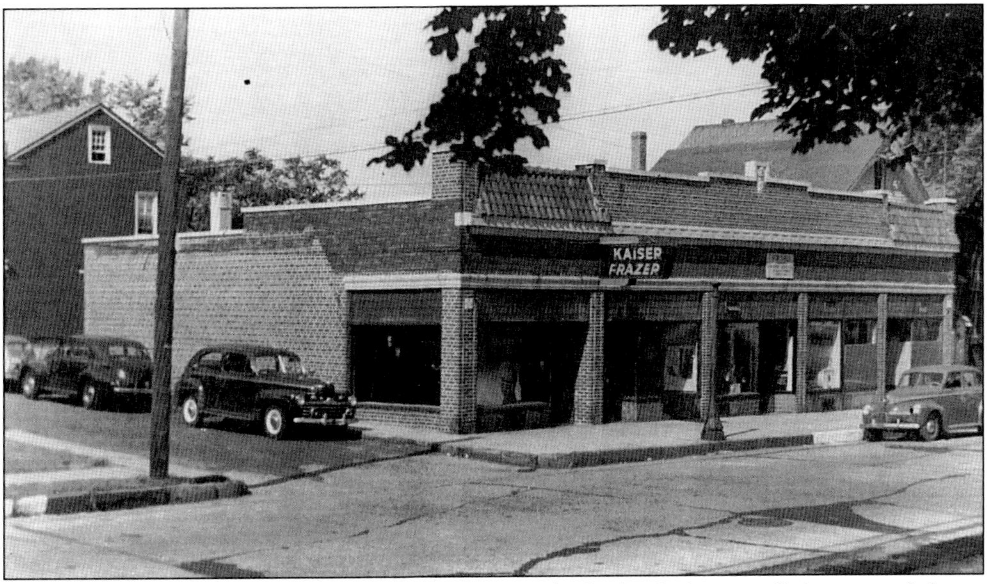

STRAUB MOTORS INC., 1949. Charles Straub Sr. and Charles Jr. began selling automobiles at the corner of Broad and Third Streets in 1947. By the time this photo was taken the showroom had been sold and Straub Motors was on its way to a larger home on State Route 35. This building was subsequently built on the lot where the first town hall and fire station had been built in 1878.

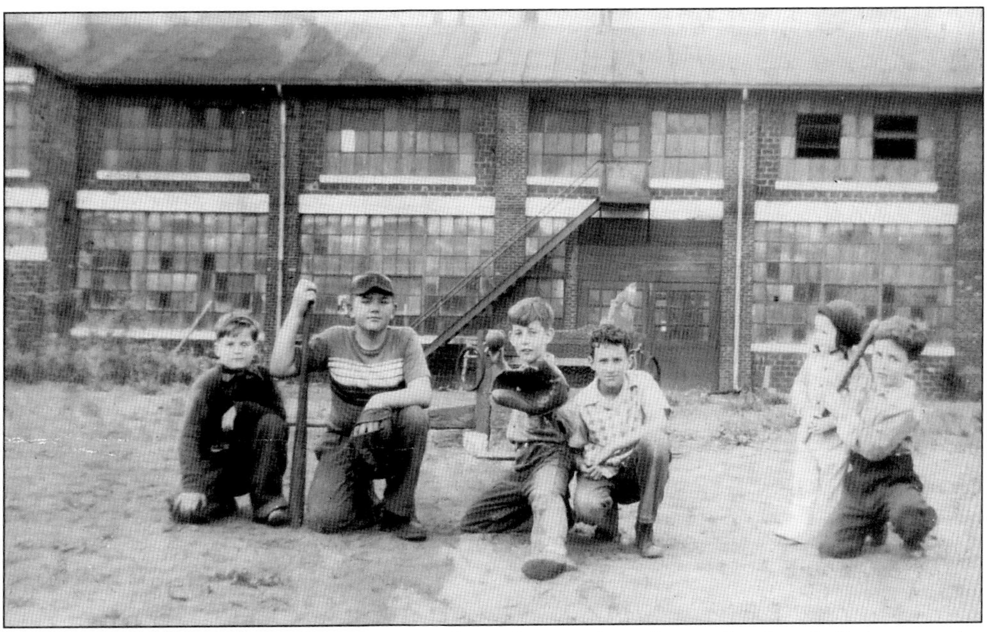

LOCKPORT BOYS, C. 1950. There was simply no better place for sandlot baseball than on the grounds of the former Aeromarine property. From left to right are John Stryker, Kent Davidson, Jimmy Shea, Frank Currier, Pete Rumsey, and Billy Mordeci. In later years, Kent Davidson served as captain of the first aid squad, Pete Rumsey was elected fire chief in 1992, and Frank "Dick" Currier served on the borough council for many years while having one of the area's most successful general contracting business.

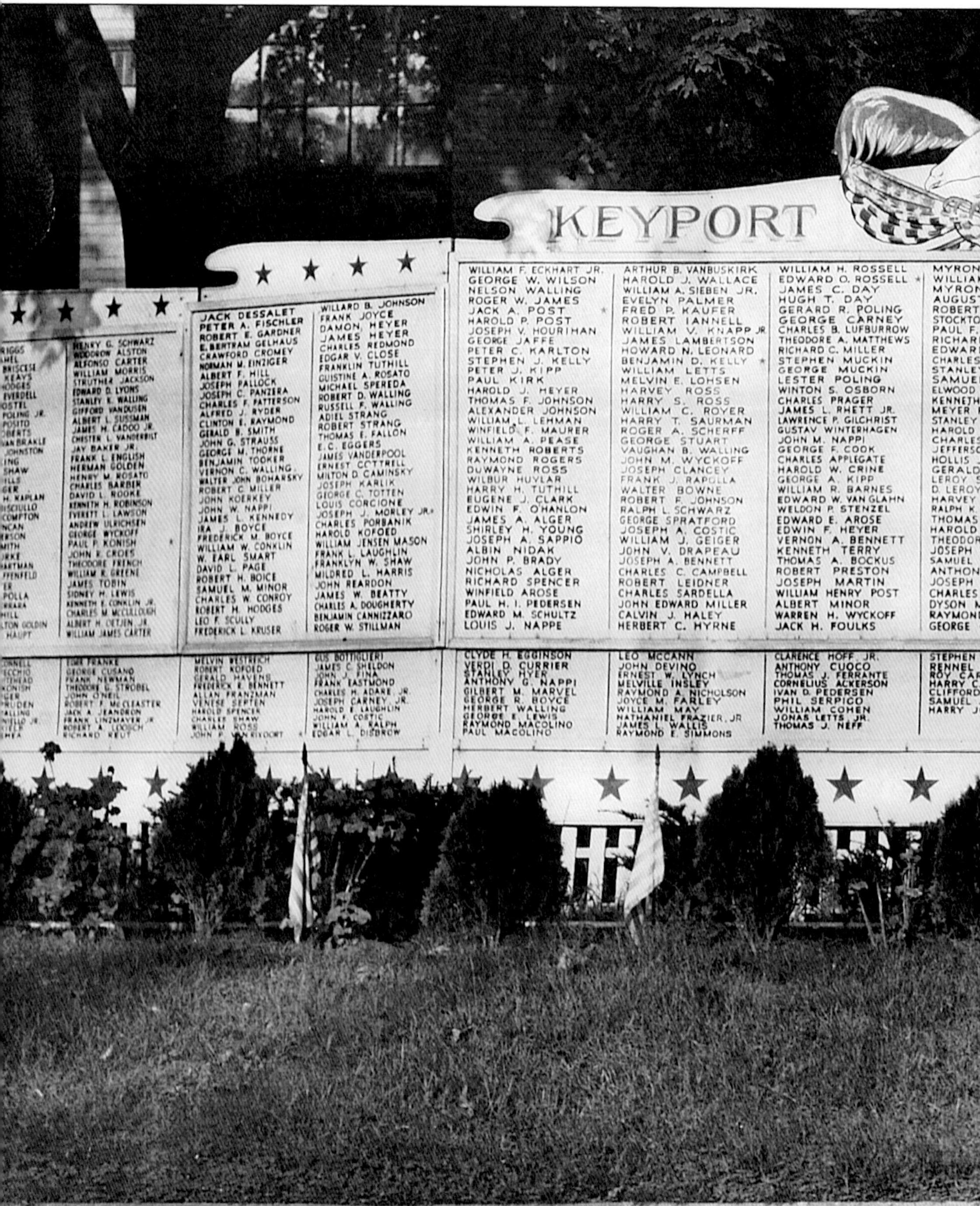

THE KEYPORT HONOR ROLL, 1945. The borough of Keyport had one of the highest percentages of enlisted personnel for a town its size during World War II. This large wooden sign was painted by Mel Hopla and erected on the grounds of the public library. The sign grew each year and by

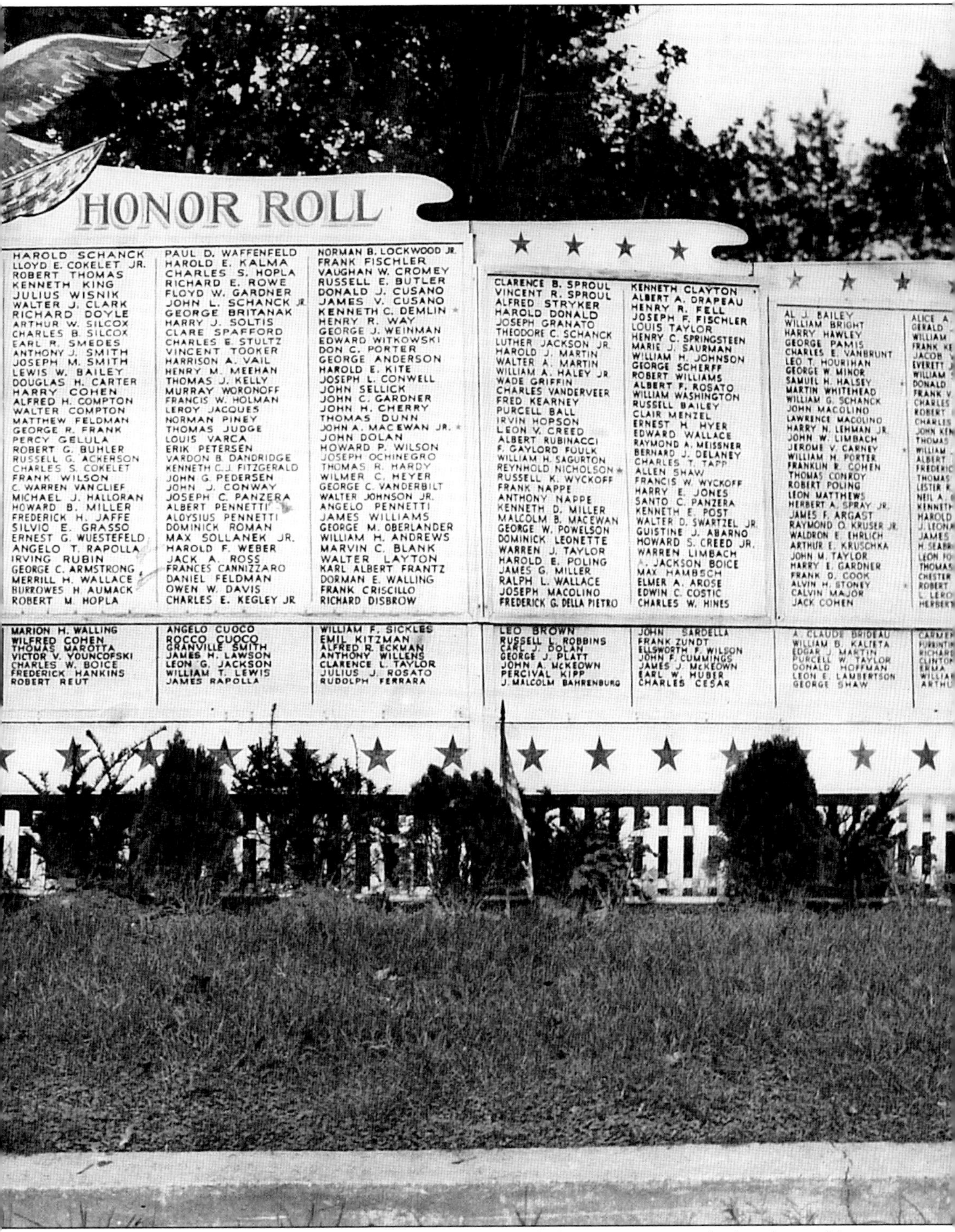

1945 it had doubled in size. The name of each man killed in action is marked with a gold star. There are nearly 600 men and women listed on this sign.

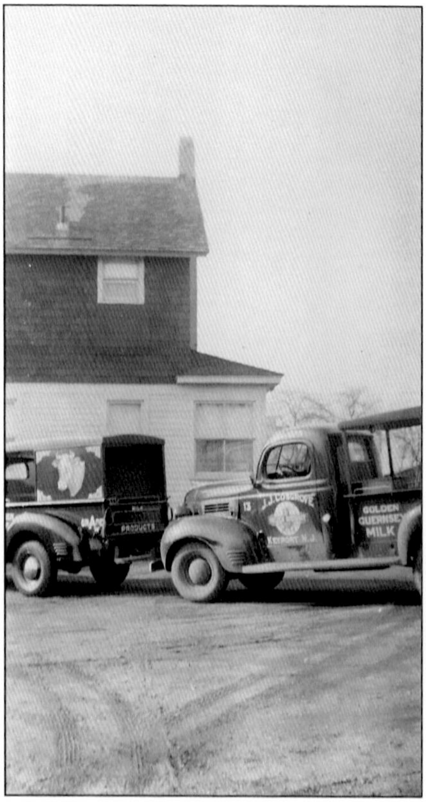

The J.J. Cosgrove Dairy. These two Dodge delivery trucks are waiting for a fresh supply of that delicious "Golden Guernsey" milk. John Cosgrove's dairy on Third Street was in operation for much of the mid-20th century, until a time when local dairies slowly disappeared from the American scene.

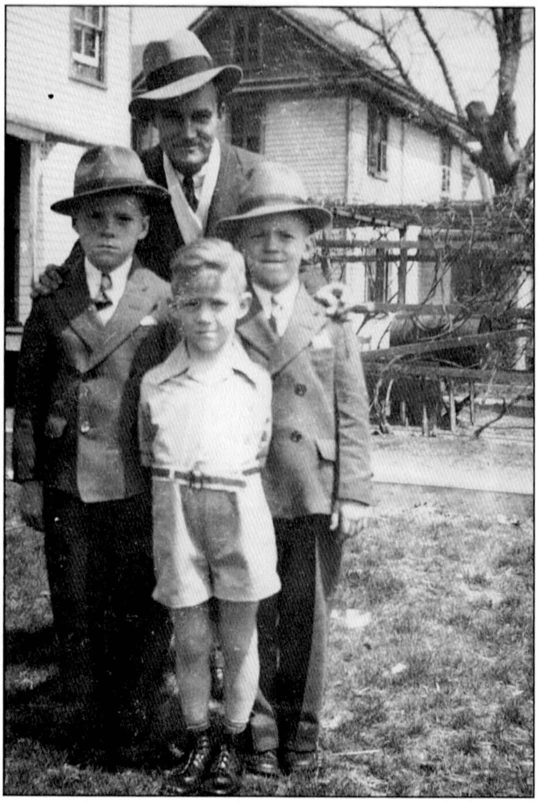

My Three Sons, c. 1947. Here, Melvin "Mel" Poling poses with his sons Robert (tallest), Frank, and James (the little one) in the rear of their First Street home. For many years Mel operated a Richfield service station at the point of Second Street near First. All three sons raised their families in Keyport, served as members of the Lincoln Hose Co., and were very active in their community.

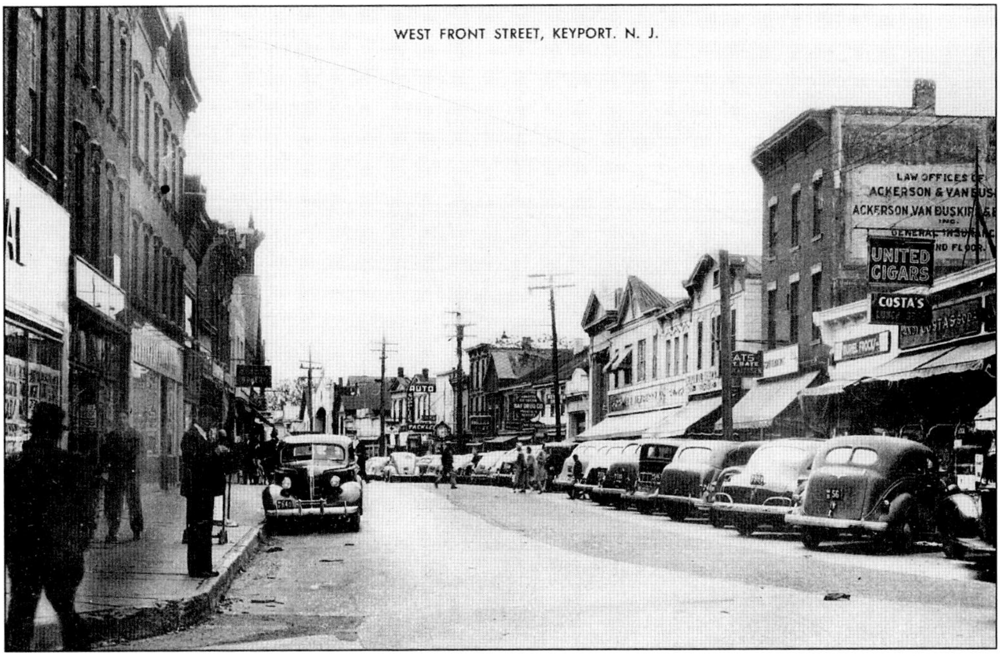

FRONT STREET, C. 1949. There were no parking spots to be found on this day as shoppers crowded the stores looking for bargains. Keyport's business district had changed little in the last 100 years, but soon older buildings would be removed and others would be altered, changing the look of the heart of Keyport.

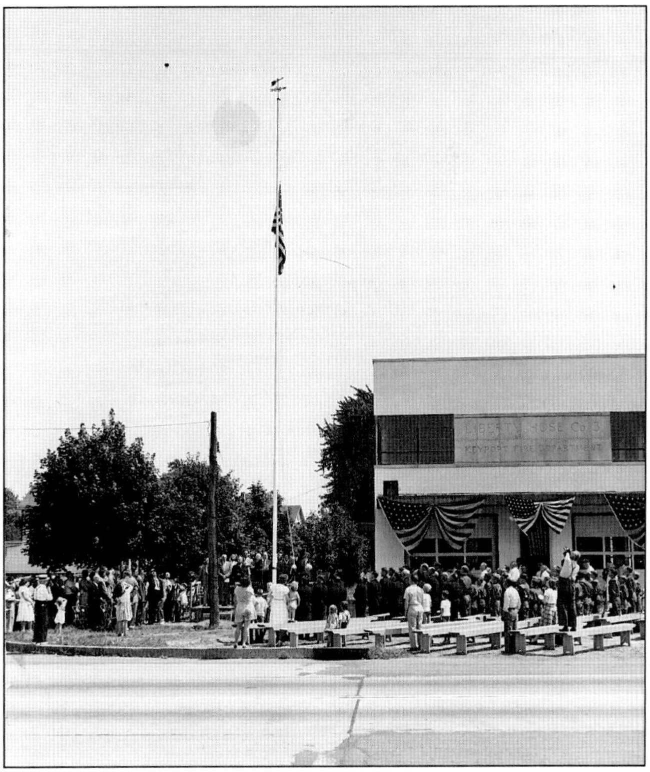

THE DEDICATION OF THE NEW LIBERTY HOSE FIREHOUSE, 1948. The day that was long overdue, moving day, finally came. The old firehouse, just around the corner, was sold and this new concrete station was built at the corner of NJ Route 36 and Atlantic Street. The new station contained a modern kitchen, double apparatus room, and a spacious upstairs hall. Just 40 years later, in 1988, this firehouse was sold and a new one built on the adjoining lot.

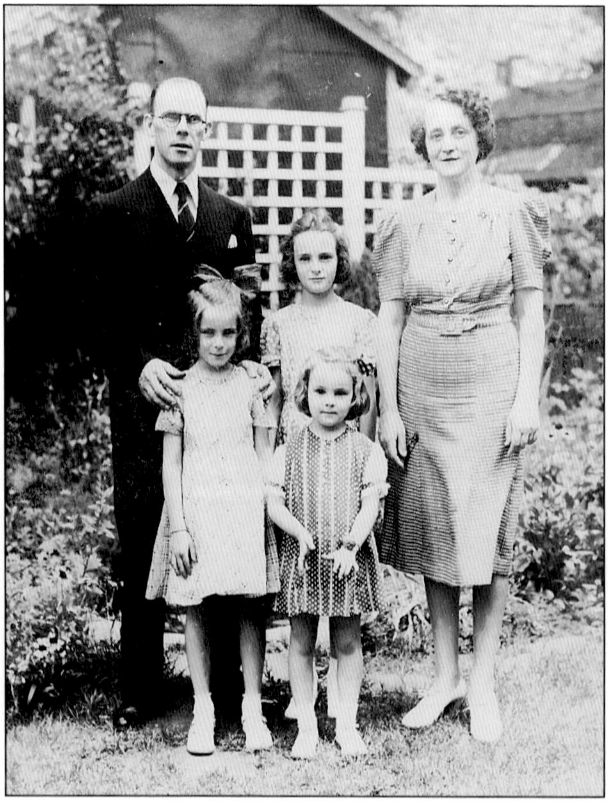

THE MUIR FAMILY, OSBORN STREET, C. 1946

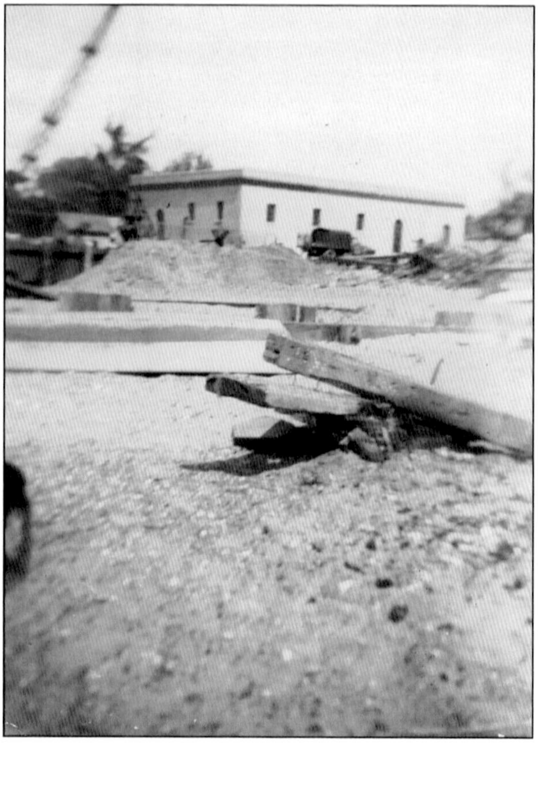

THE BEACH NEAR MYRTLE AVENUE. In the background is the old waterworks which stood from 1923 to 1985. This picture was taken as the new bulkhead was being erected for the protection of the waterworks, around 1950.

Six

1951–1960

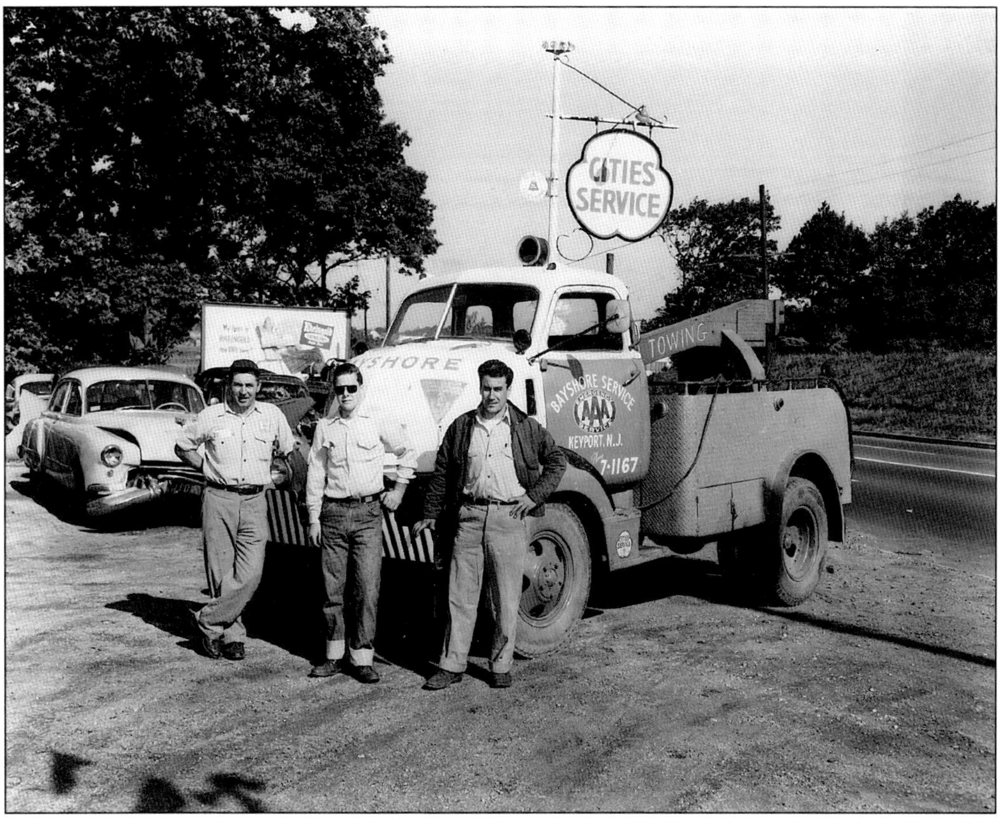

Bayshore Service, August 12, 1954. Located on State Highway 35, near the Matawan Township border, was this Cities Service gasoline station. It has been operated by the Falco family for over four decades. This classic photograph was found in the Dorn's Keyport Collection.

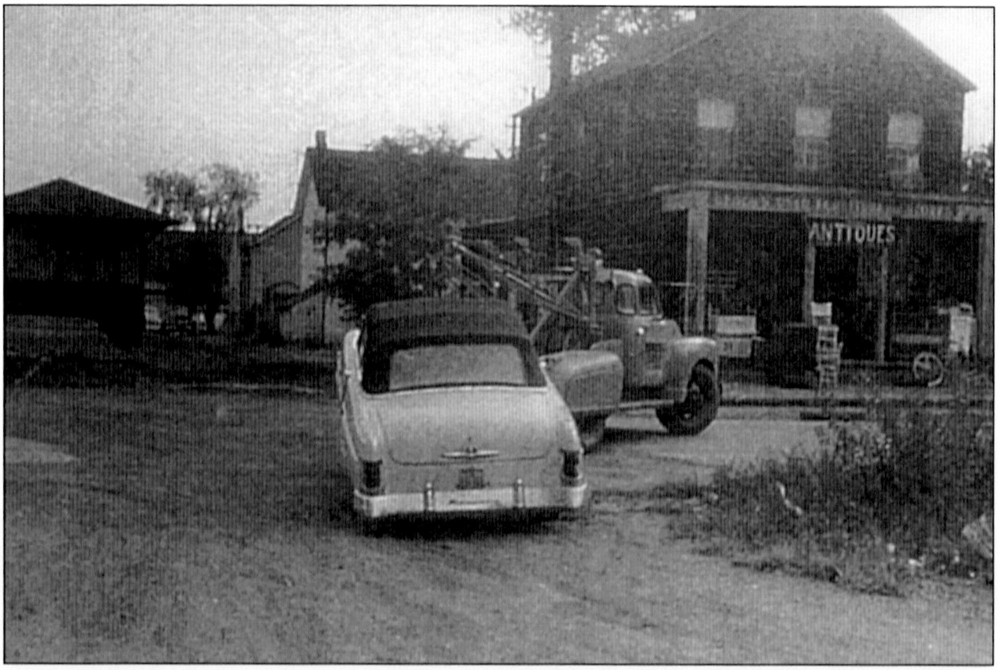

Sylvanus Lee's Store, 1957. Located at on the southwest corner of First and Waverly Streets was the store of Sylvanus and Benjamin Lee. The Lee brothers carried a full line of cigars and tobacco products and in its time the building also contained a fine pool hall. The two brothers opened the store *c.* 1870 and continued at that location into the first part of the 20th century. It was later operated by Roy Lambertson as a combination antique/junk store until the property was purchased by the Keyport Fire Patrol, who razed the century old building for a anticipated firehouse expansion in the 1960s.

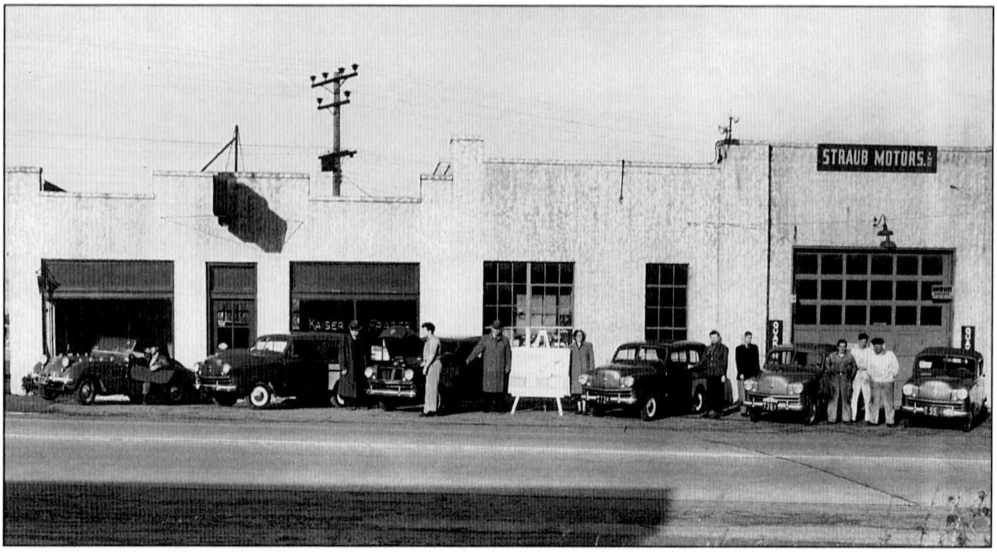

Straub Motors, c. 1951. Here is the new line of the new 1950 Crosleys. Straub had held the distributorship of the 4-cylinder Crosley since it was introduced in Monmouth County in 1946. From left to right are Robert Ferry, Charles Stryker, Mr. Straub, Charles F. Straub Jr., Nellie A. Rieth, Mary Hennessey, Jean Stadler, William Hill, Nelson Duncan, and George Hill.

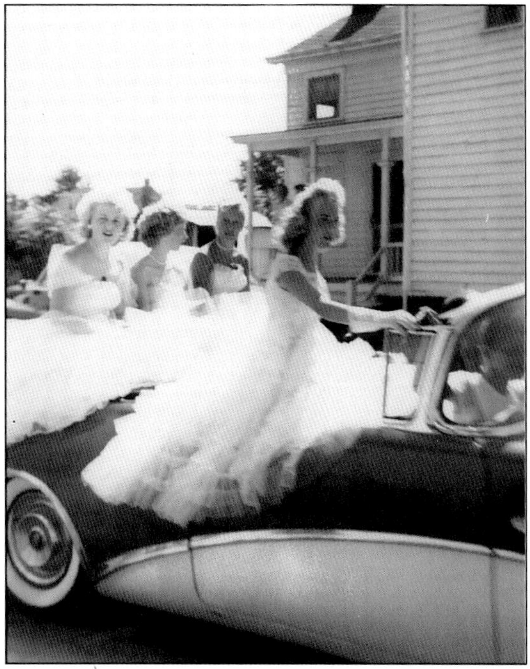

KEYPORT DAY, 1958. It was August of 1958 , Buddy Holly and Elvis Presley were topping the charts, fins were in, and Keyport Day had come again. These four unidentified women were Miss Keyport and the runners-up. They are seen cruising in a 1956 Buick, rounding the corner of Fulton and First Streets.

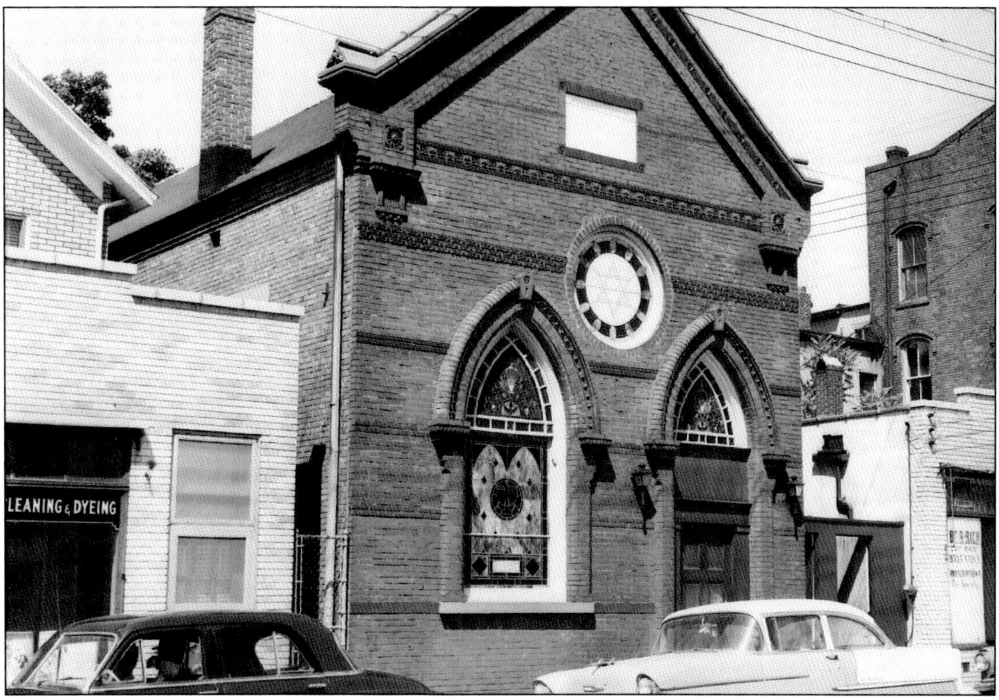

THE UNITED HEBREW CONGREGATION, 1958. The former People's National Bank was purchased by Keyport's United Hebrew Congregation sometime in 1924. The first Jewish settlers arrived in Keyport in 1860, including in their number men such as Adam Salz, A. Block, and Moritz Naftal. By 1924, over 45 families worshiped here and celebrated the ancient Jewish holidays. The large Star of David that graced the pediment has been displayed at the Keyport Historical Society since the synagogue was sold in the early 1970s.

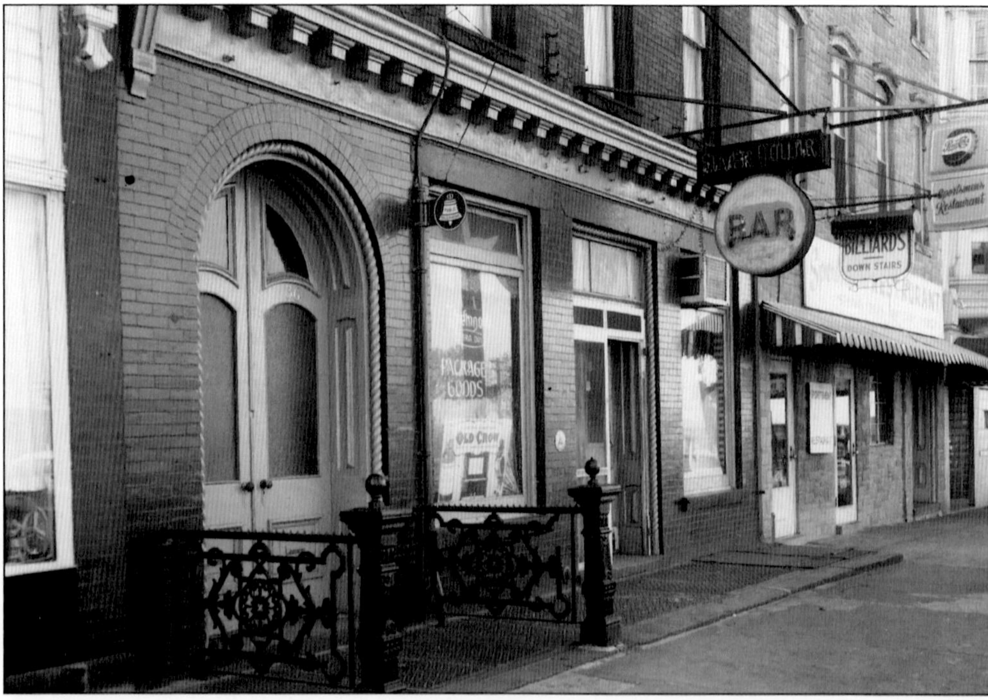

The Silver Dollar Bar. Located on Broad Street in the Maurer Building, this tavern was a busy local hangout for many years. Right next door was the Sportsmen Restaurant, operated by Willie Dillon. Next in line was the Monmouth Hotel and Lounge, and at the foot of Broad Street was the Bayside Tavern, operated by Tommy Wallace. The buildings all remain in 1998, and the Monmouth and the former Bayside (now the Passport) are still operated as local taverns.

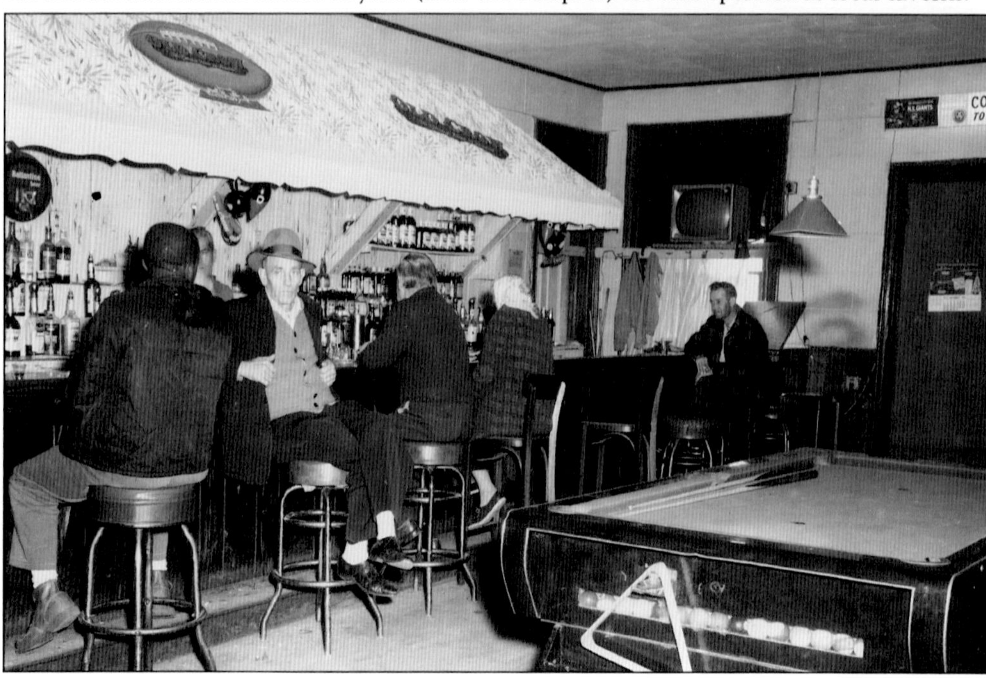

MR. SAMUEL JAMES EVANS, 1958. Mr. Evans was born in Berlin, Maryland, in 1865. He came to Keyport in 1881 to work on the bay as an oysterman. He later worked in Galbraith's Manufacturing Plant and retired in 1950, at the age of 85. When Mr. Evans was 90 years old he was hired as a night watchman at Keyport Cleaners (he never actually started work there, as the company felt he was to old, despite his insisting that he was not ready to retire). Mr. Evans is shown here two years before his death with his daughter Gladys at his family's home at 2 Spring Street.

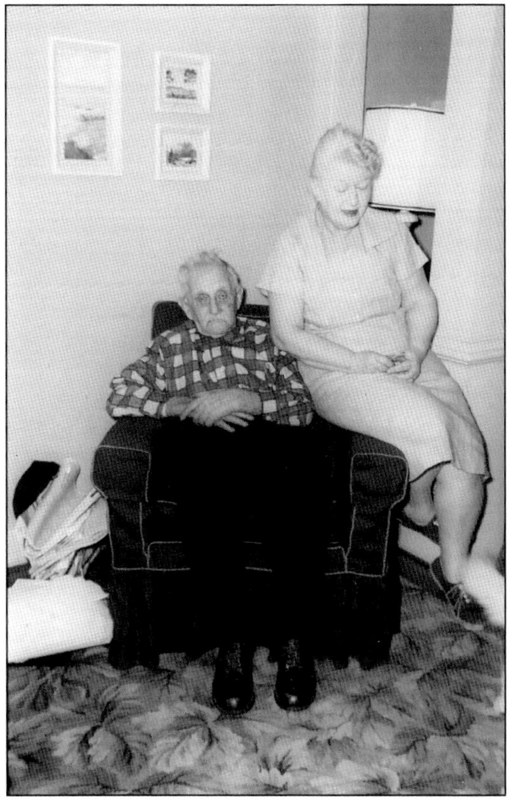

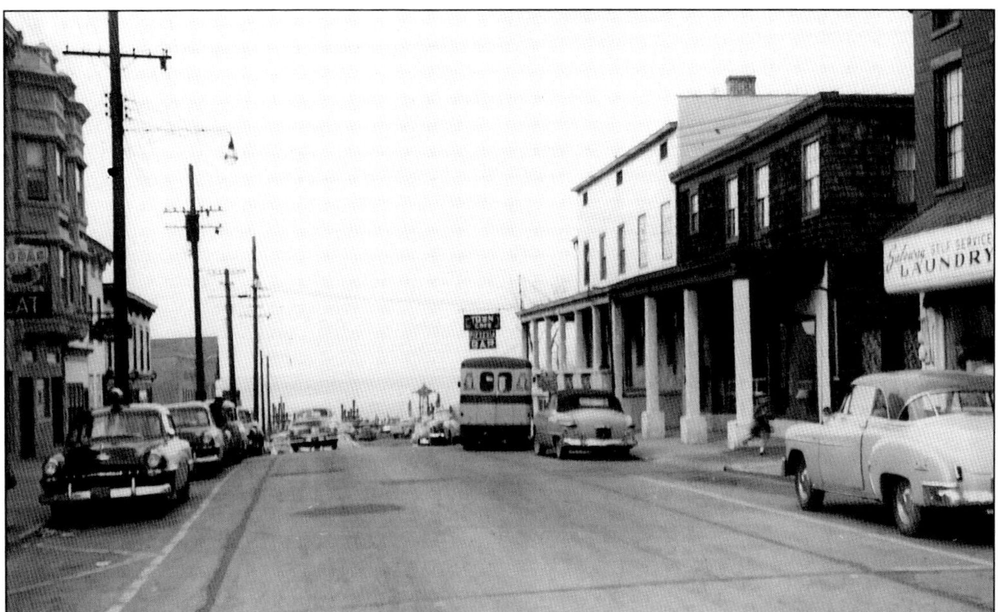

BROAD STREET, 1953. To the right is the old Raritan Inn, which, by the time this photo was taken, had seen better days. The brick structure in the foreground was built by David Warner c. 1860. To the left is one of Keyport's police cruisers in front of the old Broad Street headquarters. The police department moved into the new borough hall the next year.

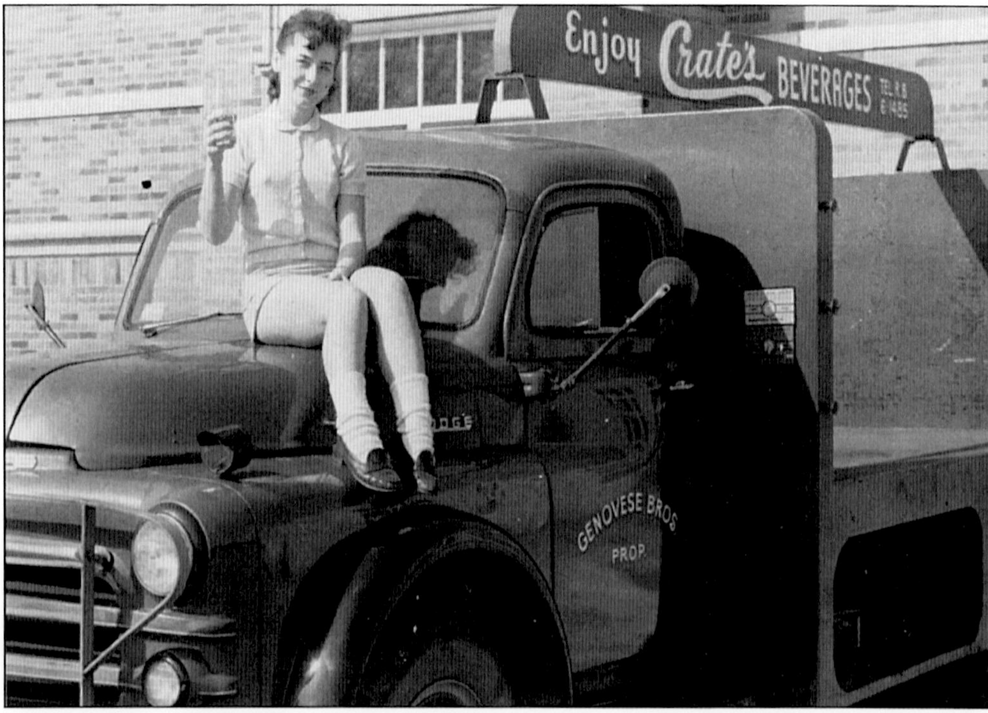

JOAN CARNEY, 1954. Ms. Carney posed for this Crate's Beverage advertisement, which appeared in the 1954 yearbook. She served as a cheerleader in high school and was known to be popular with all. In later years she married Vic Rhodes, longtime Keyport building inspector. Vic himself graduated in 1953 and was nicknamed "Cat." He was an active basketball player and king of the prom.

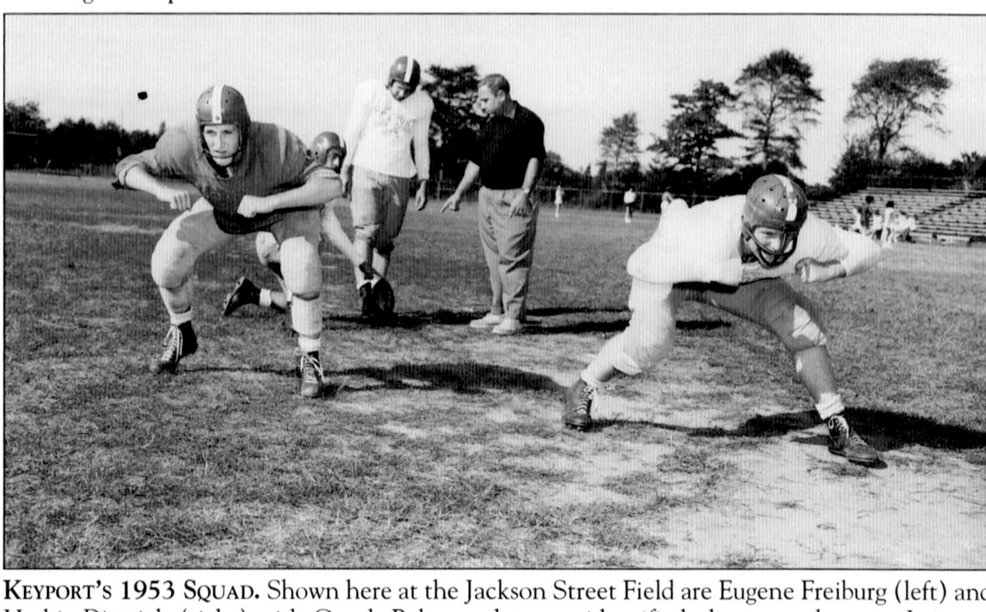

KEYPORT'S 1953 SQUAD. Shown here at the Jackson Street Field are Eugene Freiburg (left) and Herbie Dietrich (right) with Coach Baker and two unidentified players to the rear. It is not known how the Red Raiders fared that year, but in 1954 they ended the season with three wins, four losses, and two ties.

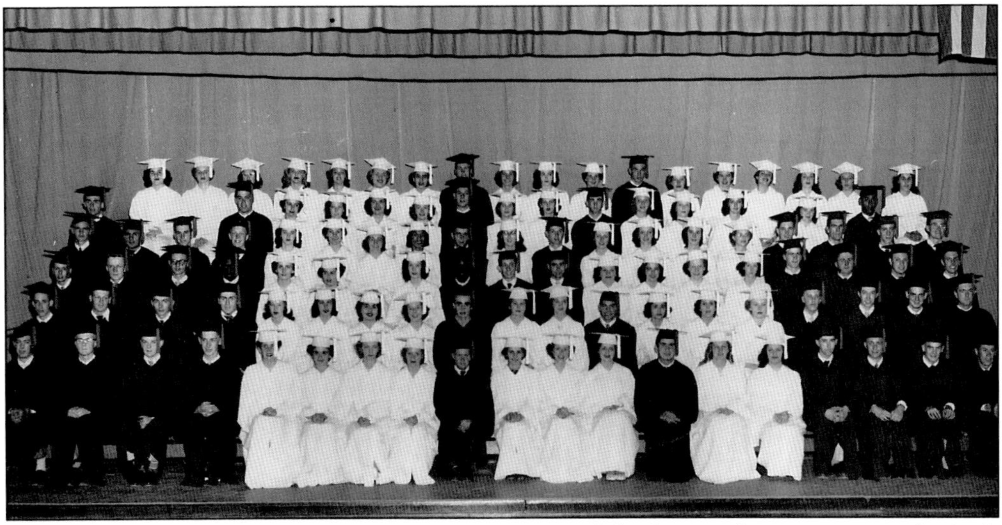

THE KEYPORT HIGH SCHOOL CLASS OF 1953. Some of the bigger classes came out the high school in the 1950s. Here 108 graduates pose in the auditorium. At the photographer's request, the graduates formed a neat "K" in the center of the bleachers. By the mid-1960s Keyport High School was overcrowded and running in double sessions to alleviate the crowding.

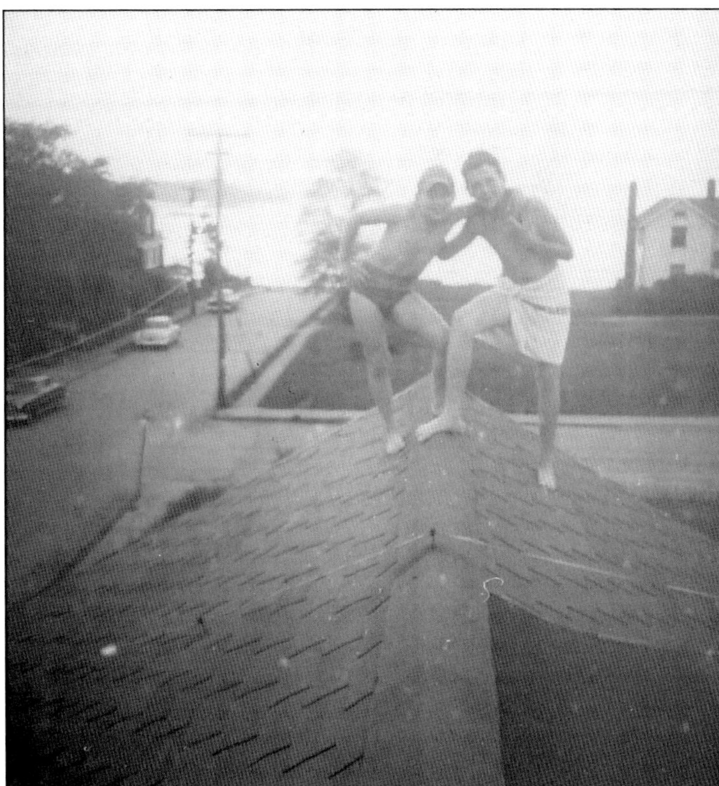

FRANK CURRIER, 1958. This photo was taken from the roof of his mom's house at the corner of Walnut and Locust Streets.

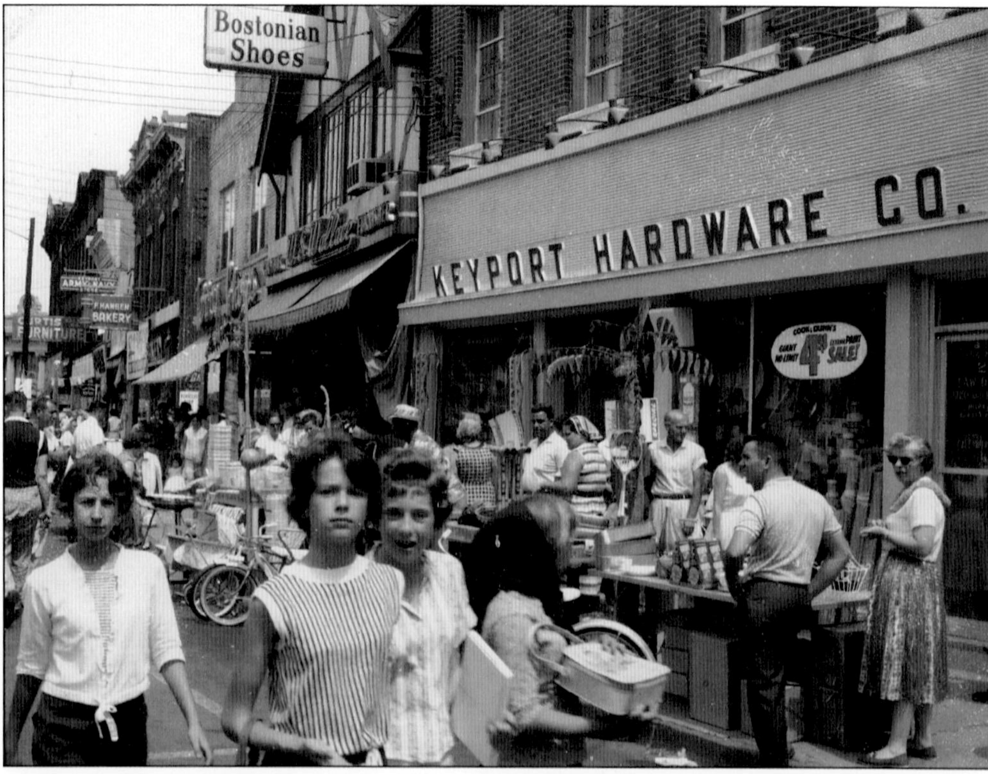

HAWAIIAN DAYS, 1960. On July 1 and 2, 1960, Keyport's sidewalk sales took on the resort island theme. Each day, from 9 a.m. to 10 p.m., shoppers could hit the beaches . . . I mean streets, as they browsed tables for bargains under the shade of large plastic palm trees, which were placed along Front Street. It is not remembered if any other sidewalk sales had such hip cool cat themes.

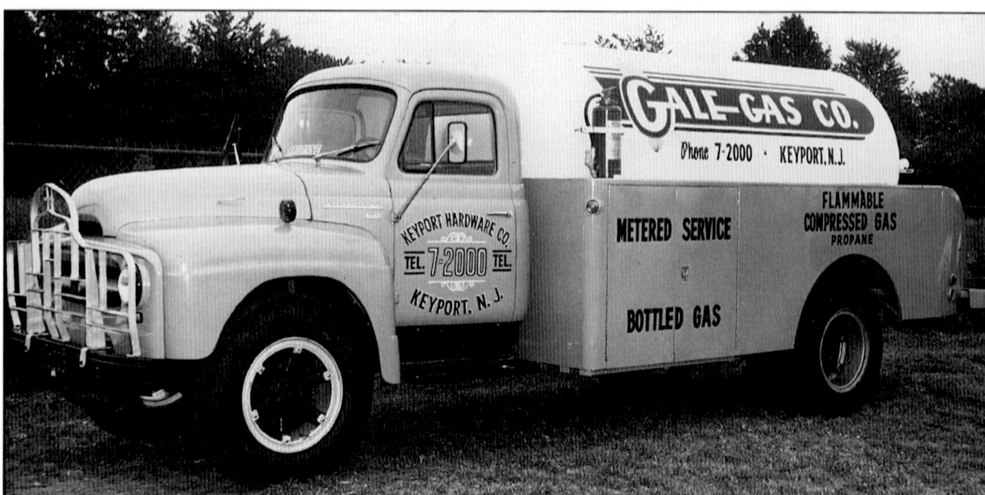

THE GALE GAS CO. The Keyport Hardware Company operated several of these International trucks in the 1950s. This R-180 model is carrying several hundred pounds of compressed liquid propane. In later years the Keyport Hardware Company sold off their interests in the propane business, concentrating mainly on industrial hardware and painting supplies.

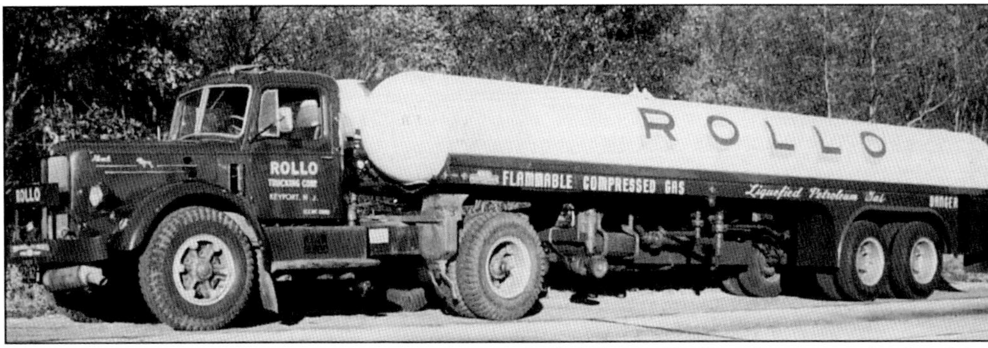

THE ROLLO TRUCKING COMPANY, 1955. Not only did the Rollo Family operate the local bus lines and the famed Rollo Post House, but they ran a successful trucking company as well. The company ran these trucks up and down the East Coast. The author's father related that while hitchhiking home from the Army in 1956, a Rollo truck passed him in Virginia. The last thing he saw were the words "Keyport, NJ" pass him by at 50 miles per hour.

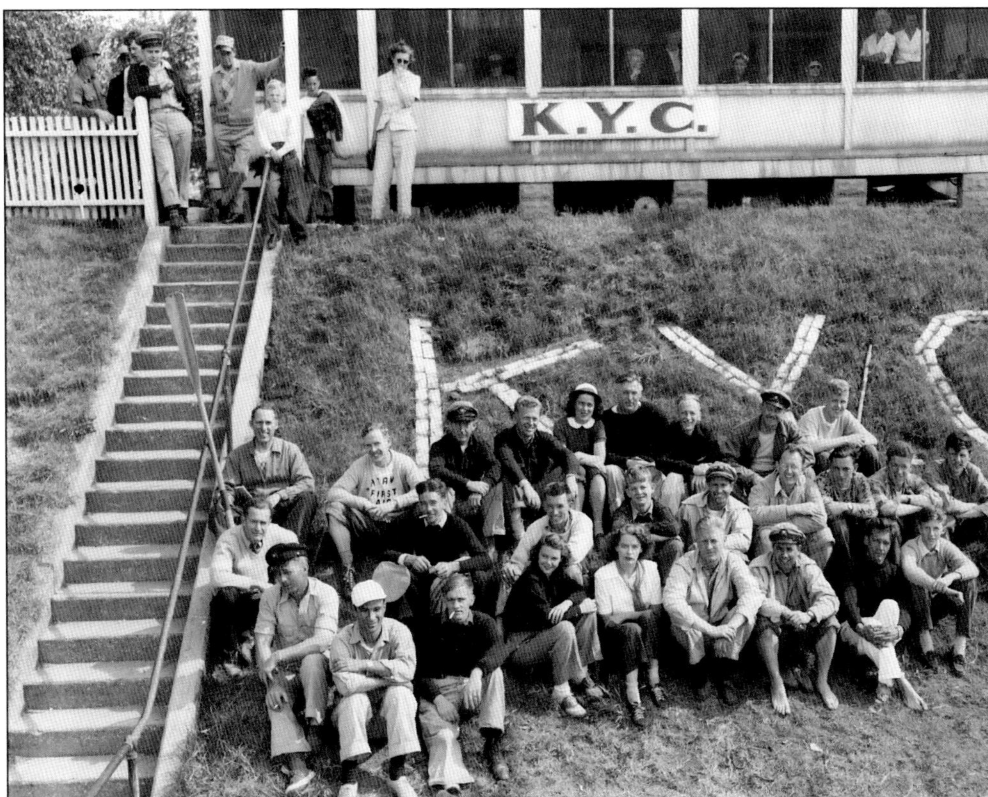

MEMBERS OF THE KEYPORT YACHT CLUB, C. 1951. This group of yachtsmen is shown sitting on the lawn of the clubhouse after a work session in the 1950s.

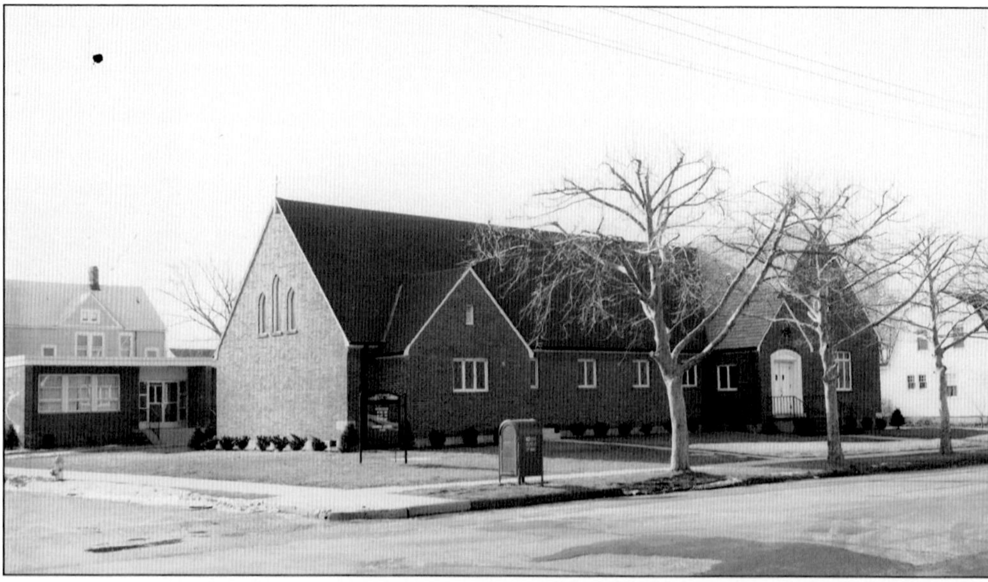

The Gethsemane Lutheran Church. In 1955 this Tudor-style church was completed at the southwest corner of Maple and Main Streets. In 1961 Reverend Frederick C. Boos began construction of the new school, which was to measure 108 by 43 feet and contain six classrooms and an office. Thirty-seven years after this image was made, the view remains the same.

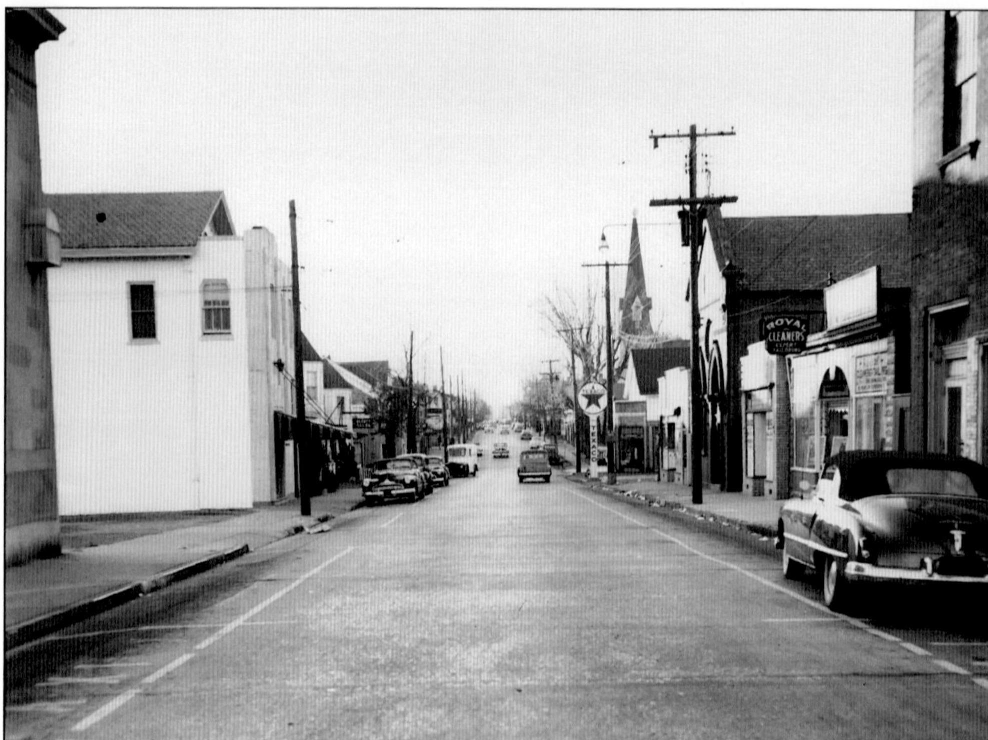

Broad Street from Front. It's early morning on Broad Street as the milk truck stops at Stanley's diner. Most store owners have yet to open their doors. Within hours Broad Street will be filled with cars and buses and scores of people making their way "up town."

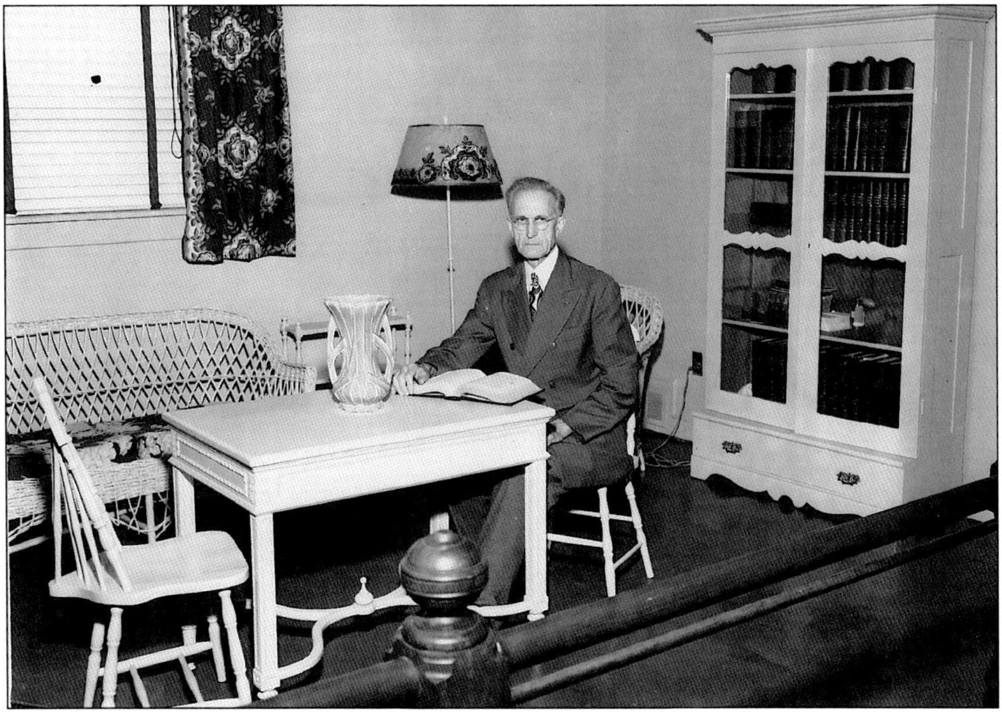

AN UNIDENTIFIED PASTOR OF THE FIRST CHURCH OF CHRIST SCIENTIST, C. 1956.

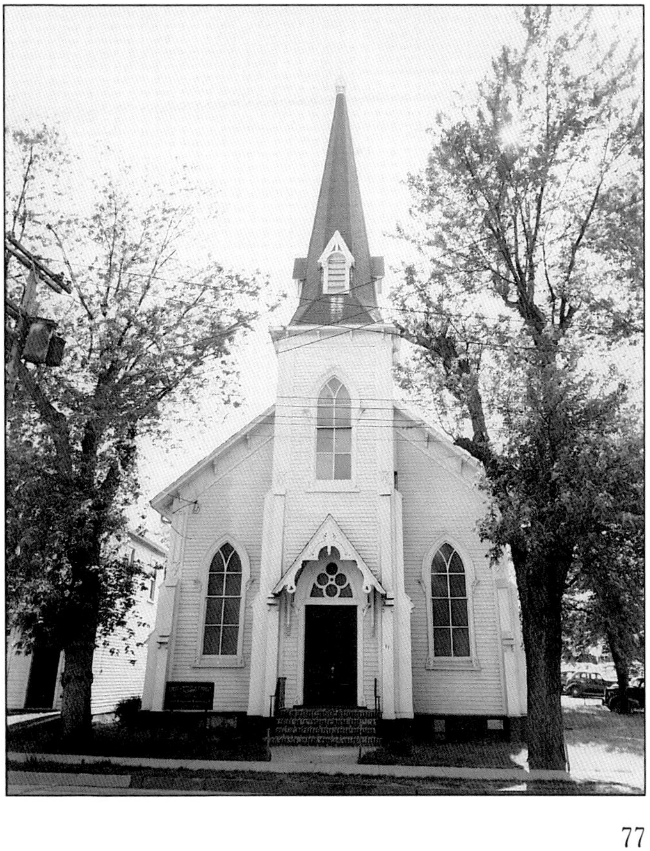

THE FIRST CHURCH OF CHRIST SCIENTIST, C. 1956. In 1953, an article published in the *World Telegram and Sun* stated "A small group of men and women in the Raritan Bay town of Keyport, whose greatest assets were faith and determination, have turned a dream into a reality." This quote refers to the hard work and dedication that the Christian Science Society showed after they purchased the former Presbyterian church at 84 Broad Street in 1953 for $33,000. The society was formed c. 1920 and met for several years in the old Scheyichbi Club on Main Street.

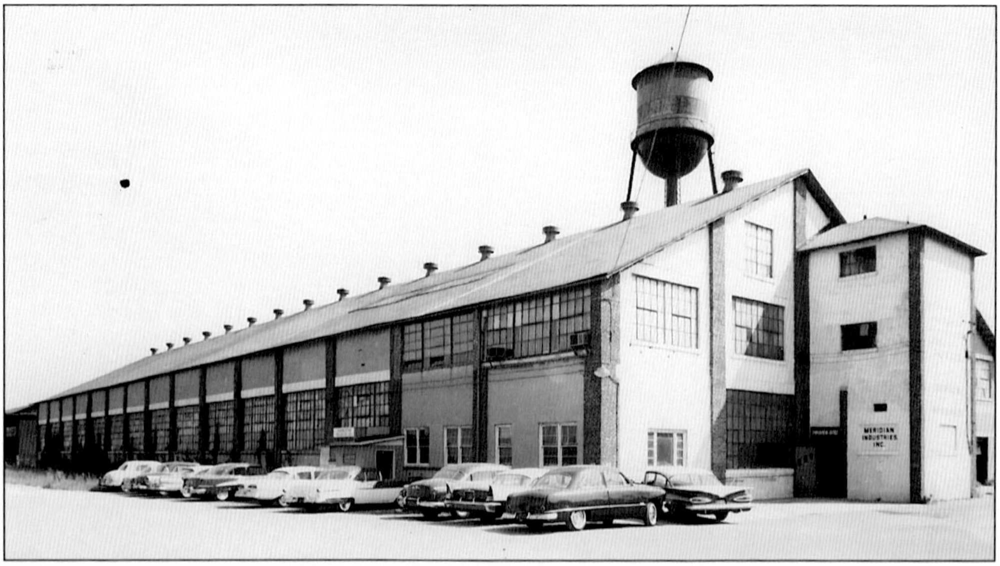

MERIDIAN INDUSTRIES, C. 1959. The Aeromarine Corporation was a distant memory by the mid-20th century. During World War II, this area was used as storage for various industries. In post-war years the Bendix Corporation arrived, Ralph Freidland began manufacturing Venetian Blinds, and soon Meridian Industries arrived. Where airplanes were once built the old "white building" was now a textile manufacturing plant. In the years that followed many small industries called the Aeromarine Complex home.

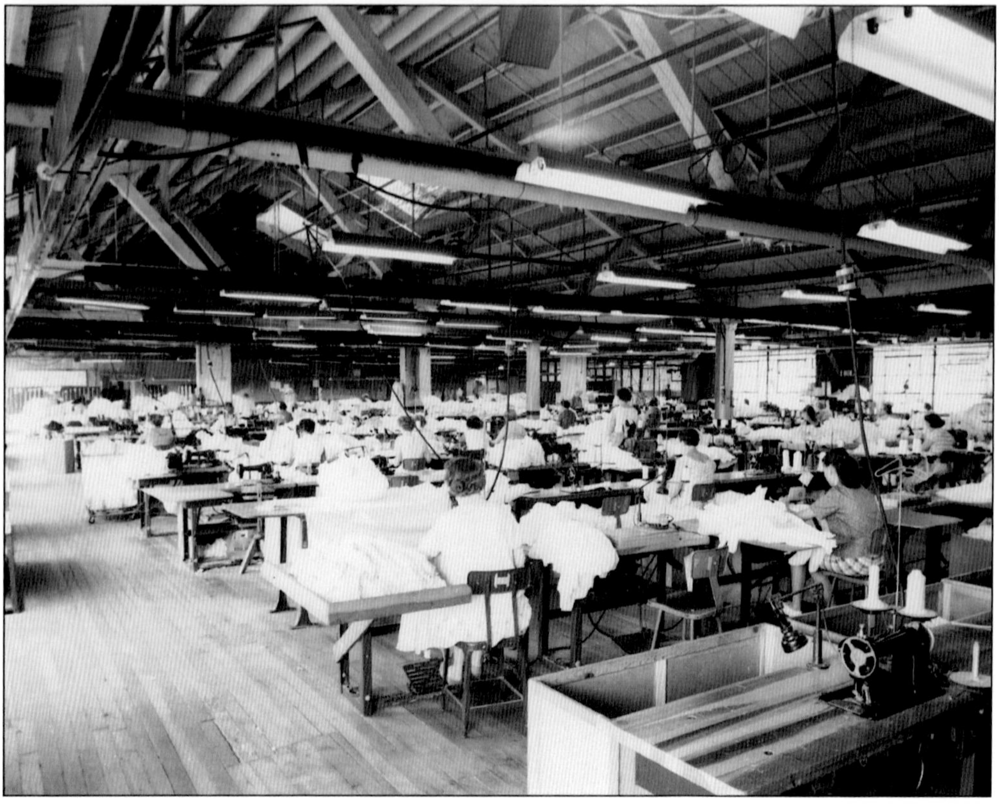

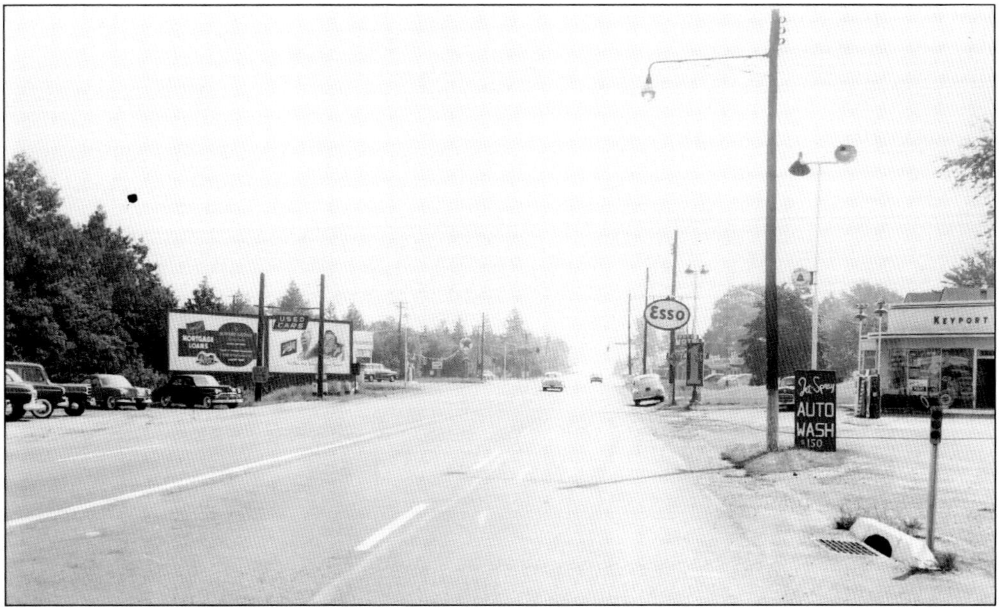

ROUTE 35, LOOKING WEST. This semi-rural area shows Bedle's Esso station on the right, while cars from Straub Motors are parked to the left. Although officially in Raritan Township, the gas station was none-the-less lettered as the Keyport Service Station.

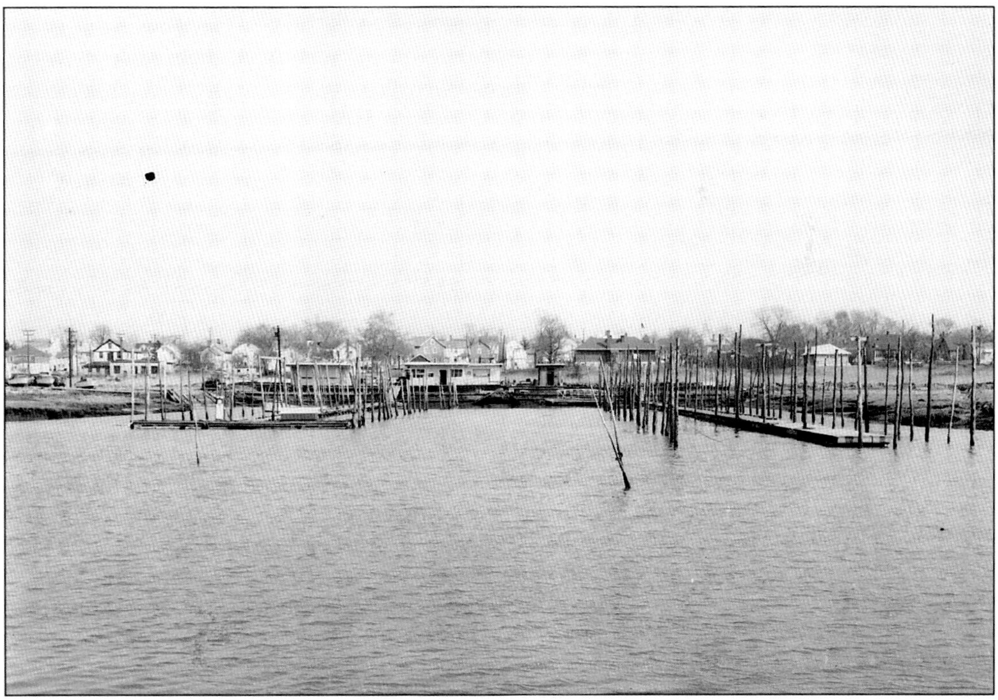

THE KEYPORT MARINE BASIN. Each winter the slips of Keyport's marinas become almost hauntingly empty. Here are some of the old docks of the Keyport Marine basin, as it appeared soon after its construction in the 1940s on Matawan Creek. The homes in the distance are situated along Washington Street. Near the center of the photo is the old brick West Keyport School.

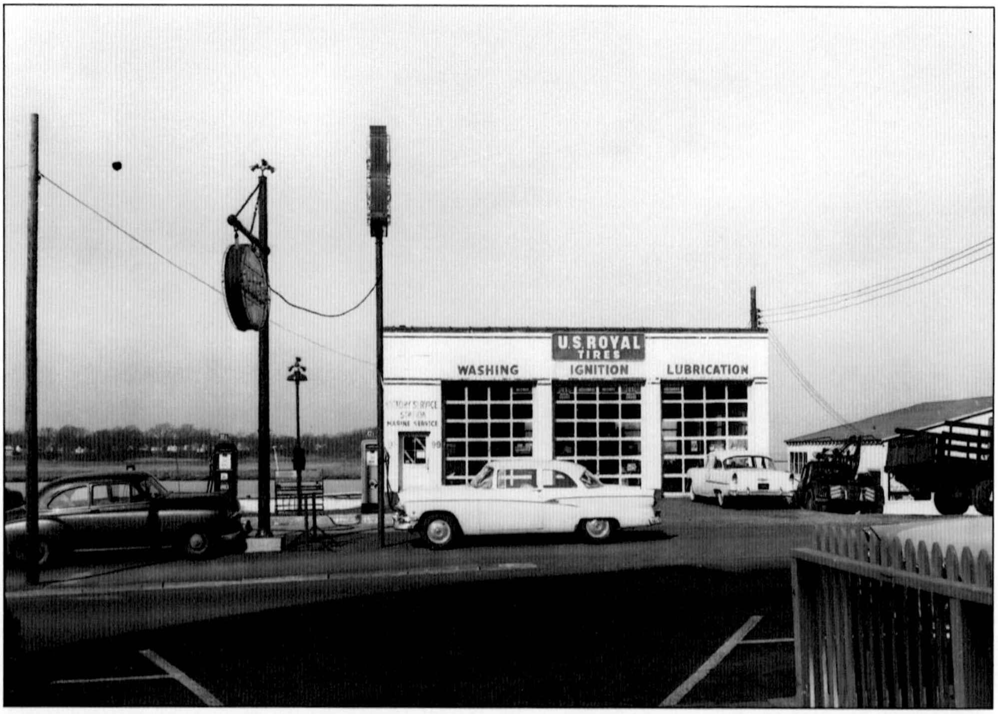

Erickson's Victory Service Station. This vintage 1940s service station once stood at 91–99 West Front Street. The station dispensed Amoco fuels and repaired all makes of cars until replaced by the post office in 1971. During the construction of the post office, under the guiding hand of Keyport Postmaster Phil Serpico Sr., this entire part of Front Street was reshaped. Does it seem like another life since you last pulled into this gas station to fill your tank?

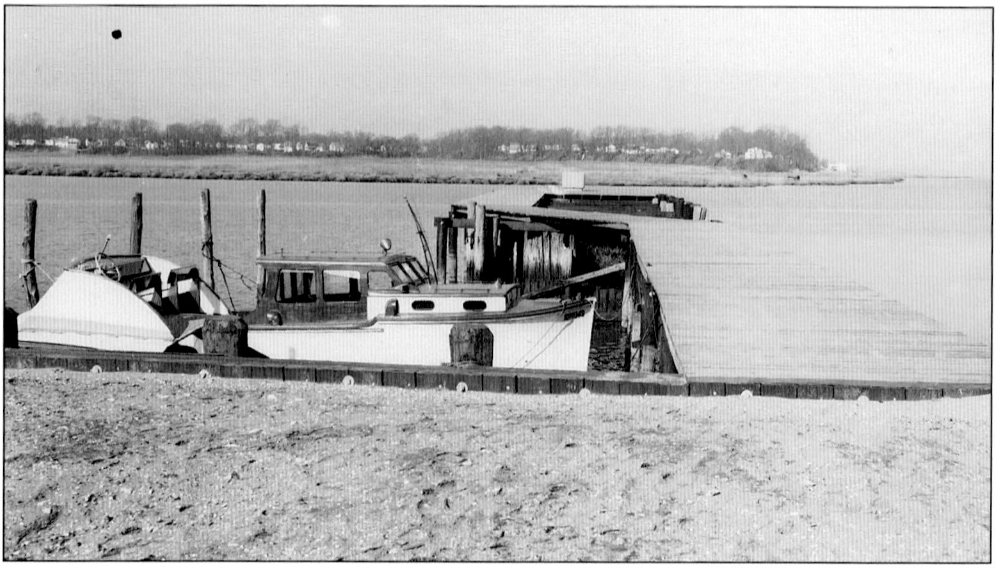

Roy Erickson's Dock. Just behind the old filling station was the gas and fishing dock. That sleek-looking boat with the enclosed cabin is a real beauty, dating from the late 1930s. This scene would today be near American Legion Drive and the municipal fishing pier.

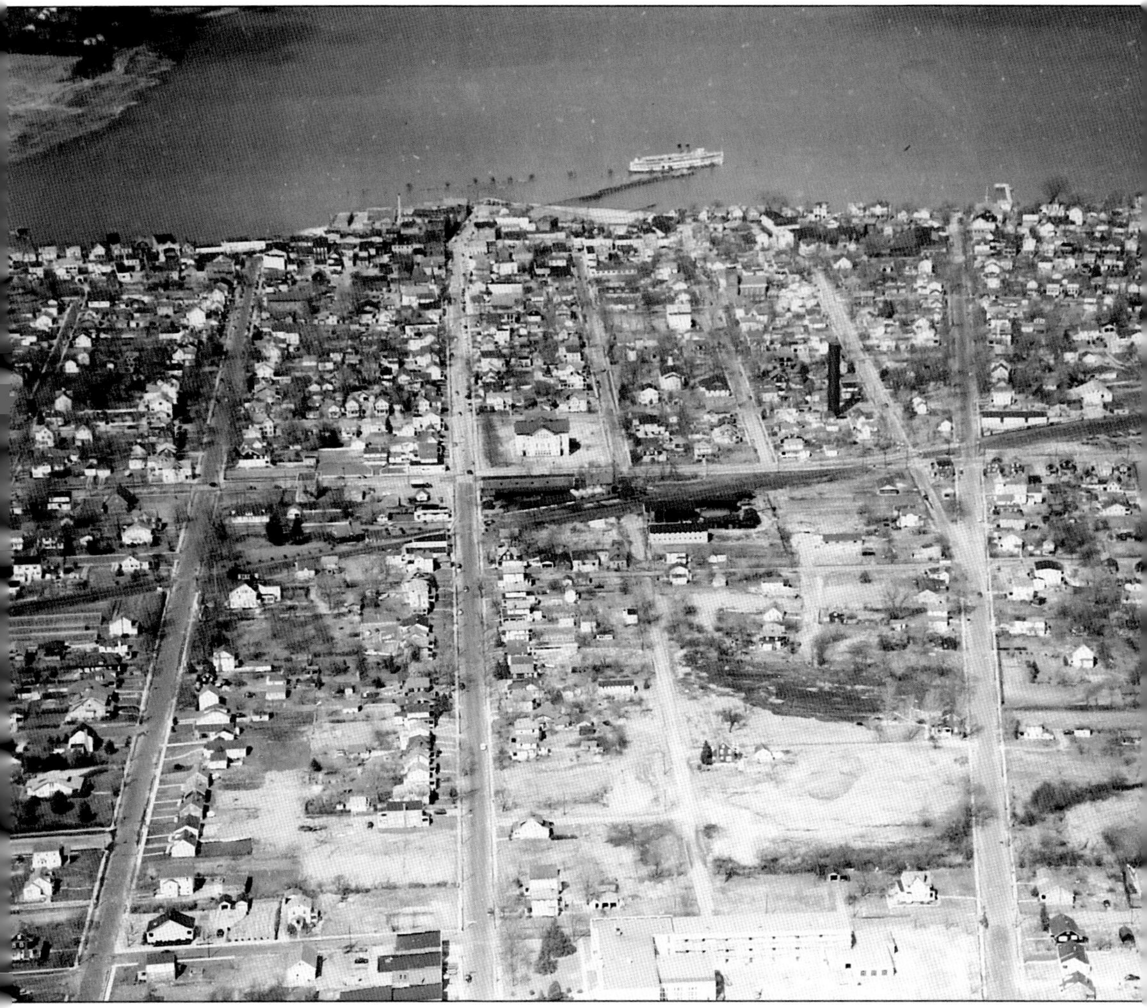

A 1950 Aerial View. With a keen eye and a magnifying glass, one can spot the many changes in this town over the last 48 years. No more steamboats, no more steamboat dock, the railroad station is gone, and so is the railroad! The old graded school has vanished and the new one rests on that large vacant lot near the bottom of the photo. Throughout our lives so many subtle changes occur that we pay no attention to, and then, later, we realize that it was those subtle changes that not only reshaped our towns but our lives as well.

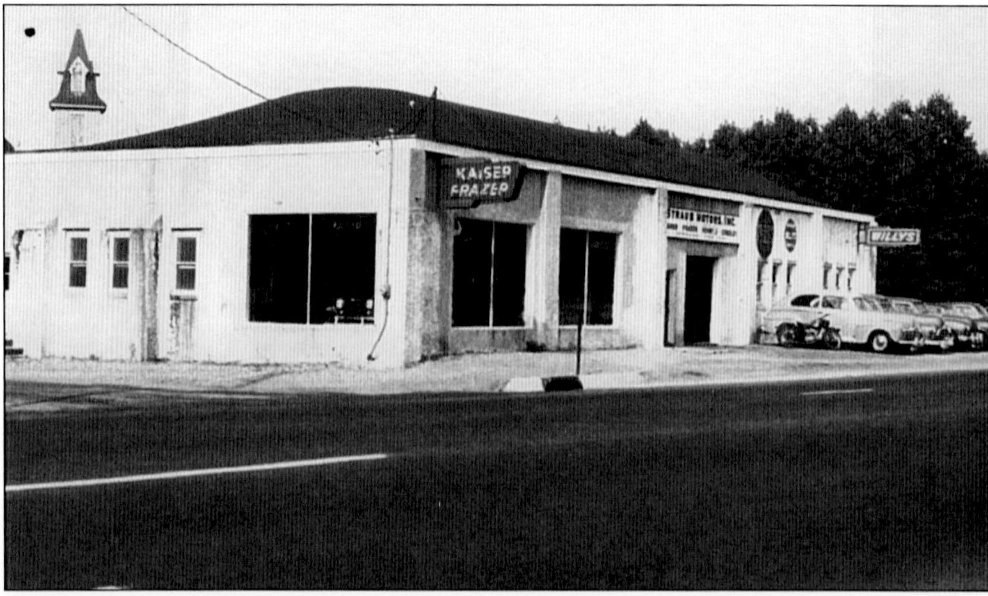

STRAUB MOTORS, ROUTE 35. These two views illustrate the new Straub Motors, constructed utilizing sections of the former Club 35, which had burned in 1949. During their years here Straub sold Desotos from 1953 to 1956, then Buicks from 1957 to 1968. It was in 1969 that Charles Jr. acquired 9 acres on Route 35 and Beers Street for the construction of a new showroom. The new showroom was constructed by taking two state-of-the-art showrooms and sandwiching them together to produce a structure that could display 45 cars. At that time it was one of the largest showrooms in the Northeast. In the photograph below, a brand-new 1954 Desoto sedan and a 1953 Plymouth rest on display in the 1949 showroom.

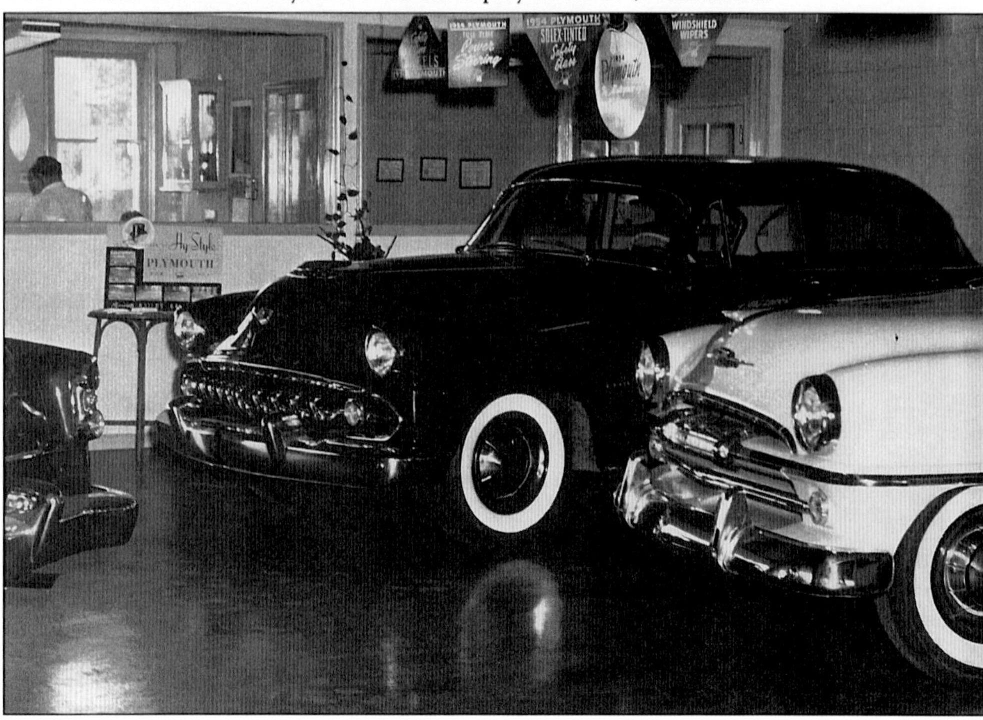

Seven

1961–1970

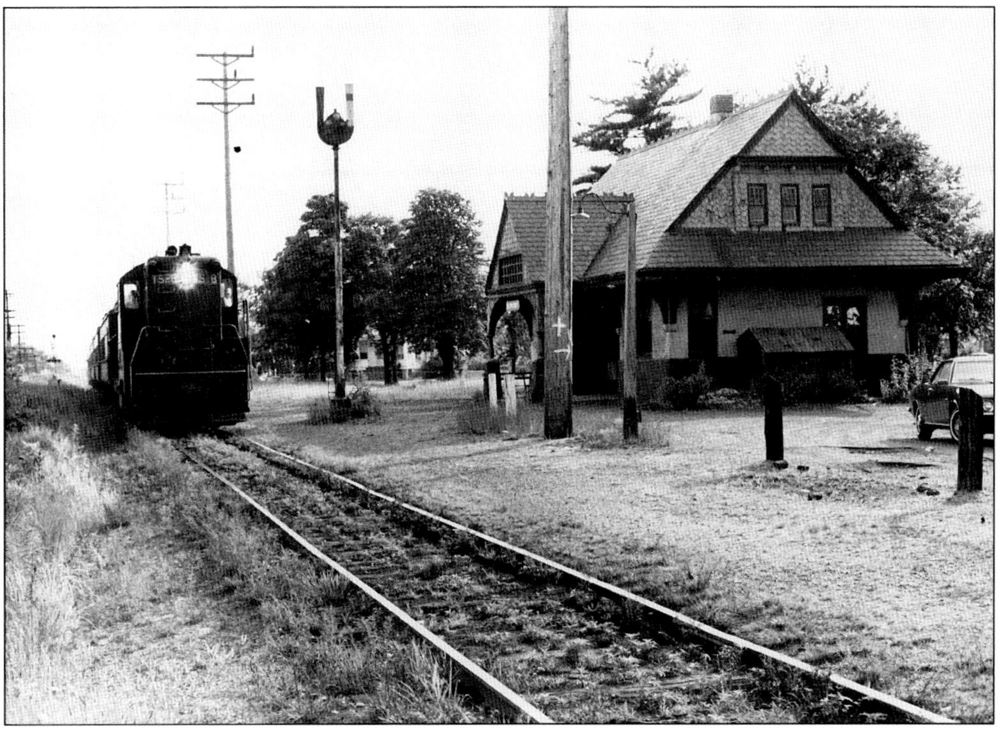

ONE OF THE LAST PASSENGER TRAINS, 1966. It all began in 1881 as the first tracks were laid through the busy little village of Key Port, on the bay. By 1966 the station was closed and service was about to be discontinued, ending nearly a century of railroading. Within two years of this image the passenger trains would rumble through town no more and the historic 1890 station would be lost to a suspicious fire.

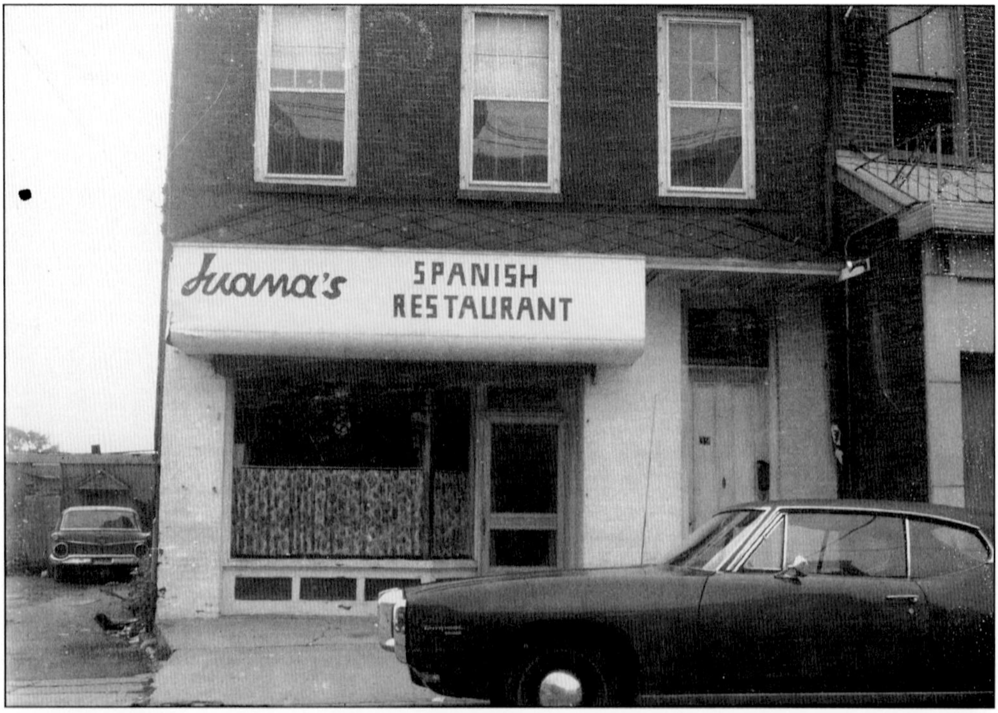

THE DAVID WARNER HOUSE, 1860. The history of this historic house had all but been forgotten when this photo was taken *c.* 1966. Mr. Warner had constructed his dwelling and tailor shop at 39 Broad Street in 1846. It was torn down in 1851 to stop the flames of the burning Pavilion Hotel from spreading to the Mansion House. He then rebuilt this house, where he resided for many years. The Warner House was razed soon after this image was made.

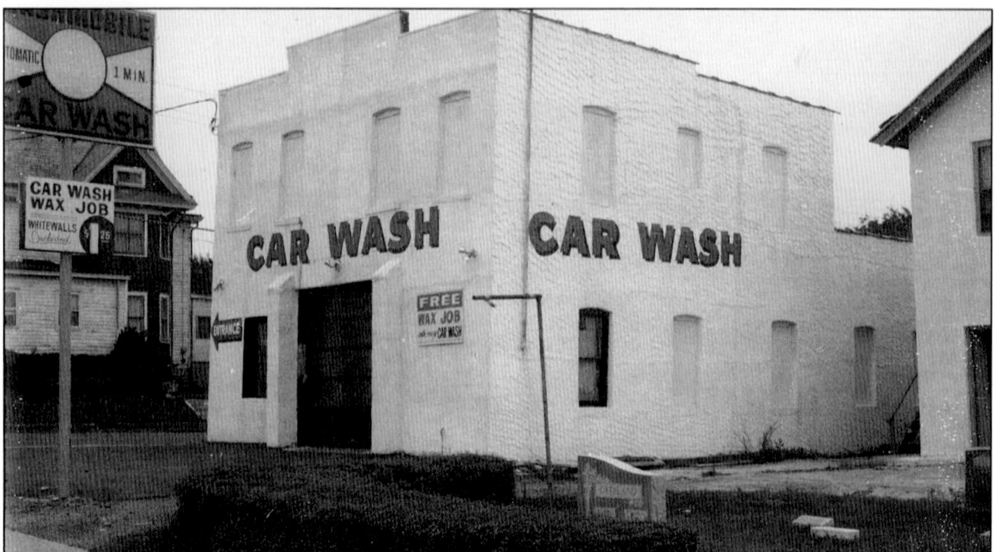

FRONT STREET CAR WASH, 1969. One of the first drive-through "automated" car washes in Monmouth County opened *c.* 1955 at the corner of Beers and Front Streets. For children it was exciting to travel through the wash, as the brushes swirled and the big fans finally blew the car dry. It still stands in 1998, although the building is slowly listing to its left side.

A Keyport Postcard, c. 1964. It is doubtful that this picture was taken in Keyport, as it appears to be a generic Jersey Shore postcard. It was, however, stamped "Greetings from Keyport, NJ." On the rear of this card was the title "Just We Two."

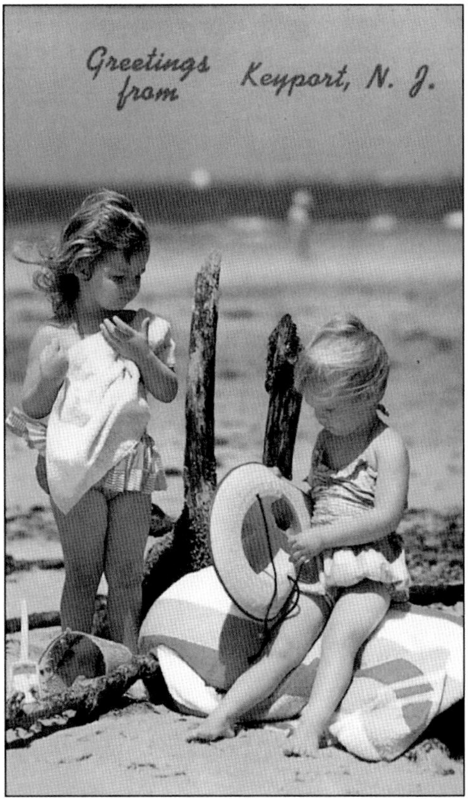

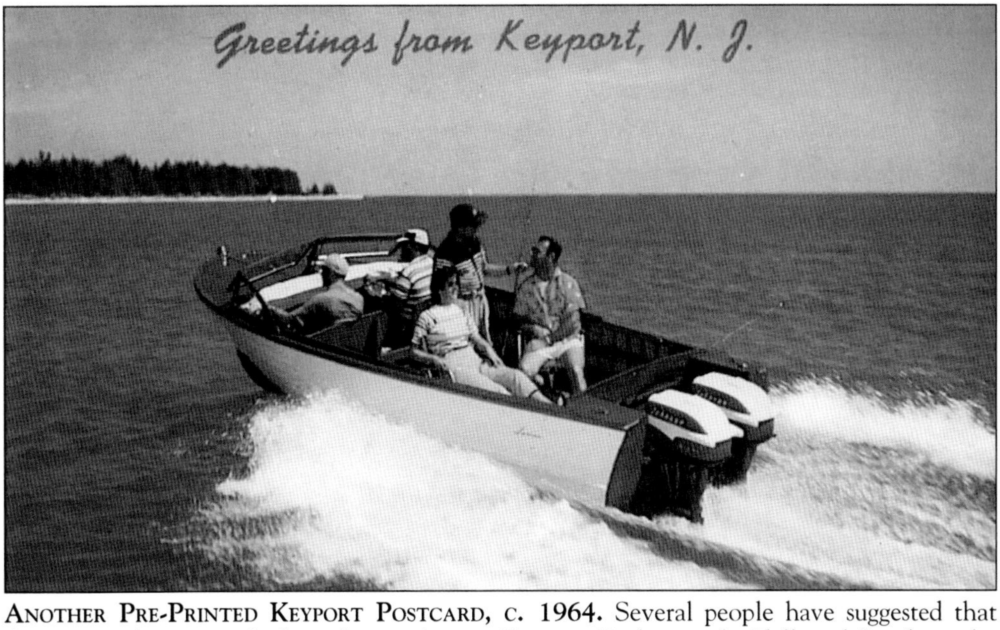

Another Pre-Printed Keyport Postcard, c. 1964. Several people have suggested that this postcard view might have been taken in Keyport Harbor, with Cliffwood Beach in the background (although there seems to be no Perth Amboy or Staten Island shore line). The scene is repeated countless times each summer as sport fishermen leave Keyport for the big catch.

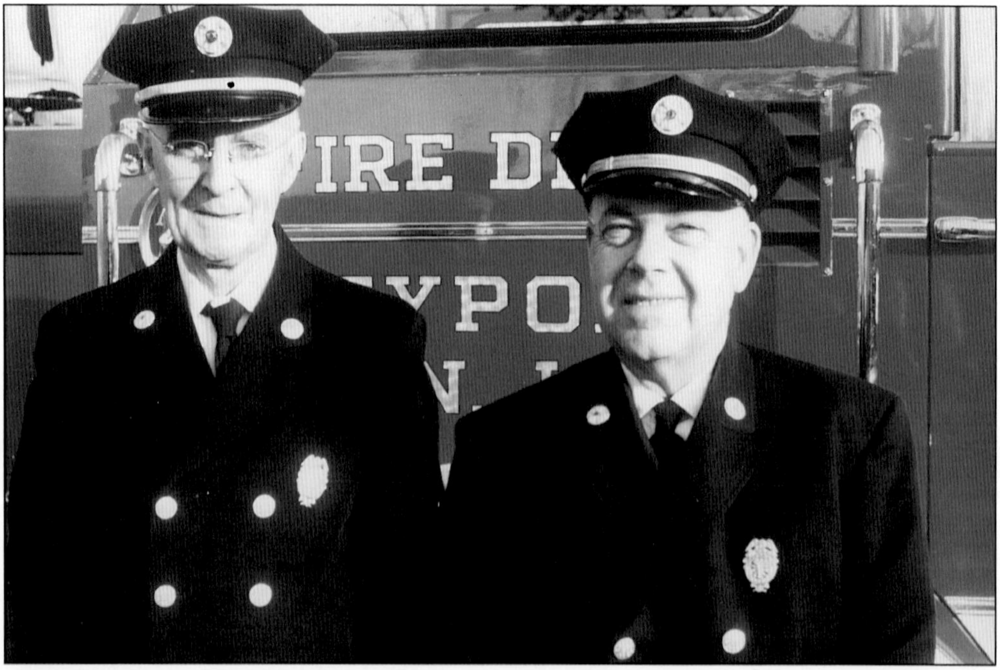

HARRY J. POLING AND ERNEST E. WALLING, JULY 1965. Harry J. Poling joined the Eagle Hose Co. after forming the Hazlet Fire Co. in 1910. He remained an active member of the department until his death on November 19, 1978. Ernie Walling joined the Liberty Hose Co. in the 1920s. He served as chief of the Keyport Fire Department in 1943 and answered his last alarm in 1981.

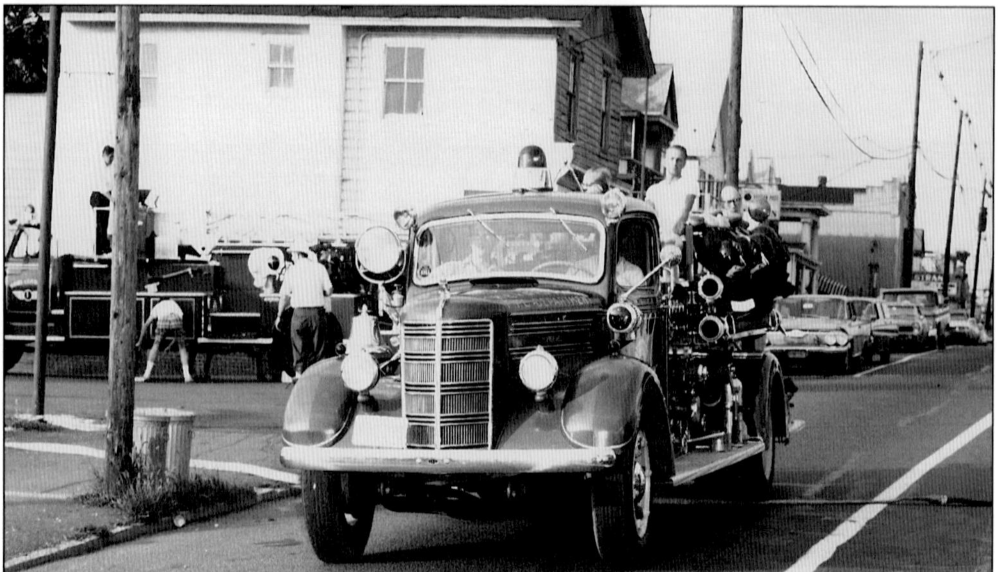

THE RARITAN HOSE CO., ON FRONT STREET. Here is the old 1946 Mack pumper that was operated by the Raritan Hose Co. until 1974. The rig is shown heading down West Front Street on July 14, 1969. This photograph was taken by James H. Atkins Jr., who, as a member of the Raritan Hose Co., served as department chief in 1990.

THE SCHIFFLI EMBROIDERY CENTER, C. 1965. This structure was built in 1951 to house the Schiffli Company's showroom and textile plant on State Highway 36 and 35. Here you could see embroidery completed on one of the world's largest embroidery machines. Wedding gowns, curtains, bedspreads, and draperies were specialties. Throughout the years many businesses passed in and out of this building. In 1998 the structure is vacant and for sale.

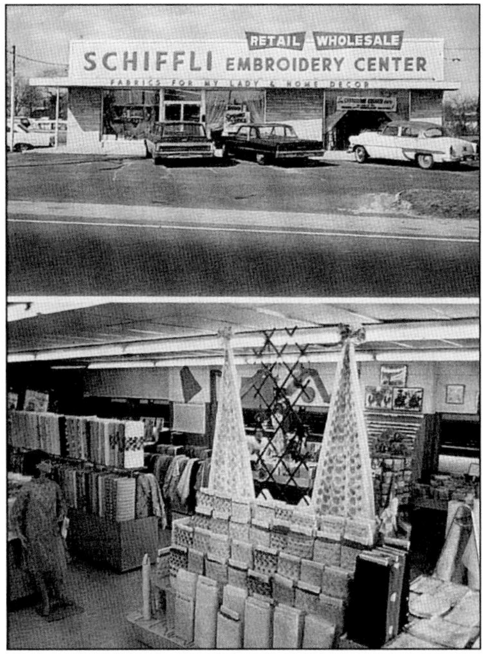

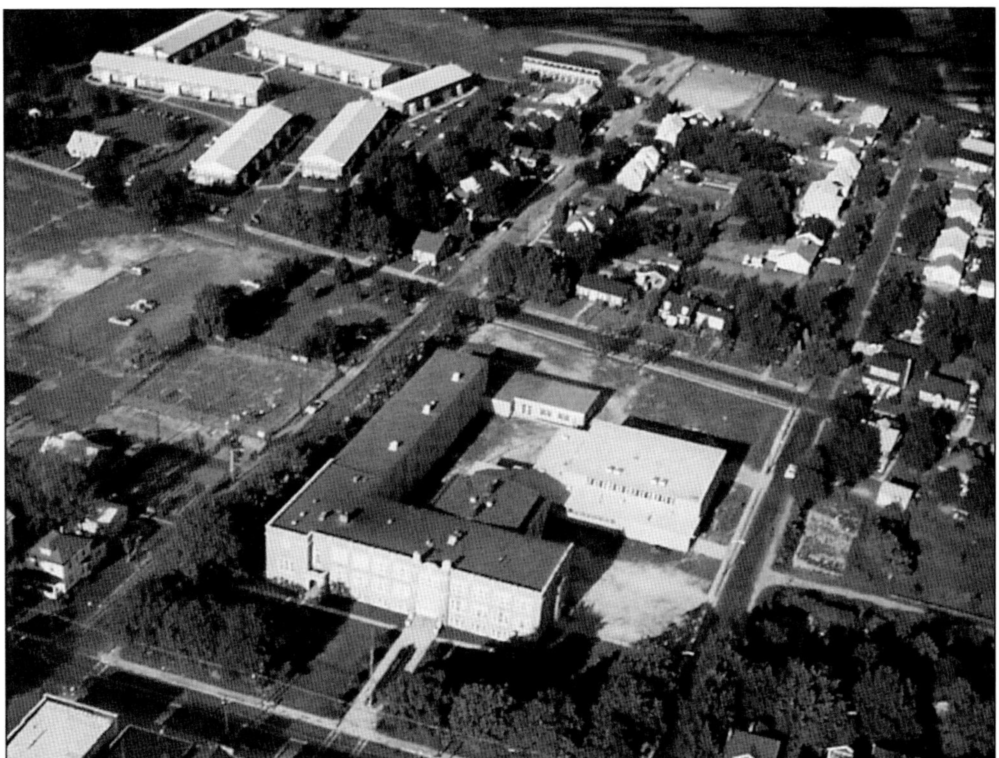

AN AERIAL VIEW OF KEYPORT HIGH AND VICINITY, 1968. This view is a nice example of Keyport's southern end of town. The area, which was primarily built up between 1910 and 1950, contains many fine single-family homes, safe tree-lined streets, and good schools within a minute's walk from just about anywhere in town.

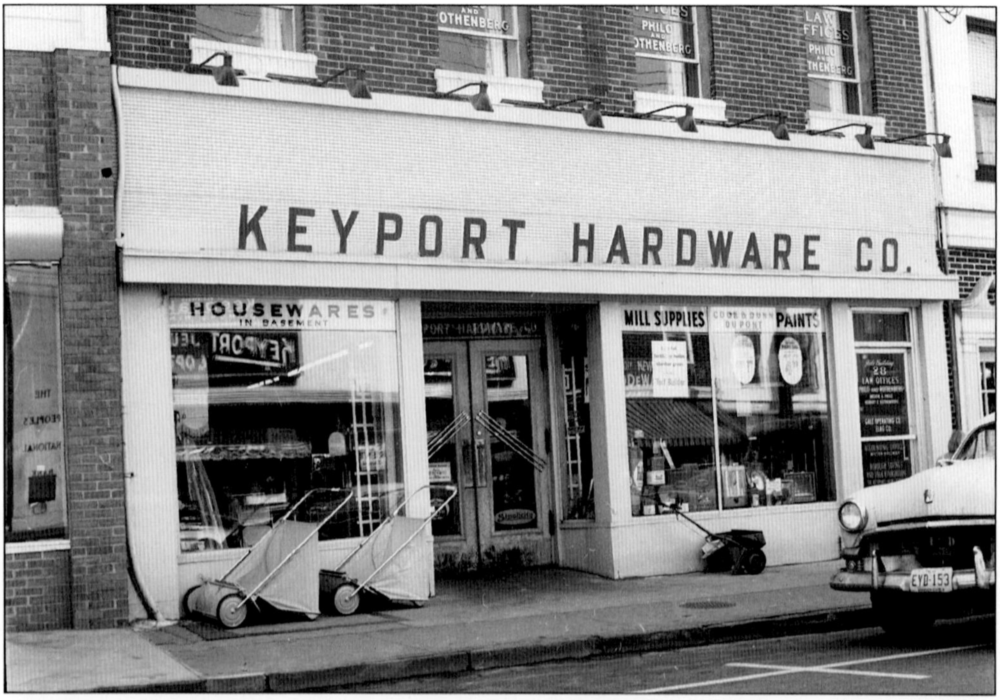

The Keyport Hardware Co., 1964. With its recently modernized facade overlooking Front Street, this building is one the oldest and tallest within the business district. Built *c.* 1870 by T.H. Roberts, it has since that time served as a dry goods and hardware store. It was for many years operated by J. Leon Schanck Sr. and later by the Gale family, who still maintain ownership in 1998.

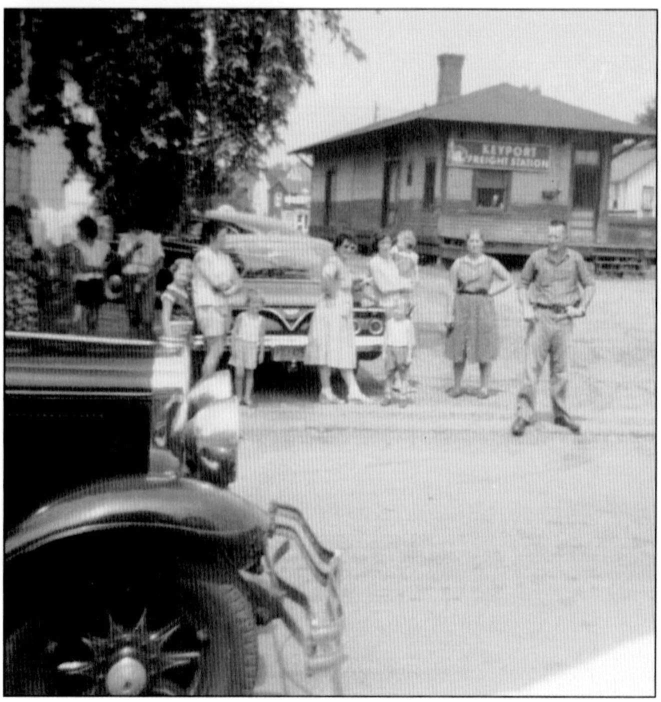

Second Street, August 1961. This unique view of the former Keyport Freight Station was captured during a parade in the summer of 1961. The freight station was removed by 1974 and the area is occupied by three single-family homes, all of which were built in 1988.

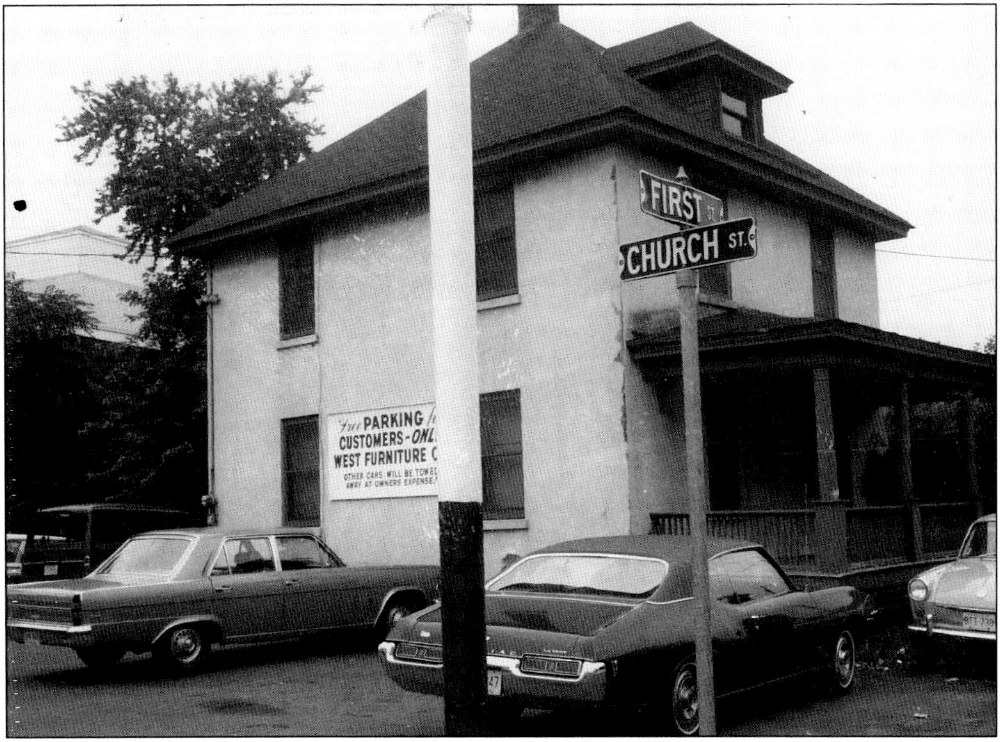

The House at the Corner of First and Church Streets, c. 1970. This "Sears Catalog" house was built around 1912 and was one of several Sears houses in the town. In this view the house—vacant and neglected—was soon to disappear. In 1986, the Hook and Ladder and Engine Companies constructed their new combined firehouse on the site.

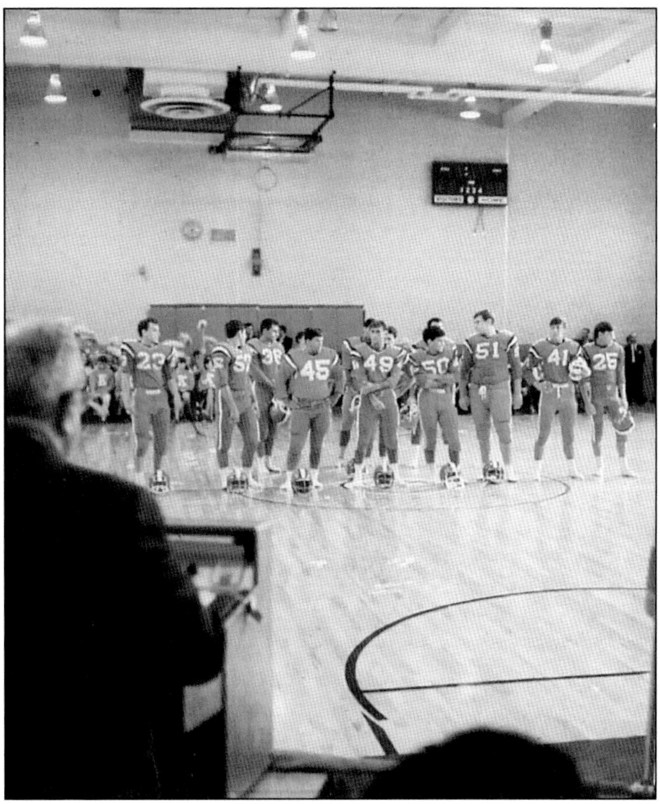

Keyport High, 1968. Everybody quiet down, please, Tuffy is about to introduce the 1967 gridiron stars. During Stan "Tuffy" Baker's career in KHS, the football team won 66, lost 88, and tied 12. In 1956 they were the Shore and Central Jersey Champions.

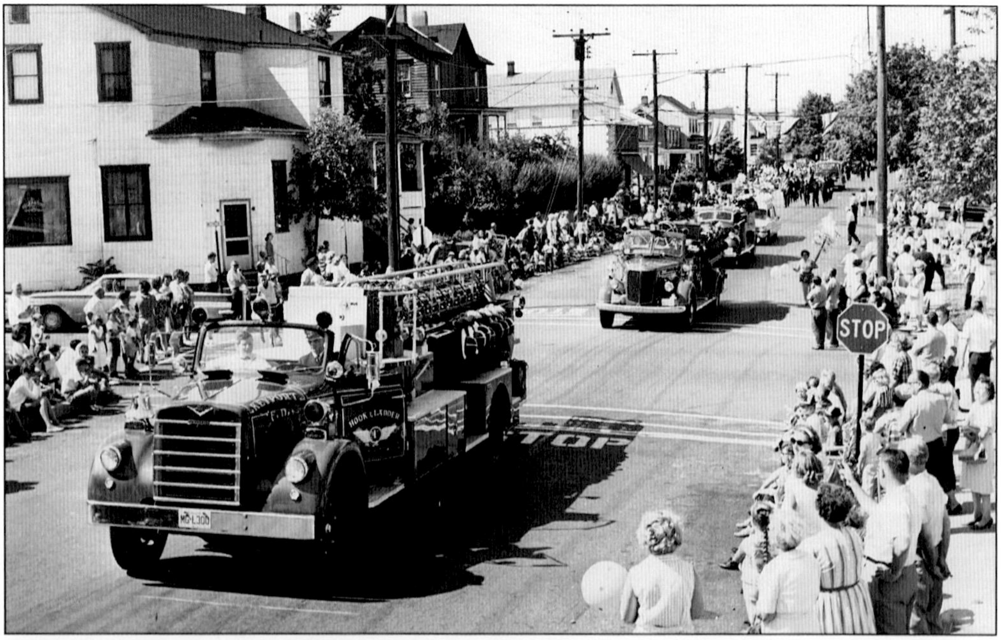

A Parade in South Amboy, NJ. The borough has always represented itself well in out-of-town parades. Here the Hook and Ladder Co., Lincoln Hose, the Fire Patrol, and the First Aid Squad slowly roll along in a well-attended parade.

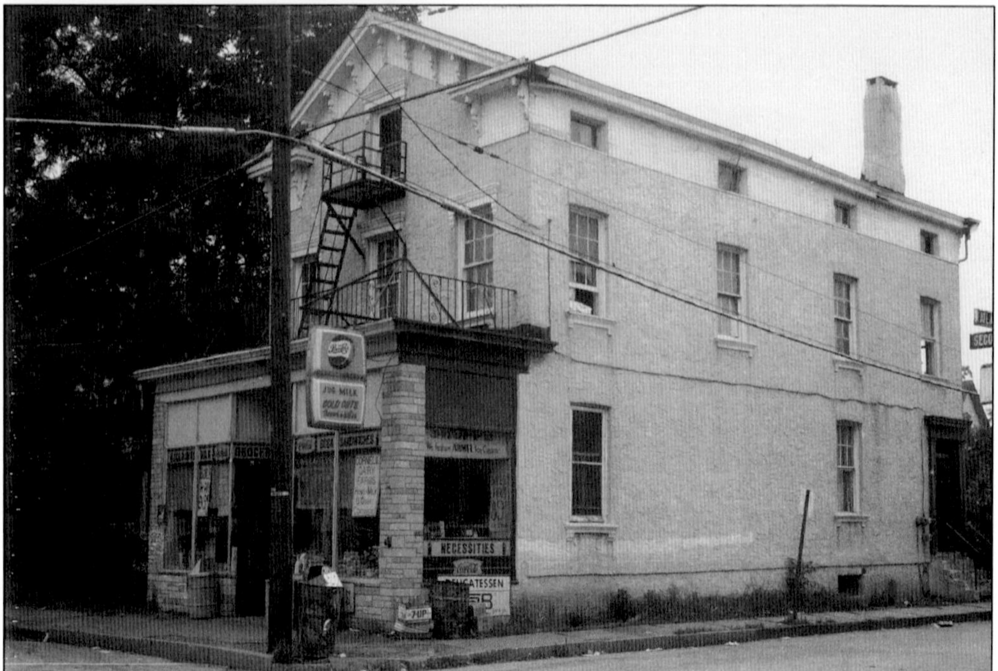

The Cornell Dairy, 1969. This fine Greek Revival structure was originally built as a dwelling during the Civil War. Located at the corner of Atlantic and Second Streets, it was later converted to a store by Mr. Storms. It remained a local corner store until *c.* 1974, when the storefront was enclosed and converted into apartments.

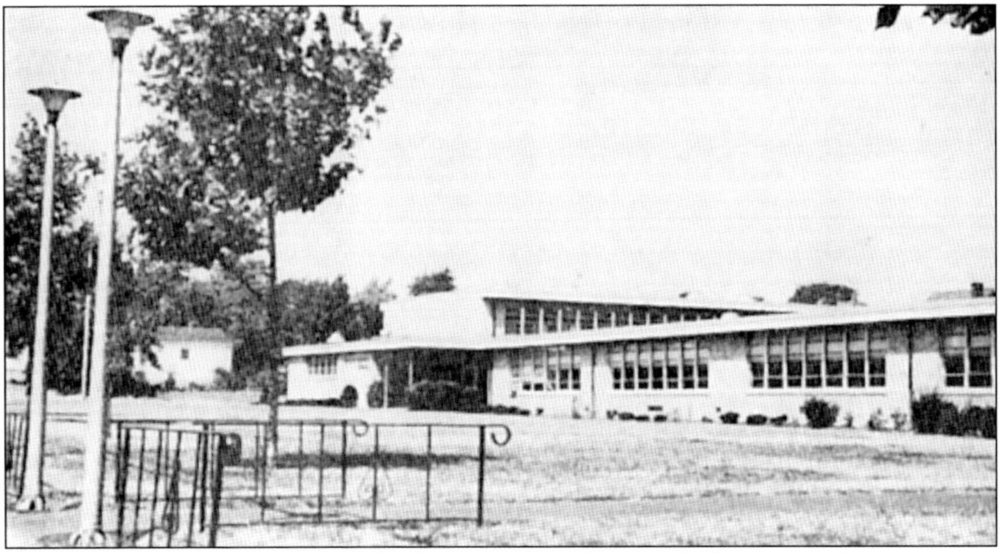

Keyport Central School, 1958. The first section of the Central School was dedicated in 1958, with approximately eight classrooms and something known as a cafetorium. The cafetorium was a combination cafeteria, gymnasium, and auditorium all rolled into one. In 1966, when the school was tripled in size, a new gymnasium was added, so no longer would the tables have to be folded up and moved for basketball games. The elementary school is still officially known as "Central."

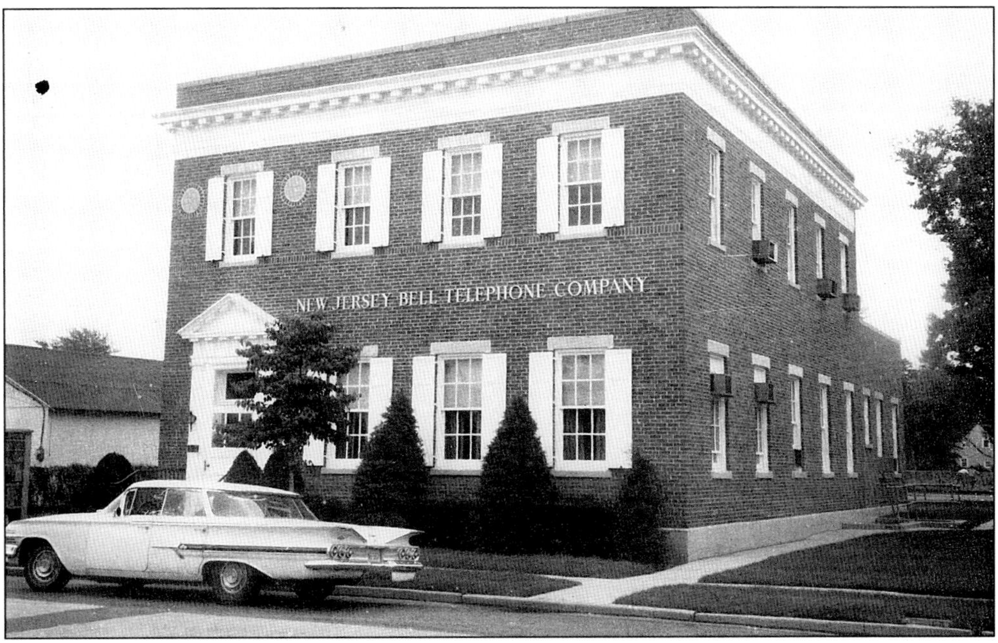

The New Jersey Bell Telephone Co. Office, 1966. This Colonial Revival structure was completed on June 12, 1931. The building, which served Keyport and Matawan, was capable of handling over 6,000 separate phone lines. When phone service was introduced in the 1880s fewer than 12 people had phones. By 1910 there were 300 phones in service and the numbers keep growing today. The building itself was later closed and replaced by a larger switching building next door. It was finally torn down *c.* 1989.

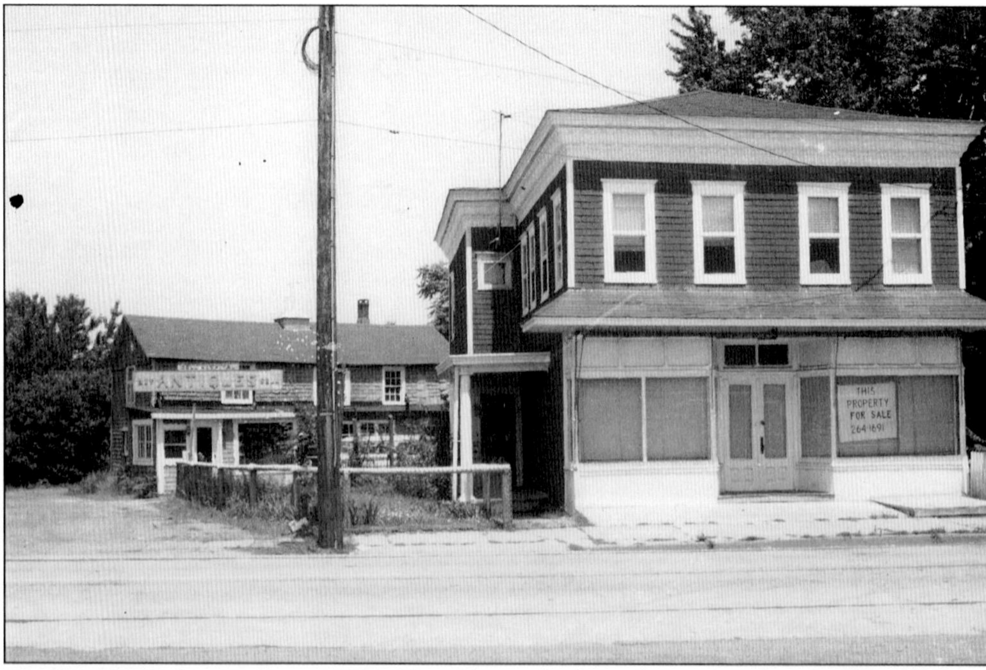

THE LEE STORE, LOCKPORT, C. 1967. The old store had seen better days (see p. 44), as it was up for sale and had just closed its doors for the last time. It sat boarded up until recently purchased by Keyport promoter Sidney Becnel, who is transforming the store into tasteful apartments which will retain the exterior charm of the old place.

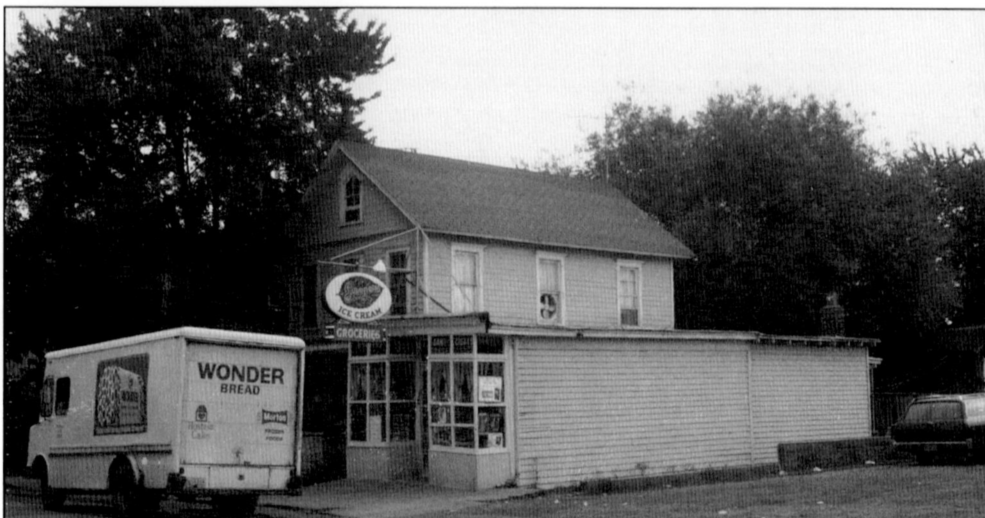

EMILY'S STORE, C. 1969. One of the most important stores in Lockport was Emily's, located on First Street near Waverly. Purchased by the Stanley Schultz family c. 1920, the store was named in honor of Emily Schultz (Snyder). Eventually, Emily took over the store and sold groceries and all kind of goodies until about 1993, when the store closed its doors. It is interesting to note that the Breyer's Ice Cream sign, which had hung over the store for nearly 50 years, was promptly picked up by Breyer's! This was the spot for cold drinks and those tasty little goldfish candies, which still cost only 2¢ even into the 1980s.

Eight

1971–1980

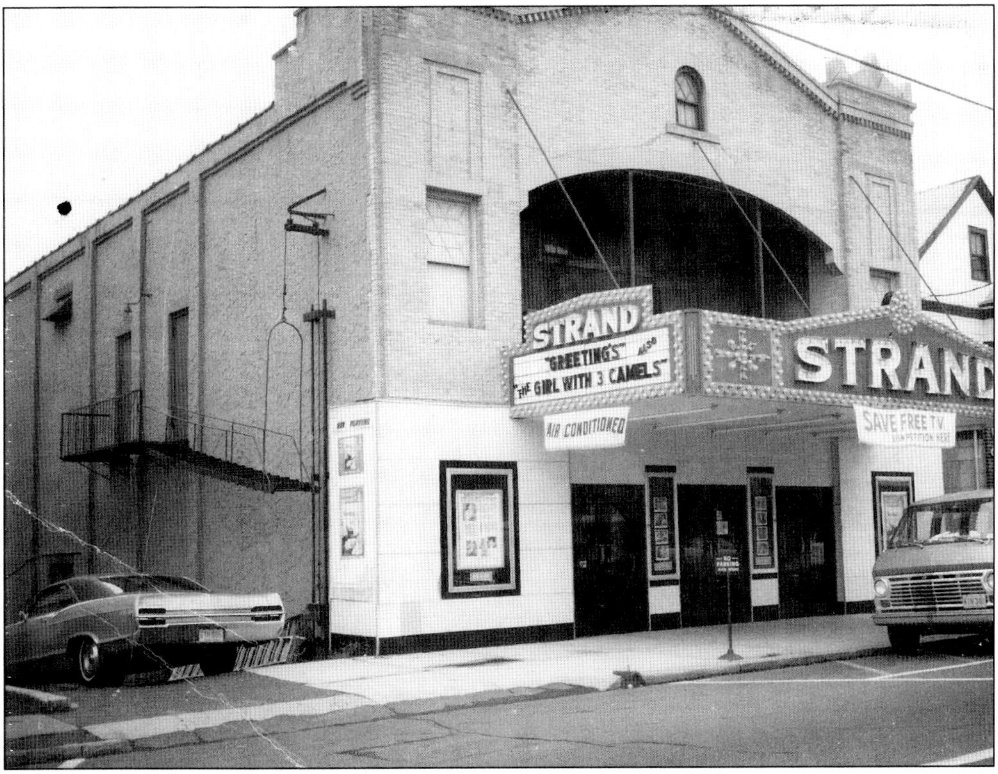

The Strand, c. 1971. By the mid-1960s, Keyport's downtown theatre was showing XXX adult movies. No longer would generations of Keyporter's spend Saturday afternoons at the matinee. The town had hit bottom by 1971 as the real estate market had faltered and many of Keyport's historic buildings were neglected, destroyed, or burned in a decade that proved to be a turning point for the town.

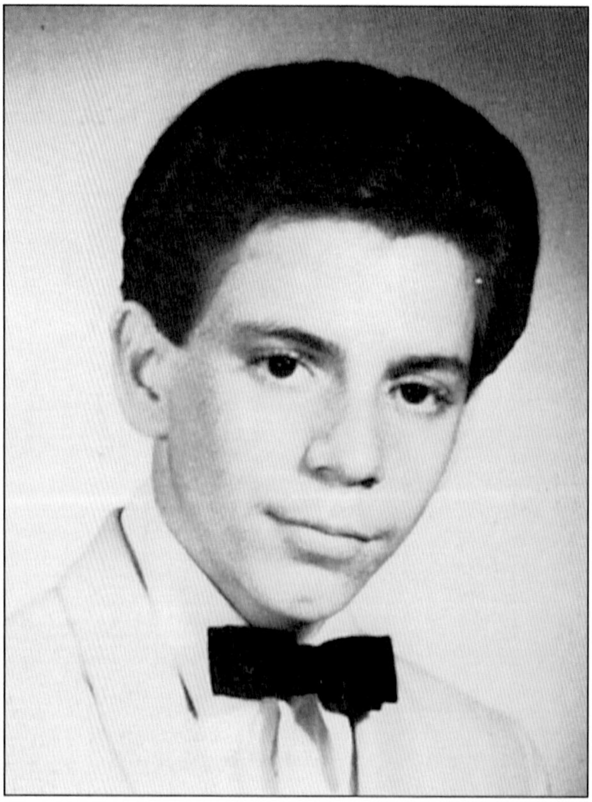

SPEC. 4 DENNIS J. GATTI. Three months before he was due to return from southeast Asia, U.S. Army Spec. 4 Dennis Gatti was killed in action while serving with the 198th Light Infantry Brigade in Vietnam. Dennis was born in Newark and graduated from Keyport High School in 1968. Mr. Gatti was the son of Mrs. Connie F. Mongiello of 3 Monroe Street.

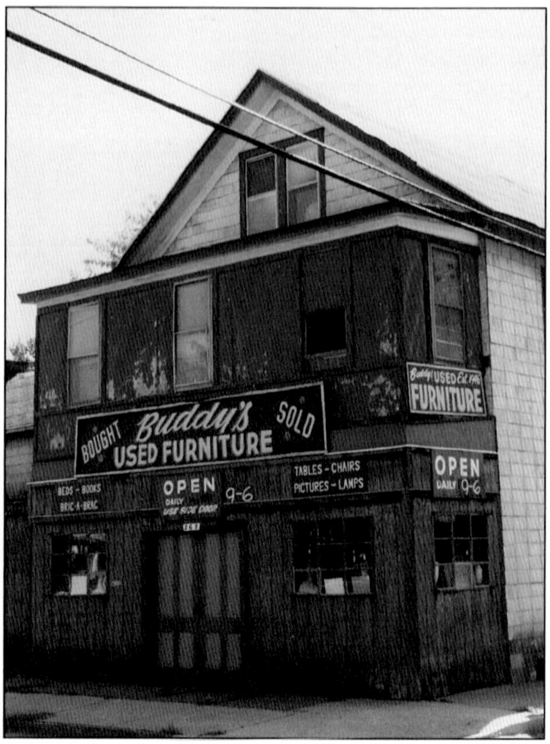

BUDDY'S, C. 1980. For anyone searching for a lamp, couch, or just about anything else that could be considered furniture, Buddy's was the place to go. Buddy Emmons lived and worked in this store, located at the corner of First and Fulton Streets since the turn of the century. It was originally operated as the Fulton Cash Market (see p. 13). Buddy himself operated the place until his death *c.* 1994.

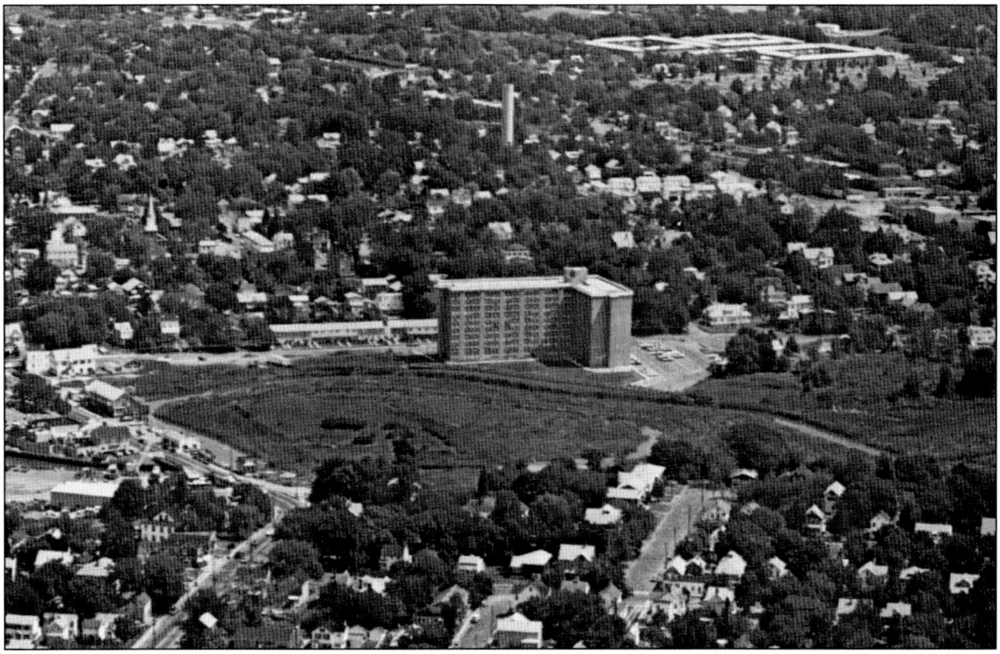

A Bird's-eye View, 1976. These two photos almost encompass the entire town. In the summer of 1976 we were enjoying fishing at the bulkhead, soap box derbies, and celebrating America's birthday.

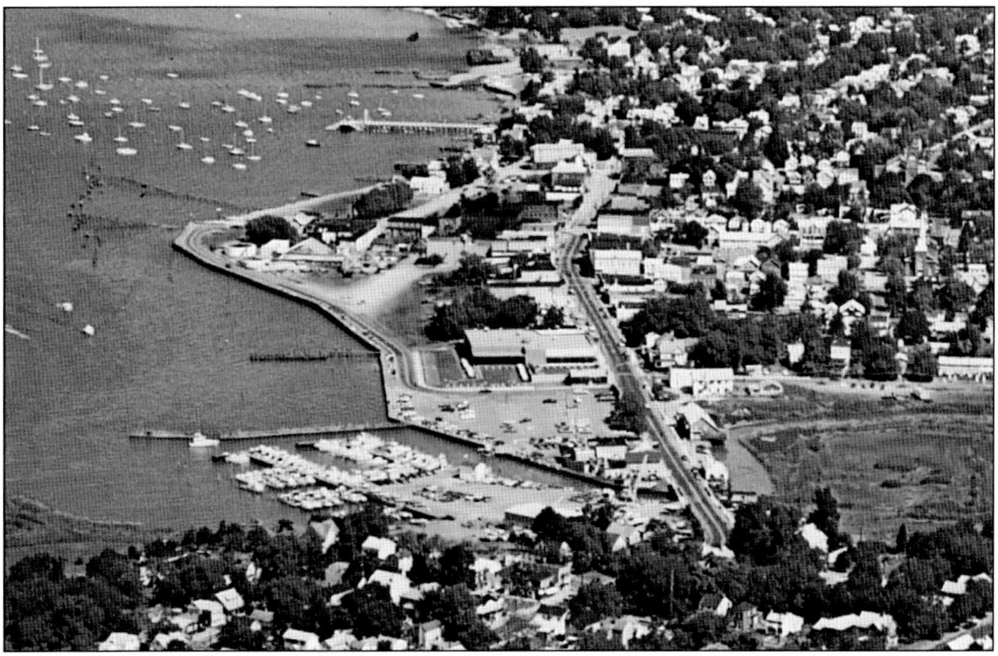

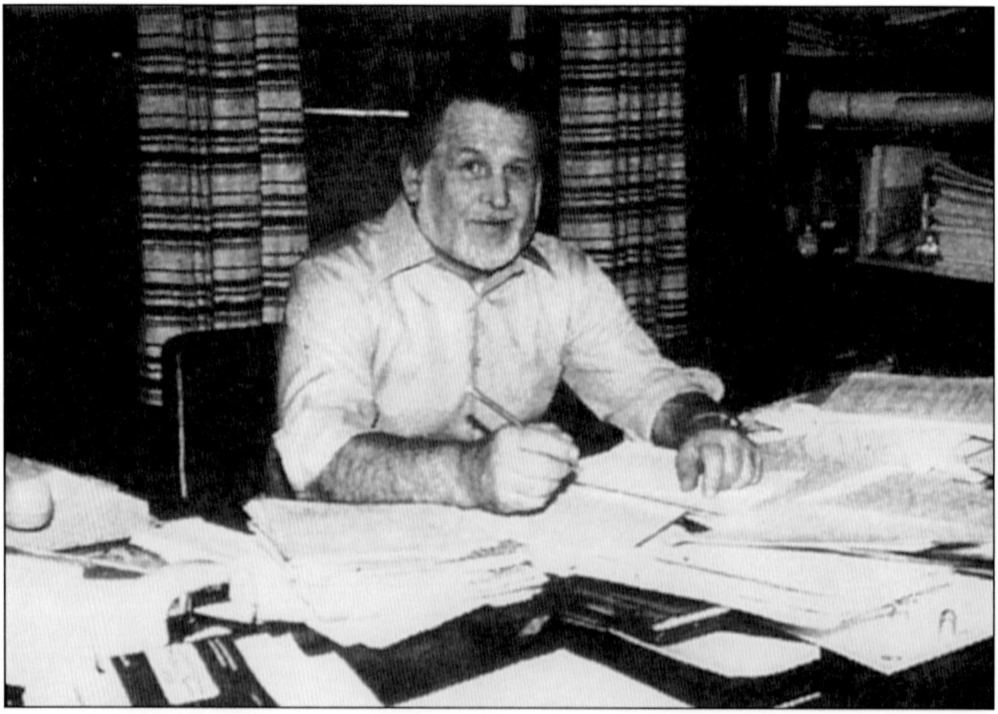

Mayor Richard W. Bergen. Mayor Bergen served Keyport for eight years at a time when the town was beginning to see light at the end of a long tunnel. During his tenure the commercial fishing boat the *Dolphin* M. came to Keyport waters, the first commercial fishing boat in Keyport waters in nearly 50 years. Not only was Richard Bergen mayor, but he also served as a well-respected high school industrial arts teacher for many years.

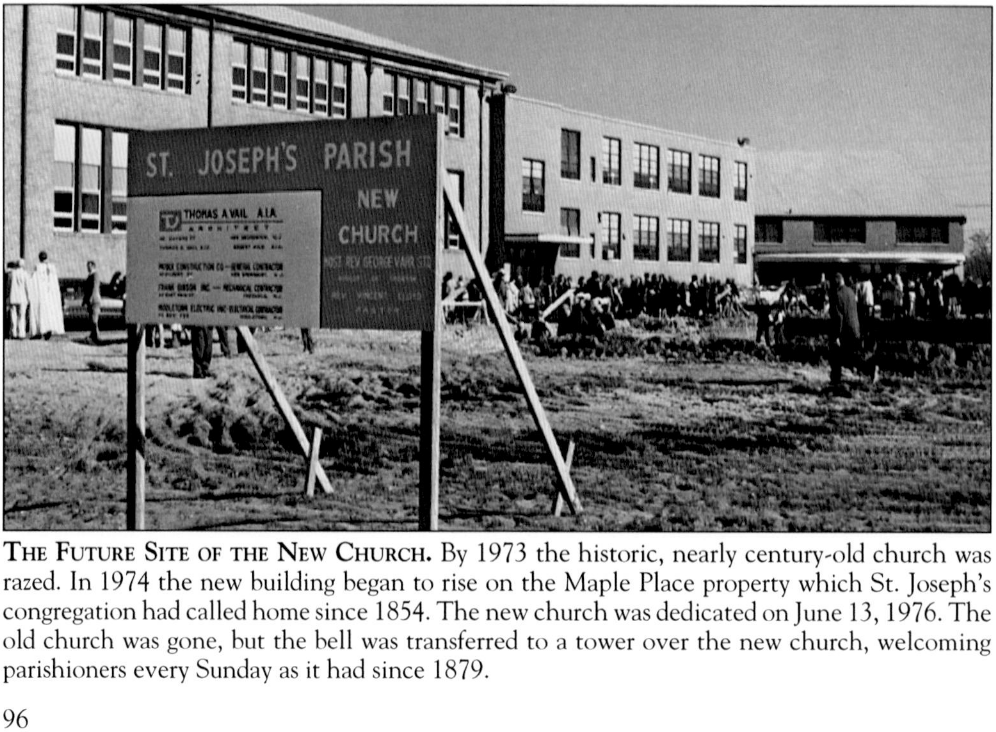

The Future Site of the New Church. By 1973 the historic, nearly century-old church was razed. In 1974 the new building began to rise on the Maple Place property which St. Joseph's congregation had called home since 1854. The new church was dedicated on June 13, 1976. The old church was gone, but the bell was transferred to a tower over the new church, welcoming parishioners every Sunday as it had since 1879.

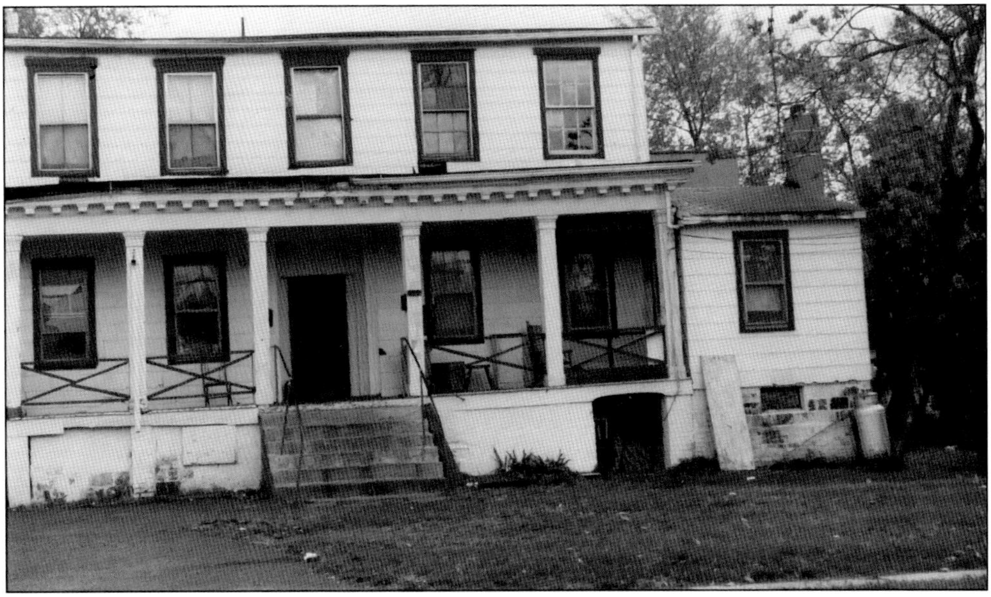

MAJOR'S LOUNGE AND RESTAURANT, C. 1980. For many years Major's slogan was "Where the City meets the Shore." Major's was begun in 1937 by Frank Major Sr. and his children, Frank Jr. and Mary Alice. Major's has played an important role in entertaining Keyport. One of the special guests of the place used to be Juanita Long Hall. Hall, who was born and raised in Keyport, became a famous singer and starred in the 1950s movie *South Pacific*. She played the character Bloody Mary in that film and sang the solo "Bali Hai."

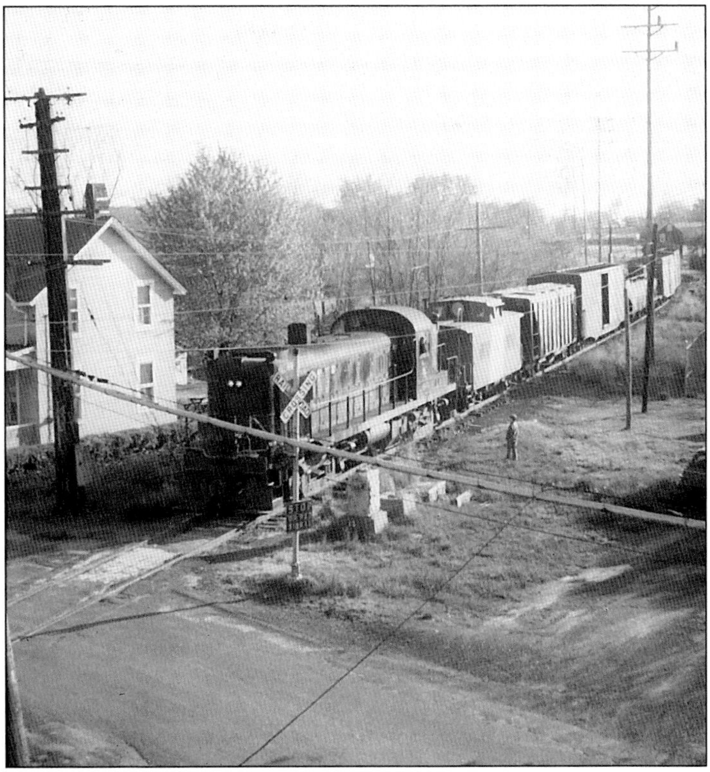

THE FULTON STREET CROSSING, JUNE 1972. This photo was taken by local railroad historian and Keyporter Tom Gallo. Freight trains were still running twice weekly into the 1970s to the IFF complex in Union Beach. The trains could travel no more than 10 or 12 miles an hour, due to the rails being nearly 100 years old in some places.

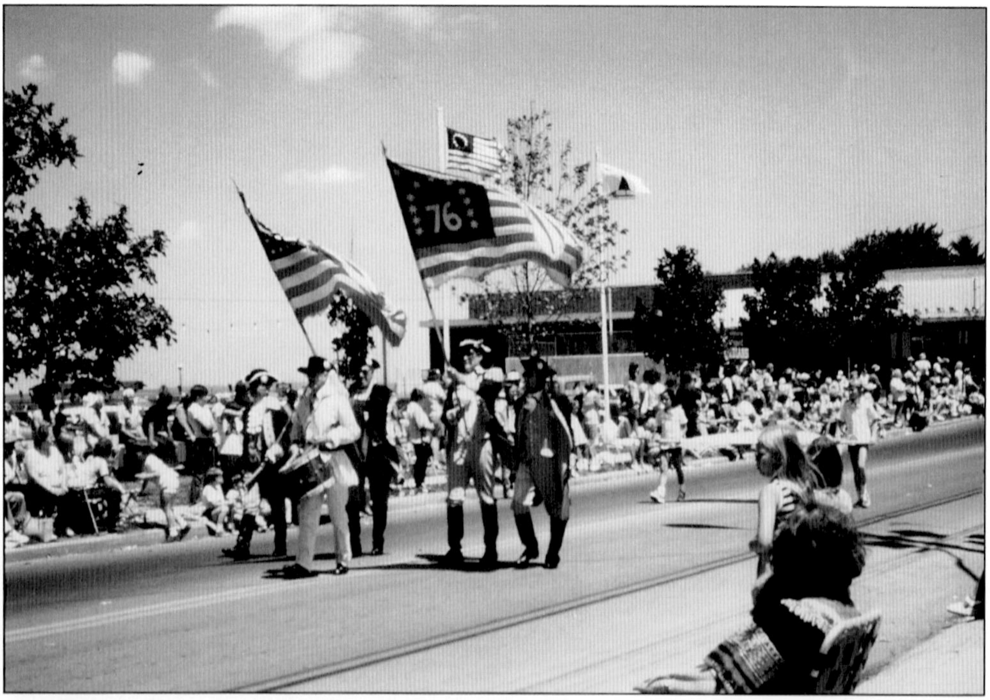

The Bicentennial Celebration. All throughout the summer of 1976, Keyport had weekly events planned. The biggest of these was no doubt the bicentennial parade. Months of planning finally came together as thematic floats, bands, and, of course, colorful fire trucks all made their way through the borough streets. The bottom float depicts the whaleboat raiders who were active during the revolution, under the command of Adam Huylar.

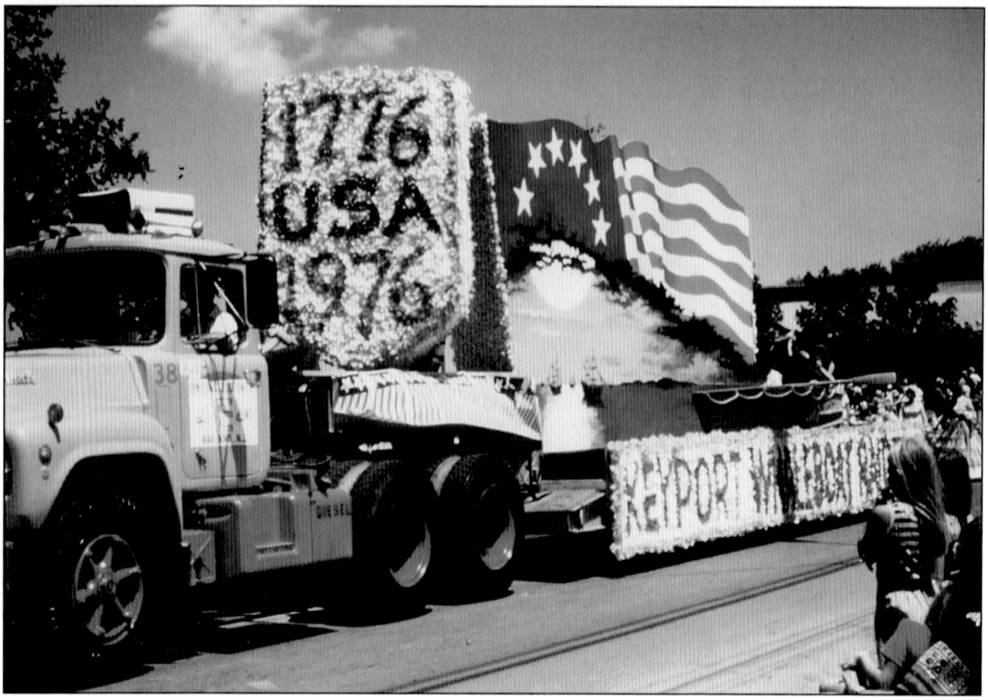

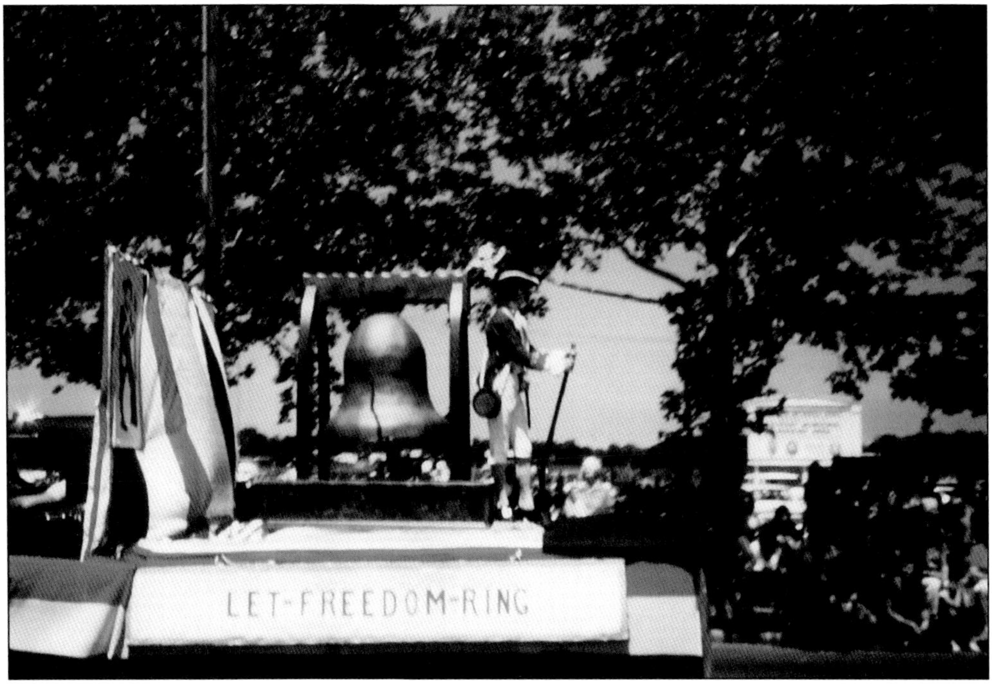

THE BICENTENNIAL CELEBRATION. Here, two more floats roll down West Front Street during the big parade. The top float represents the Liberty Bell, while the bottom float is reminiscent of the Washington's crossing the Delaware.

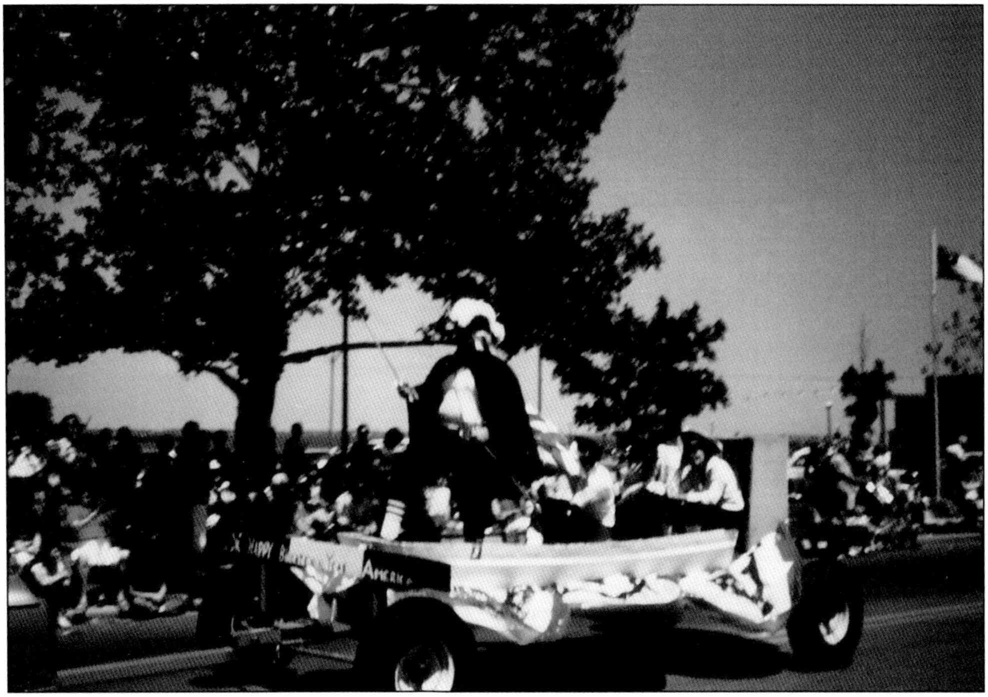

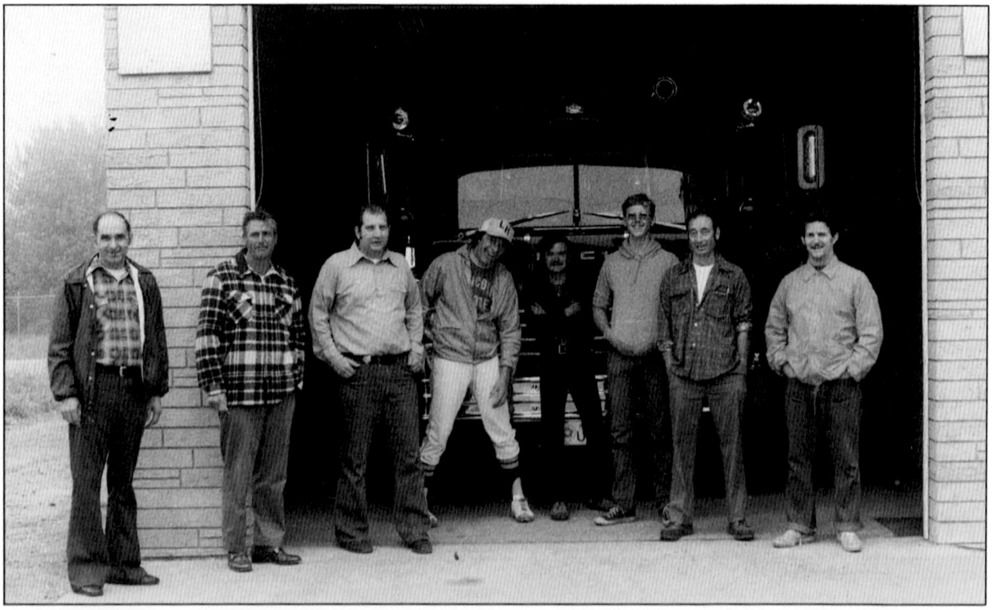

LINCOLN HOSE MEMBERS, 1978. Eight members of the Lincoln Hose Company were caught on camera hanging around the station one Saturday afternoon. From left to right are Dominick Panzera, Sam Minor, John Kovacs, Anthony Youncofski, Jim English, Randy Hicks, Rich Poling, and Jim Poling. John Kovacs served as department chief in 1974 and Jim English was elected chief in 1996.

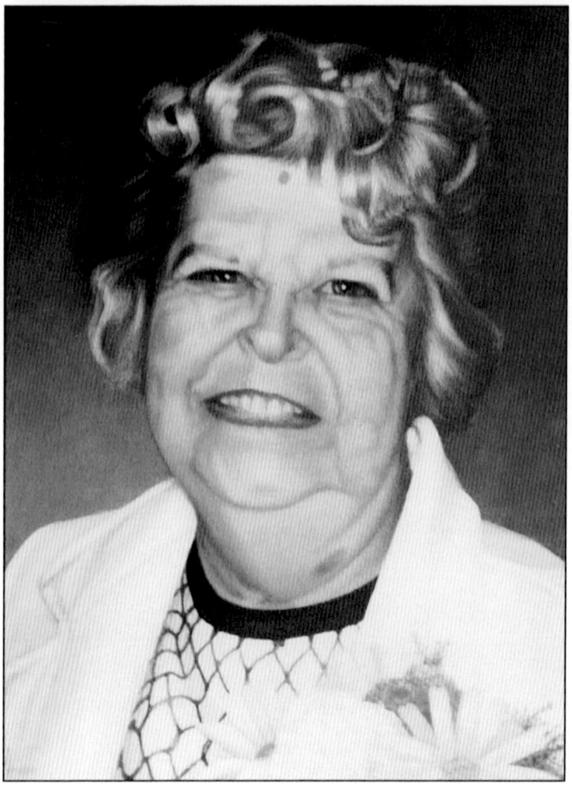

VERA A. CONOVER. One of the strongest advocates of the Keyport Historical Society was Vera Conover. She was the daughter of William and Annie (Seabrook) Conover, born on May 12, 1896, in their Main Street home. In 1972, Vera's dream came true as the Keyport Historical Society was officially formed. Vera Conover lived to see the museum of the society dedicated in 1976. Sadly, Vera passed away on November 2, 1977.

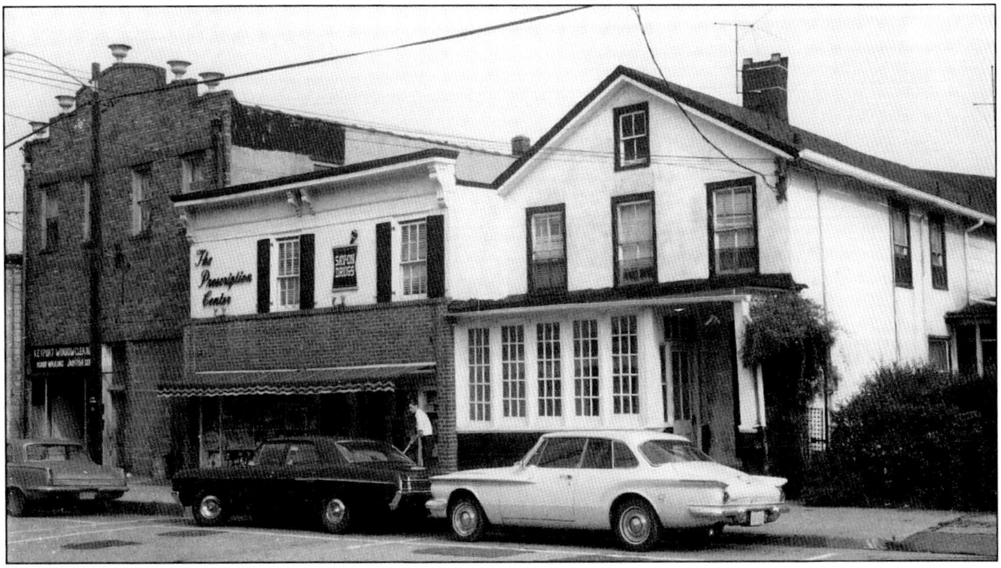

EAST FRONT STREET, *c.* 1965. To the extreme right of this photo is the old Palace Theatre. During the 1930s this was one of Keyport's finest theatres. Rarely did the theatre advertise in local papers, choosing instead to utilize advertising space in the New York City papers. Next in line was the Sav-On Drugstore, operated for many years by Jack Miesler. The historic theatre was razed *c.* 1971, while the drugstore moved further west on Front Street in the late 1980s.

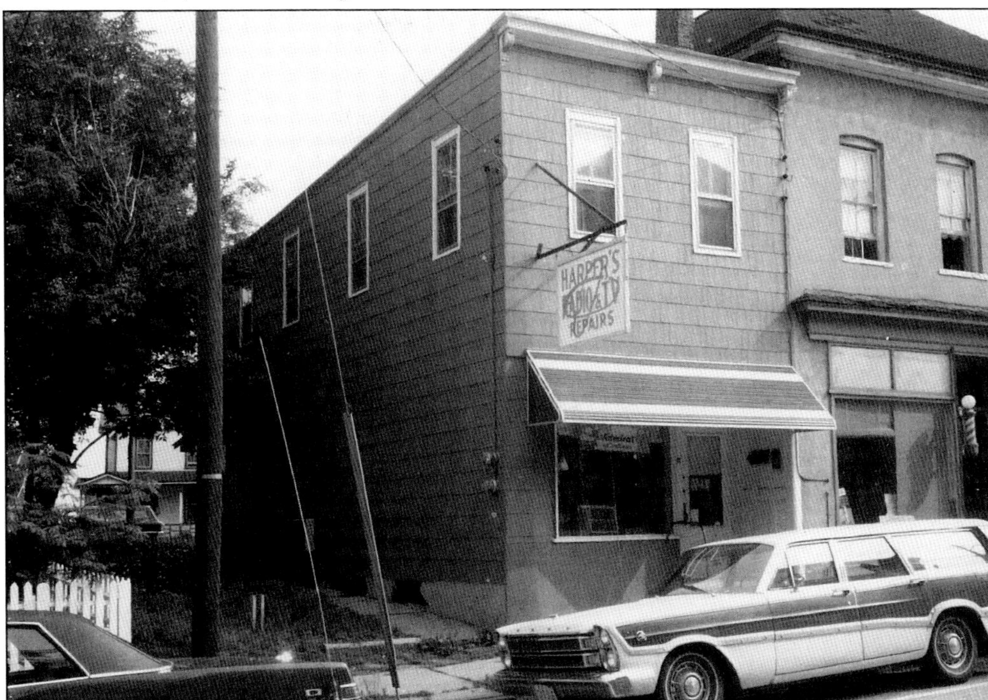

HARPER'S RADIO REPAIR, *c.* 1965. This long, narrow store has stood on East Front Street near Church for well over 100 years. It has been home to many commercial establishments over the years; however, it has always been rented, even when other small stores sometimes sat vacant for years.

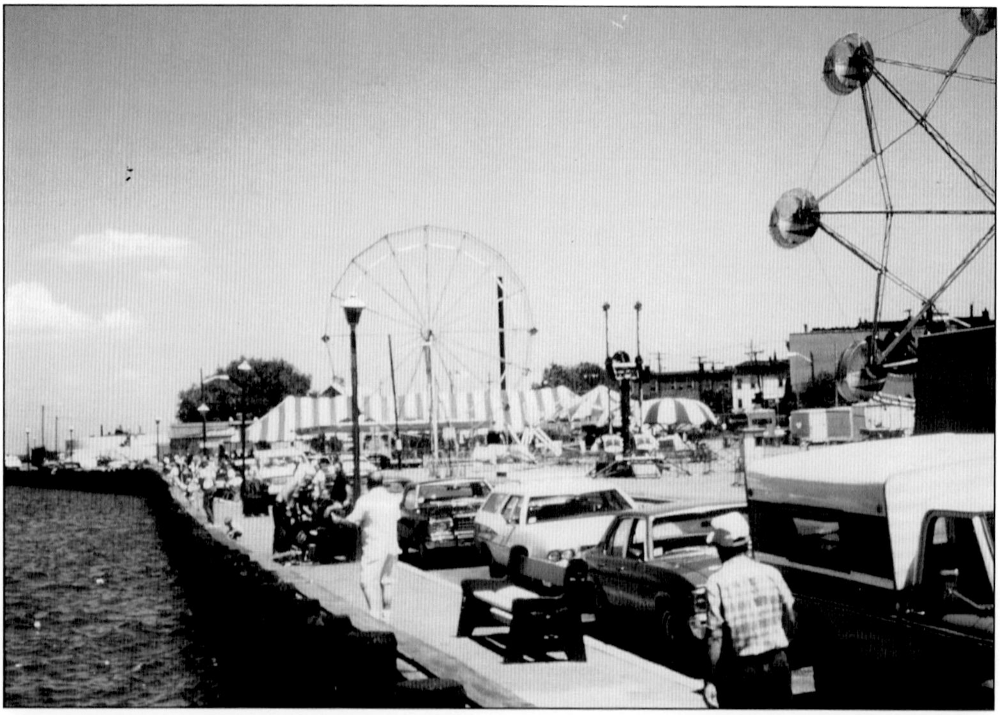

THE 1976 KEYPORT FIREMEN'S FAIR. Each July the municipal parking area on American Legion Drive is transformed into a week-long carnival. The Firemen's Fair is used as the major fund-raiser by the borough's seven fire companies for operating expenses throughout the year. It is also a well-attended event for local people looking for tasty seafood, great fireworks, and good old-fashioned summertime fun. The fair has been run annually since 1966, when it was begun by former-chief Frank "Jr." VanPelt.

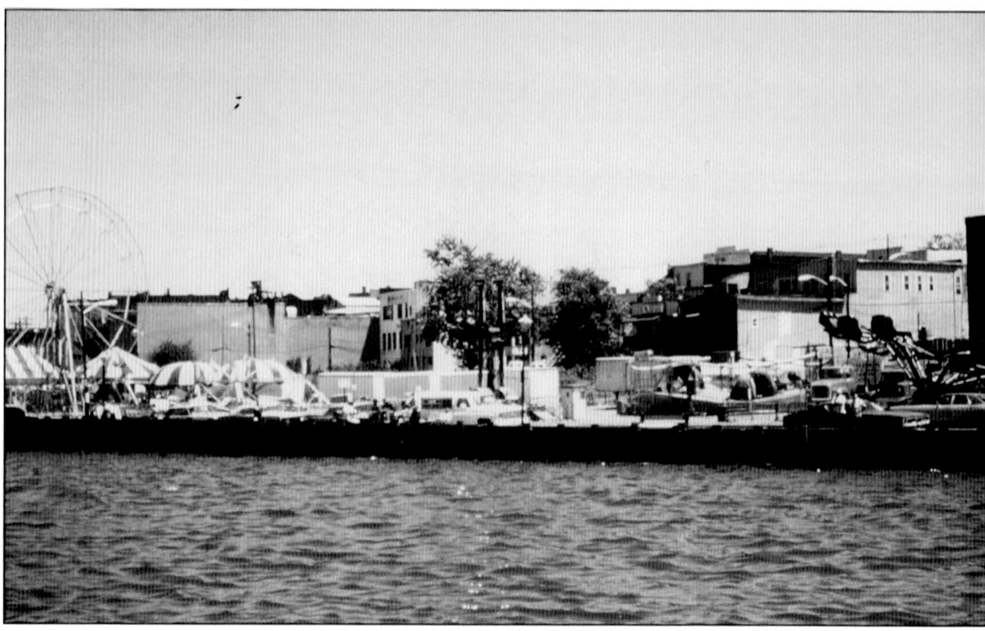

ANOTHER VIEW OF THE 1976 KEYPORT FIREMEN'S FAIR.

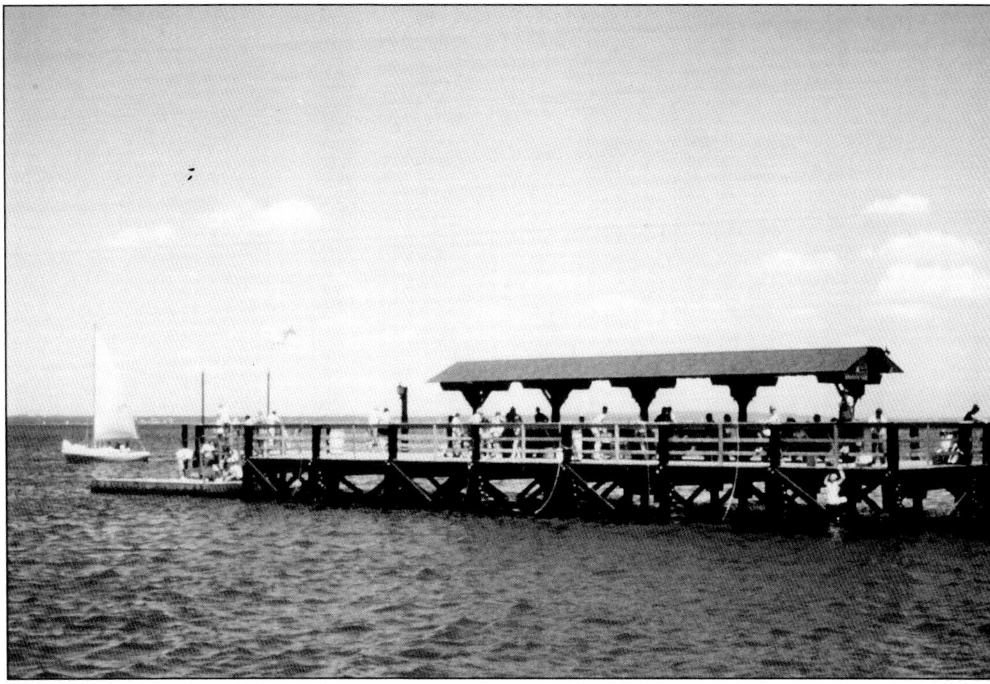

The William Ralph Municipal Fishing Pier. Dedicated in 1976, the pier was later renamed in honor of Mayor William Ralph, who was instrumental in securing the funding for the pier and other projects, such as Cedar Street Park.

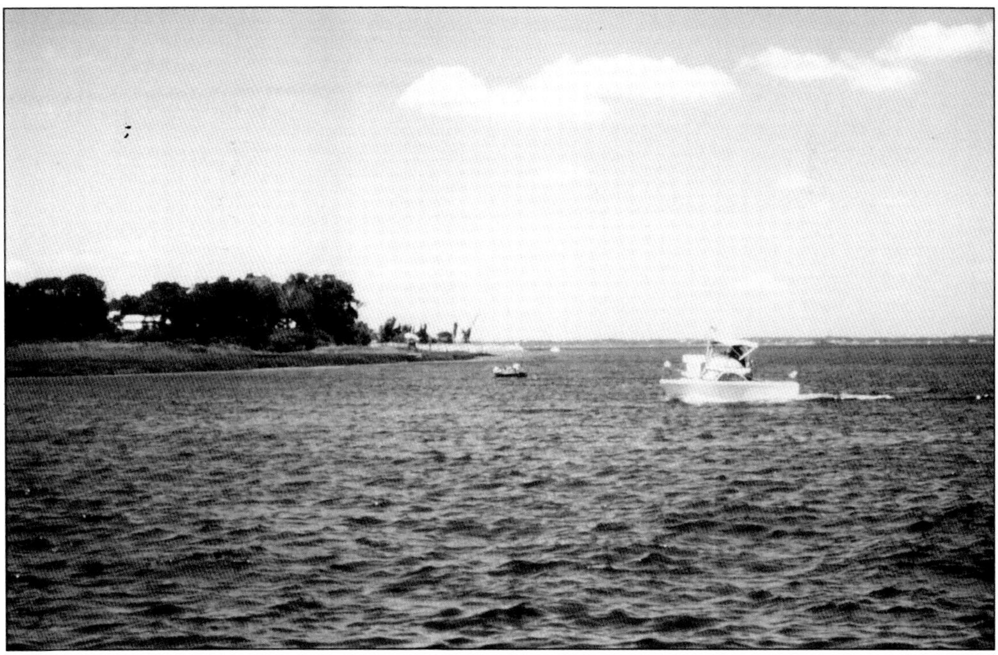

Keyport Harbor, 1976. In just 100 years the boats found in the bay had changed from schooners and steamboats to simple sailboats and small pleasure craft. The bay itself had changed from being a means of making a living to being a place where people went to escape what they did for a living.

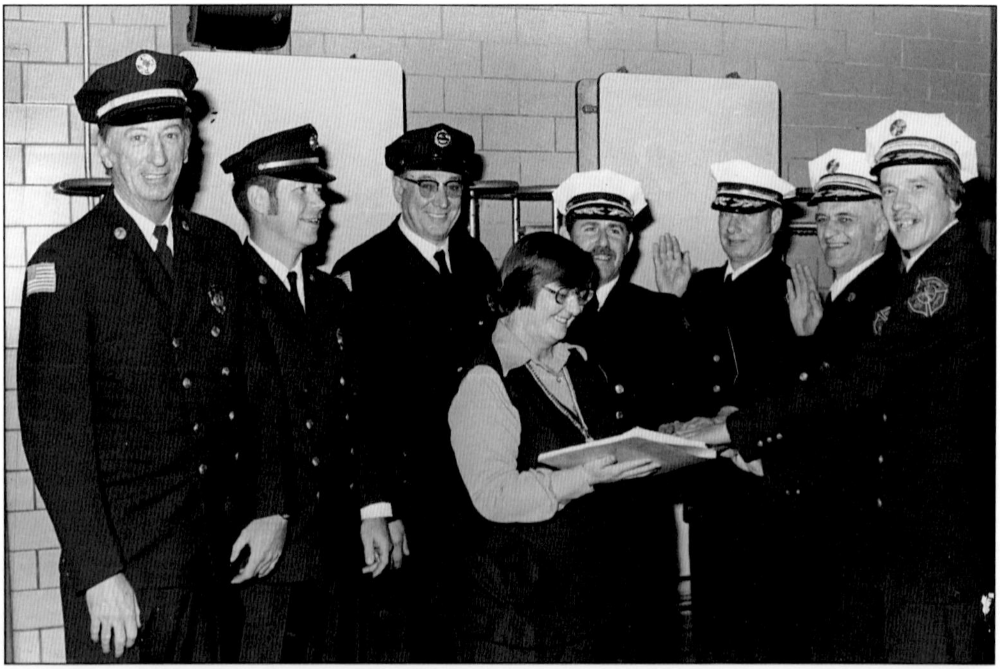

CHANGING OF THE GUARD, 1976. Each January the borough holds its reorganization meeting in the Central School Auditorium. During this time the new board of chiefs is sworn in for the fire department. From left to right are Bill Nagle (chief 1975), Ray Walling (1972), Fire Inspector Jud Ellison, Third Asst. Ed Levine, Second Asst. Bill Brockie, First Asst. Leo McCann, and Chief Harry Aumack II. Officiating the ceremony is Borough Clerk Barbara Tice.

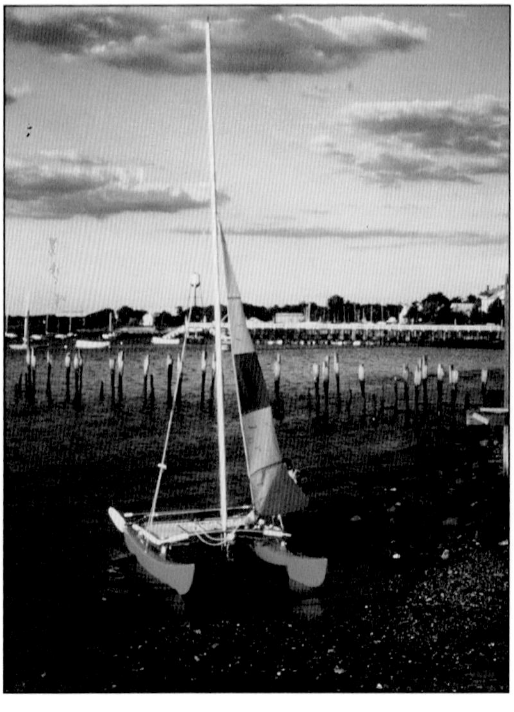

A CATAMARAN ON THE BEACH AT THE FOOT OF BROAD STREET, 1976.

Eight

1981–1990

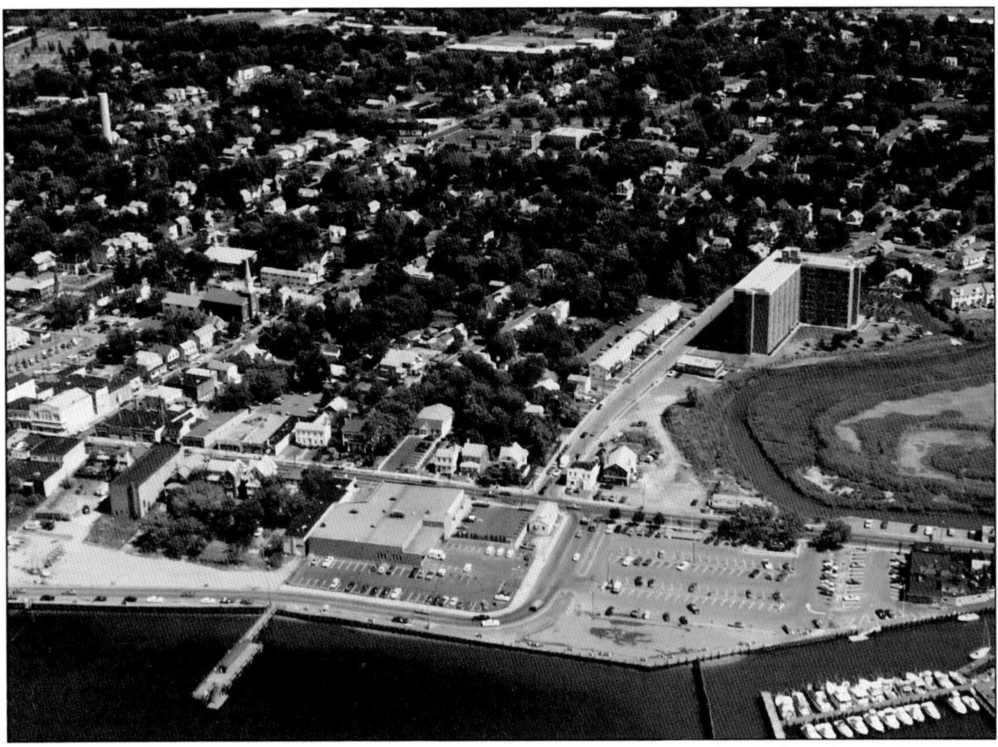

DOWNTOWN CHINGARORA, 1986. Over 156 years had passed since the little village of Key Port was laid out by several men of the Key Port Company. Leonard Walling, the man responsible for naming the town, later regretted choosing the name of Key Port and wished he had kept the Indian name of the place, Chingarora. Unable to change it, he built a vessel of that name in the 1850s.

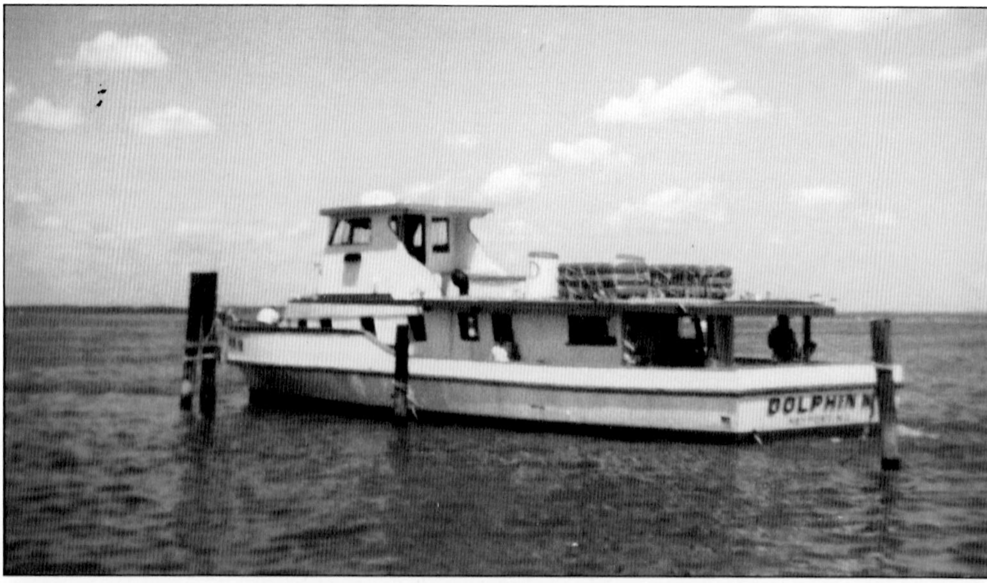

THE *DOLPHIN* M., c. 1982. Many a late night fishing party left Keyport in the 1980s, bound for some good Blue fishing farther out in the Atlantic. For most of the early 1980s the *Dolphin* left Keyport twice daily for charter fishing trips. In the winter of 1987 she sank at her mooring, was later refloated, and soon after disappeared from Keyport. Several years later a new charter boat, the *Captain John*, took the *Dolphin*'s place and continues to run from Keyport throughout the summer of 1998.

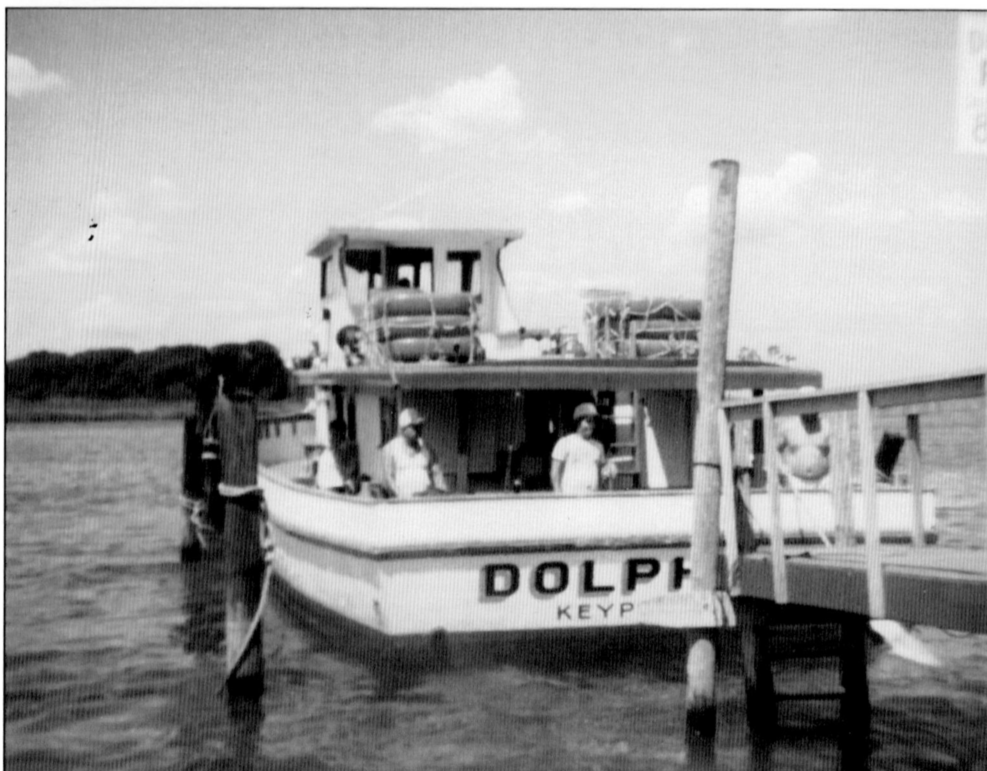

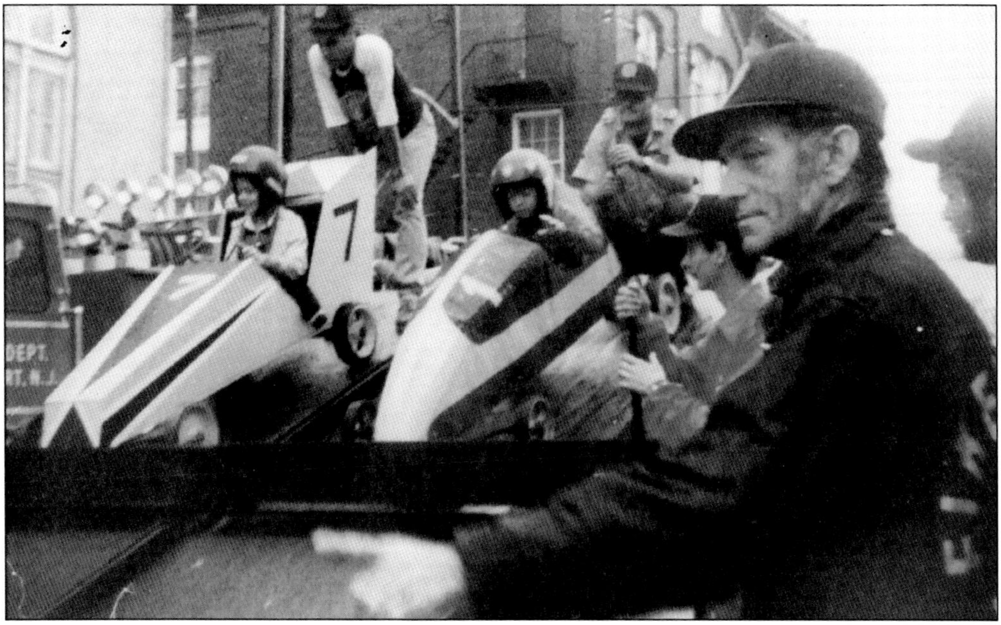

A Keyport Soap Box Derby, 1984. Keyport's soapbox derby was held during the 1950s and again resurrected in the early 1980s by Bob Ferry Sr., a member of the Keyport Fire Patrol who originally sponsored the derby. By 1985, the Keyport Fire Department adopted the derby and Bob Ferry was joined by Gene Regan, jointly operating the derby for several years. Each year the course was the same—down the "Big" East Front Street Hill to the finish line. In the top photograph, Bob Ferry gets ready to give the starting signal to let the racers go. In the bottom photograph, Dan Regan edges out Matt Wasser in a big 1980s race.

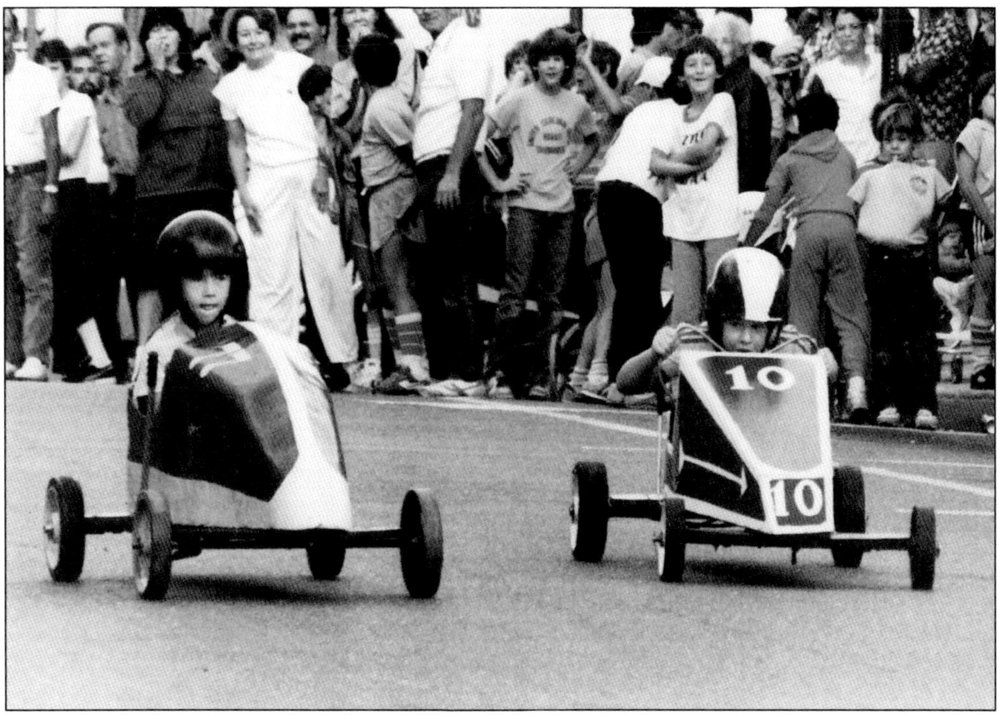

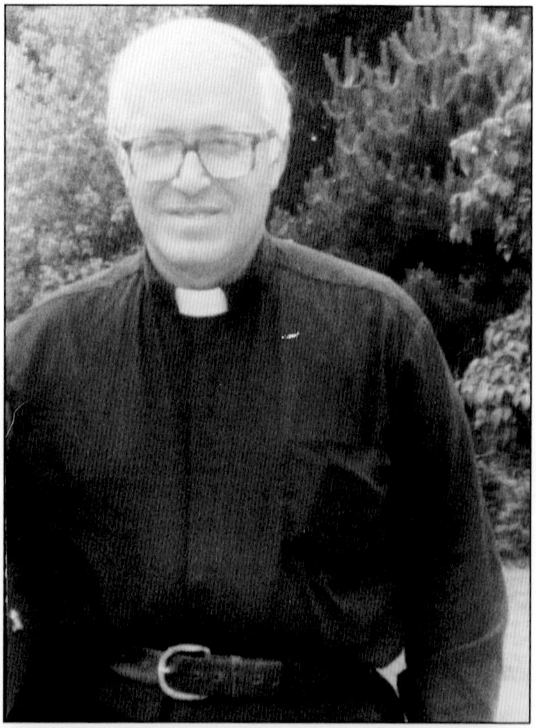

FATHER NICOLI LODO, C. 1984. Father Lodo came to Keyport in the early 1970s and began a Roman Catholic Church originally known as the Immaculate Conception. By 1976, that church had grown substantially in membership and was meeting in the old First Aid Squad building at 128 Broad Street. In 1979, the congregation (which had by then become Jesus the Lord Roman Catholic Church) purchased several lots surrounding the old church and constructed a new church to accommodate its still-growing membership. Father Lodo was a friend to all and because of his diligence and fine leadership, Jesus the Lord Church then became the second Catholic Church in Keyport History.

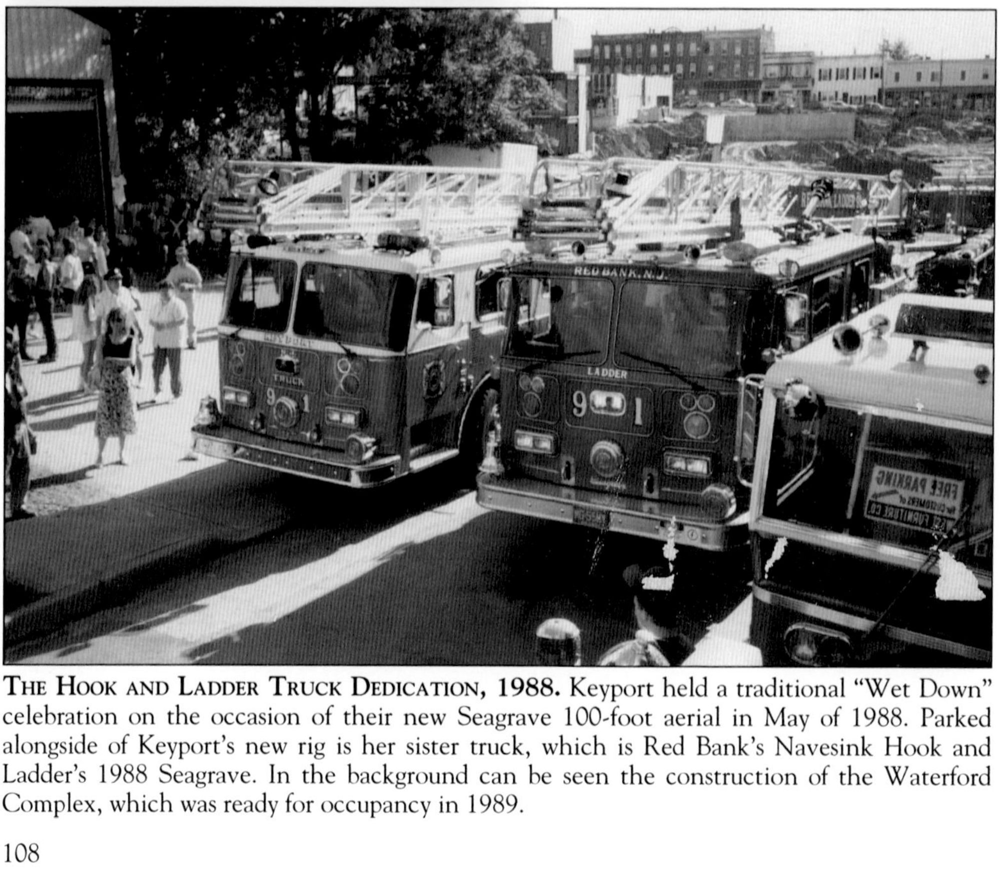

THE HOOK AND LADDER TRUCK DEDICATION, 1988. Keyport held a traditional "Wet Down" celebration on the occasion of their new Seagrave 100-foot aerial in May of 1988. Parked alongside of Keyport's new rig is her sister truck, which is Red Bank's Navesink Hook and Ladder's 1988 Seagrave. In the background can be seen the construction of the Waterford Complex, which was ready for occupancy in 1989.

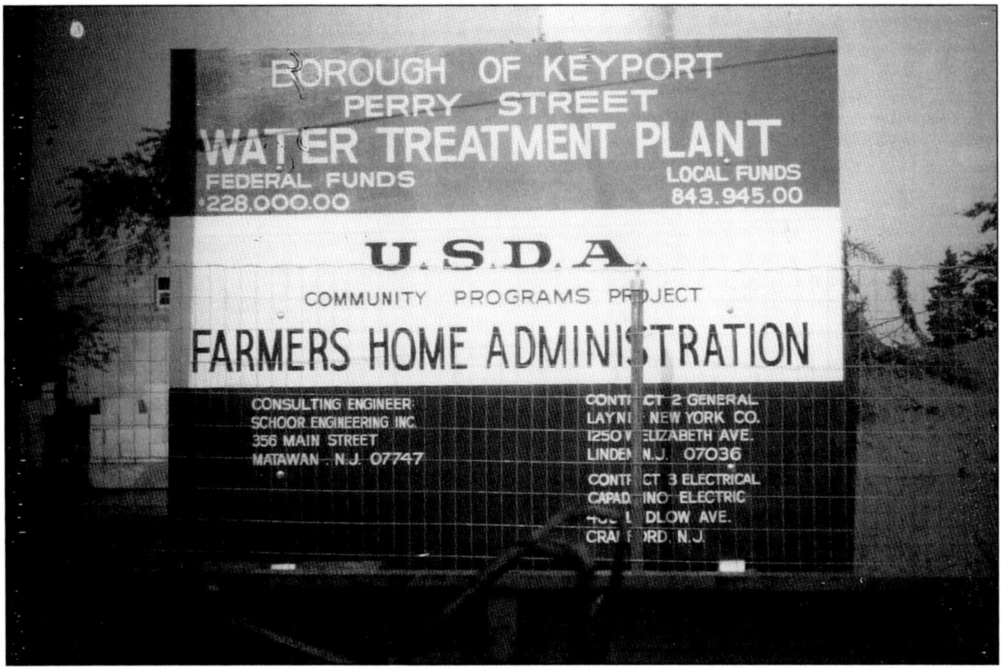

THE WATER TREATMENT PLANT, 1980. Ground was broken in 1980 for the construction of the new water plant, which was to be built on Perry Street near Route 35. The plant was built to replace the old Cedar Street Water Works, which had been in use since the early 1920s. No longer would the place be known as the nostalgic sounding "Water Works," but would now be called a high-tech water treatment plant.

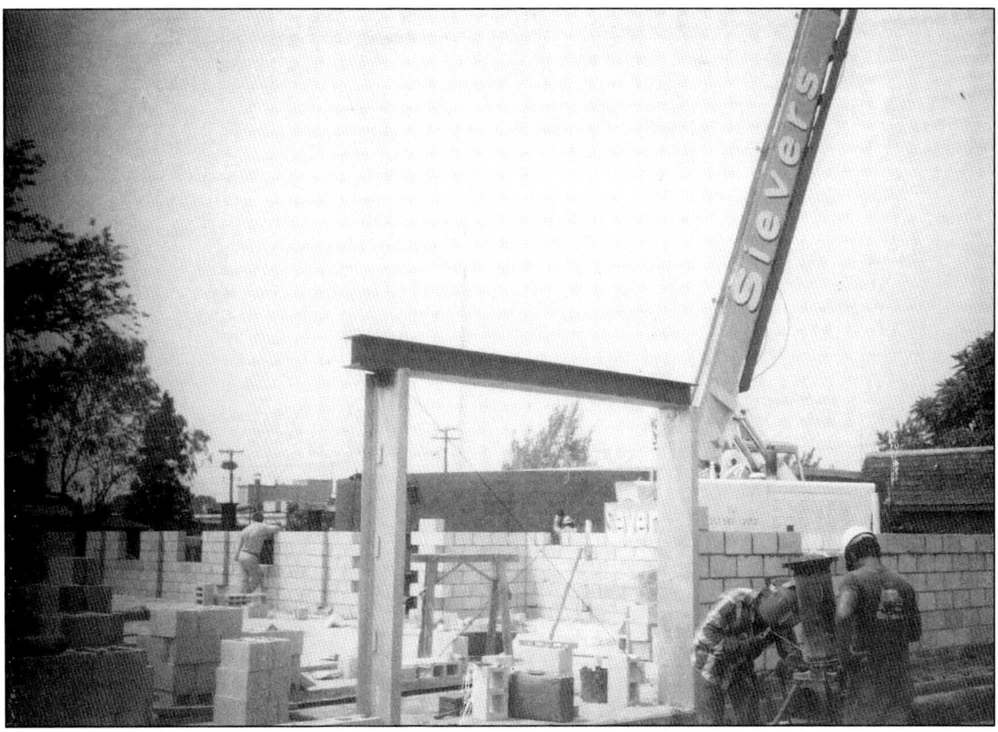

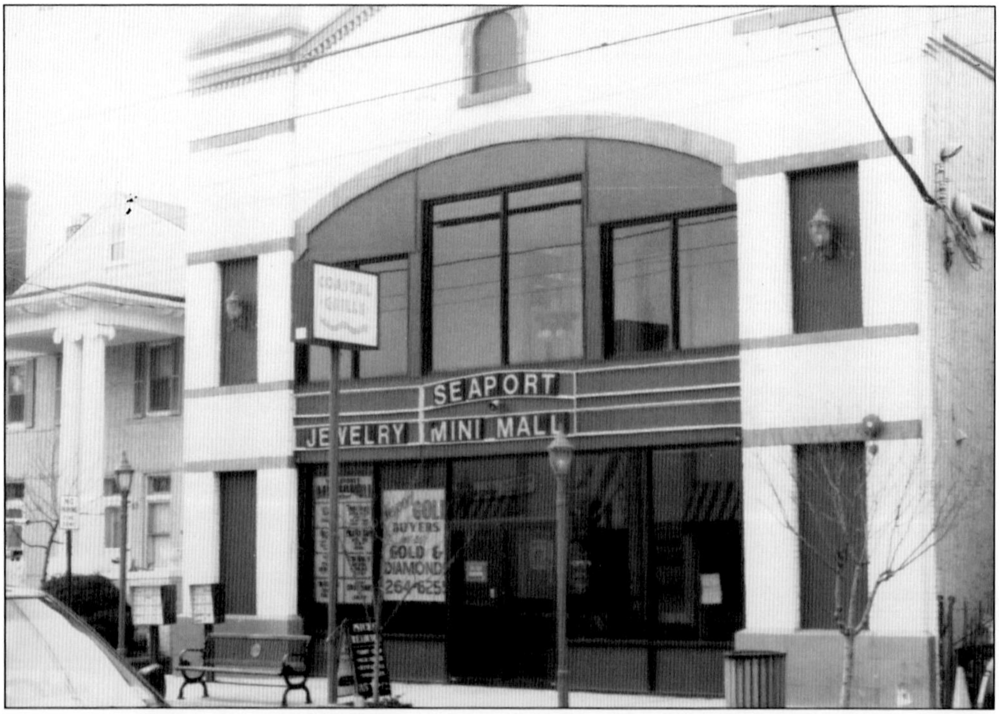

The Seaport Mini-Mall, 1987. The last film to be shown in the old Surf/Strand Theatre was *Popeye*, with Robin Williams and Shelly Duvall. After its re-emergence from use as an adult theatre, it was known briefly as the Movies at Keyport. Simply unable to compete with the larger theatres, the place closed down soon after. It was then remodeled into a mini-mall, After housing a series of floundering restaurants, the place is now known as the Bulkhead Bar and Grille. The Bulkhead, with its great food and outdoor deck, is operated by the Merla family—Josie, Charlie, and Joseph.

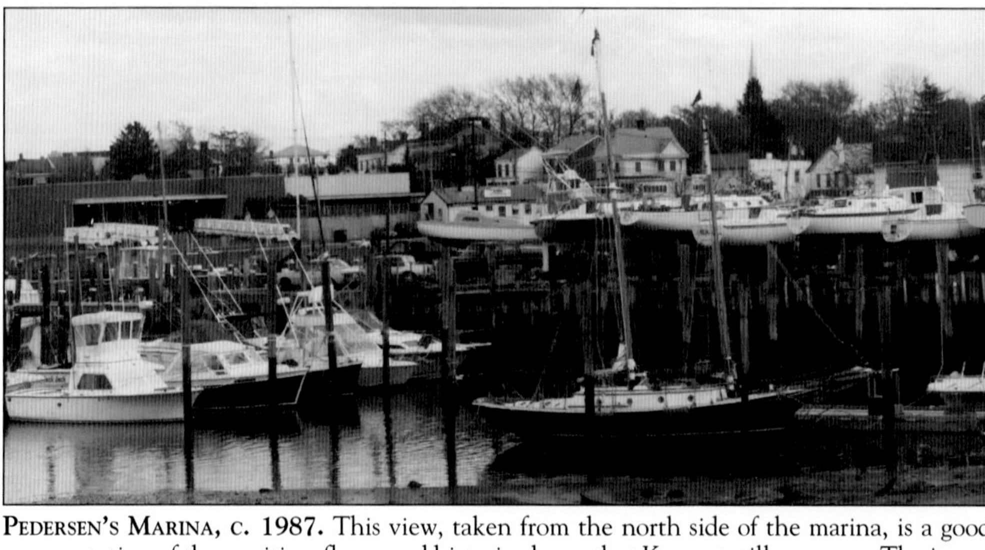

Pedersen's Marina, c. 1987. This view, taken from the north side of the marina, is a good representation of the maritime flavor and historic charm that Keyport still possesses. The image was taken in the early autumn, as only a few vessels remain in the water. In a few weeks all the boats would be on land and the owners would be winterizing their craft until the next spring.

FRENCHY'S MEAT MARKET, C. 1987. Keyport's last family-owned butcher shop was located along the south side of Front Street until 1995. The building, vacant for some time, was later to become one of the many antique stores that settled in town.

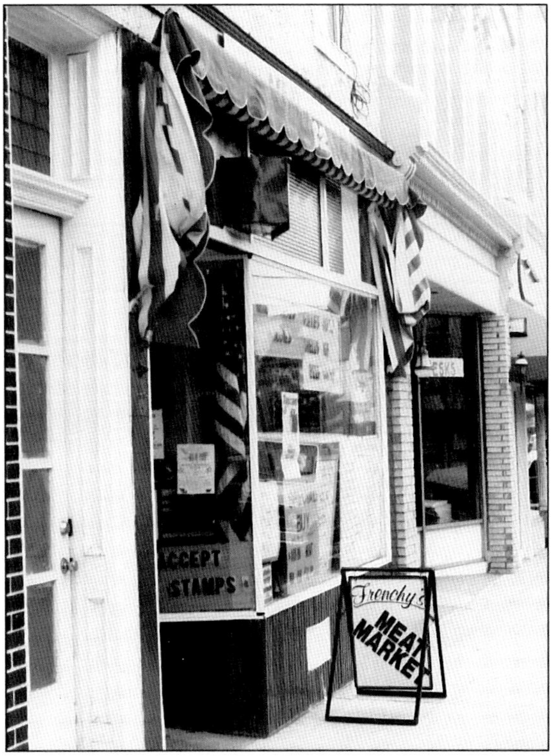

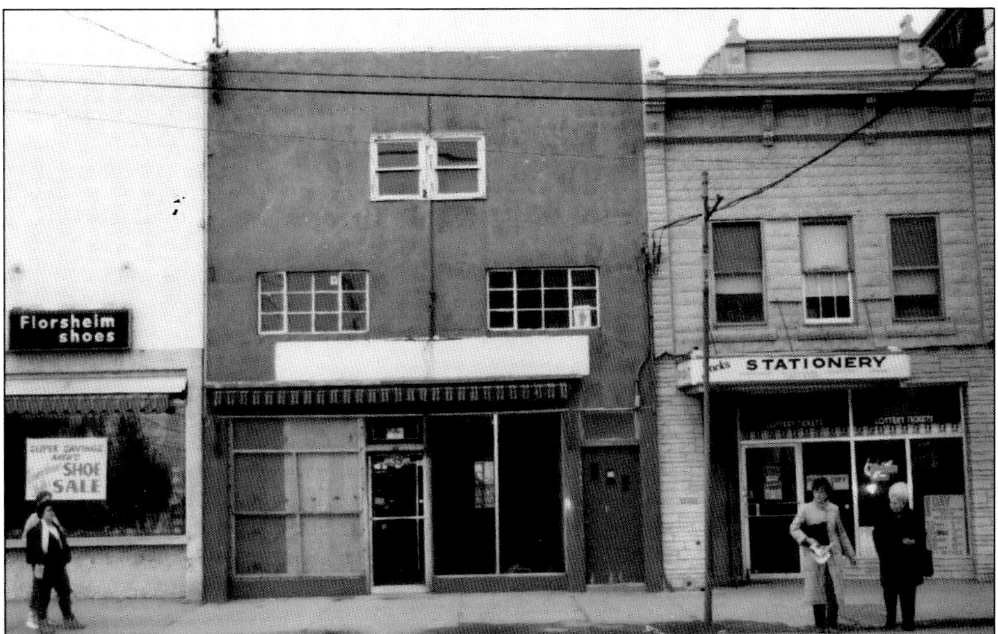

FRONT STREET AT MAIN, 1986. The last eyesores in Keyport's shopping district would be remodeled soon. Led by Keyporter Kathy Shaw, the business district was given a complete facelift, including new signage, paint, and benches. Trees were placed along Front Street from Beers to Broad Street. The beautification process continues in 1998.

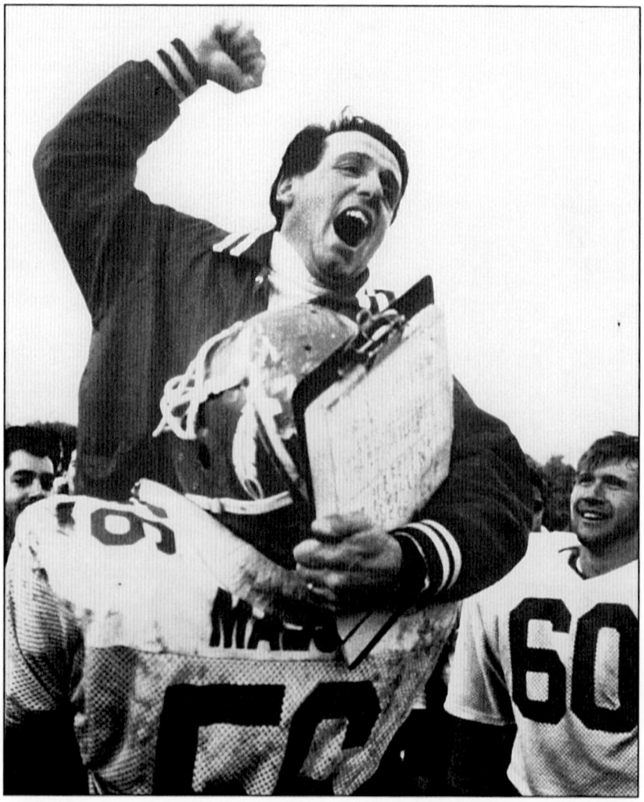

Champions, 1987. It was a cold Saturday afternoon when Keyport traveled south in December of 1987 for the big showdown against Asbury Park High School. Keyport was predicted to lose by almost everyone, in what was to become the most memorable day in Keyport athletics. Mike Ciccotelli, Bob Crader, and Brian Brady coached the team, led by seniors such as Lou Tomasello, Efrain Cabrera, Jerold Jeffcoat, Greg Stillwell, George Mazur, Frank Currier, Mike Sage, Steve Antonucci, and Robert Aumack, to a 20-12 victory over Asbury Park. It was headlines for Keyport, as they had coveted the Central Jersey, Group C Championship.

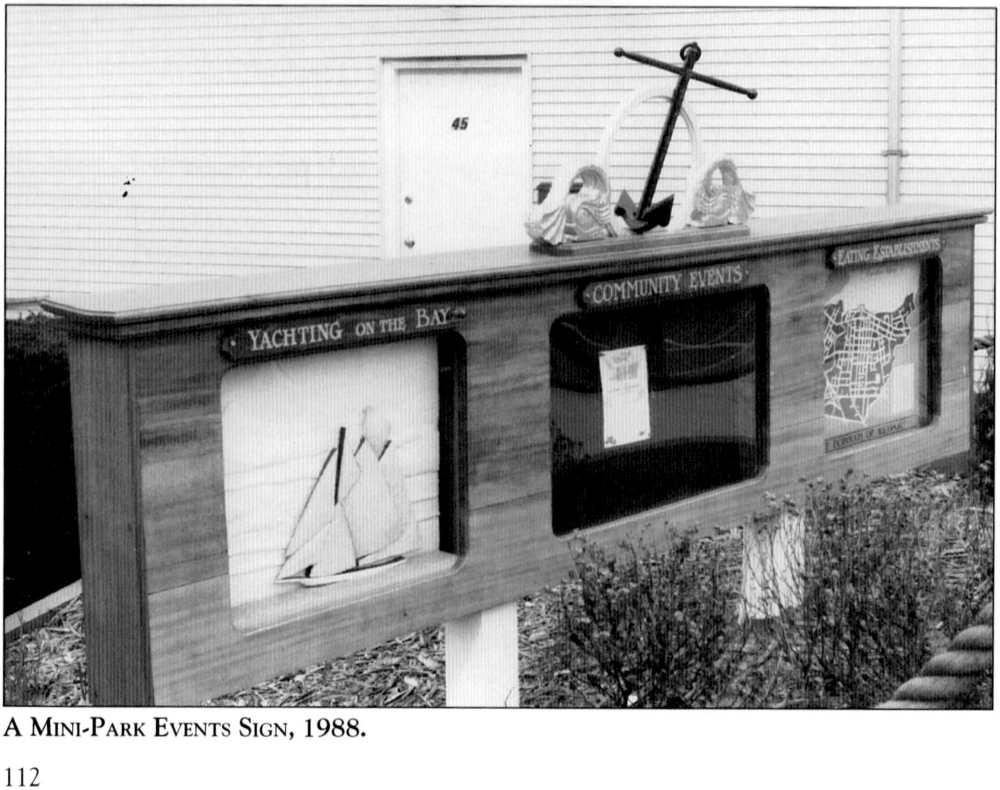

A Mini-Park Events Sign, 1988.

A Future Firehouse Sign, 1986. In 1985 both the Keyport Hook and Ladder Company and the Keyport Engine Company were looking to move to new locations. The ladder company's firehouse was over 100 years old, and the engine house was fast approaching its centennial. It was decided to build a shared firehouse on property on First Street. The new building, which was known as Consolidated Fire Protection, was dedicated in 1986 and continues to serve the companies today.

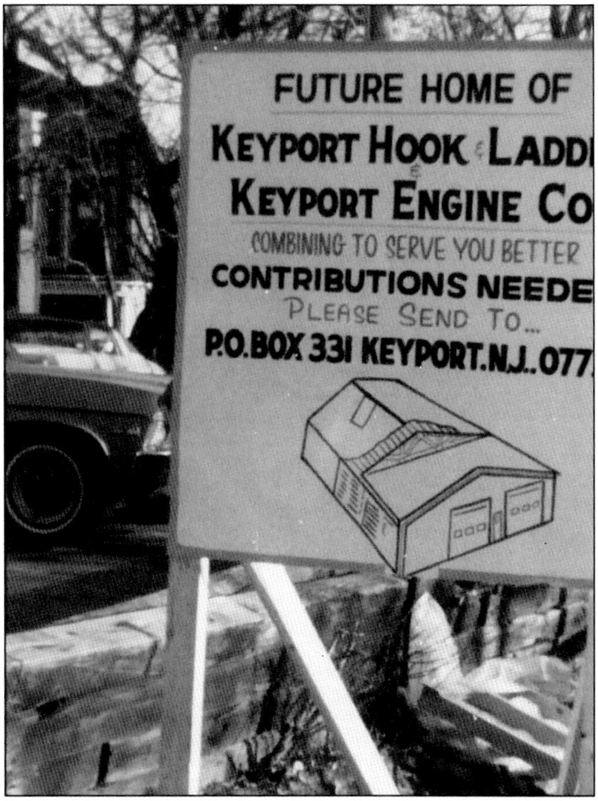

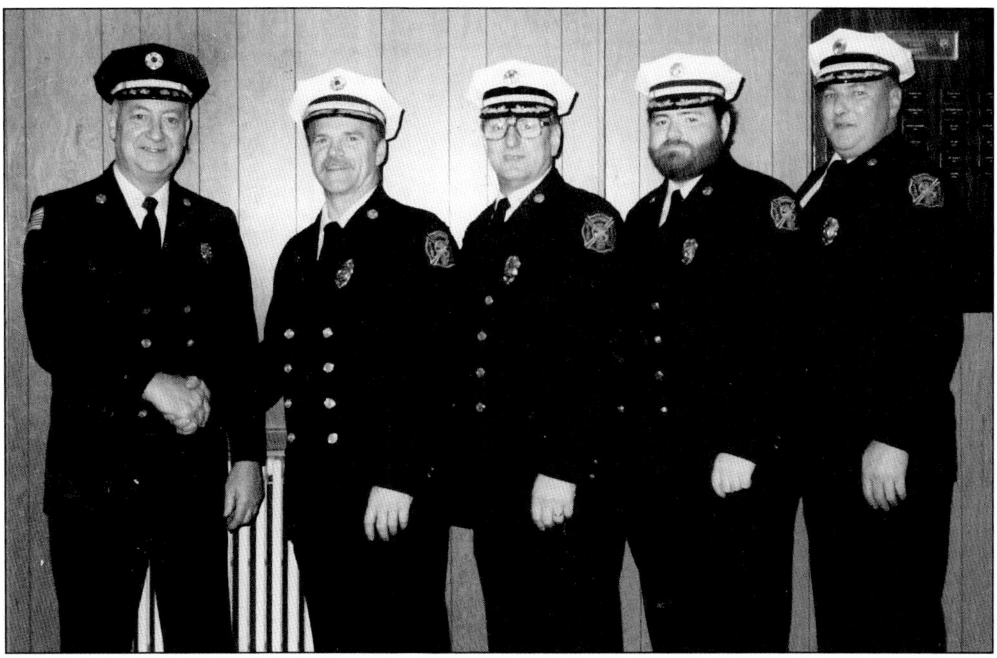

The Passing of the Chief's Hats, 1985. From left to right are outgoing 1984 Chief John Jones, 1985 Chief Robert Poling, 1986 Chief Julius Rosato, 1987 Chief Robert Ferry Jr., and 1988 Chief John M. Brandauer.

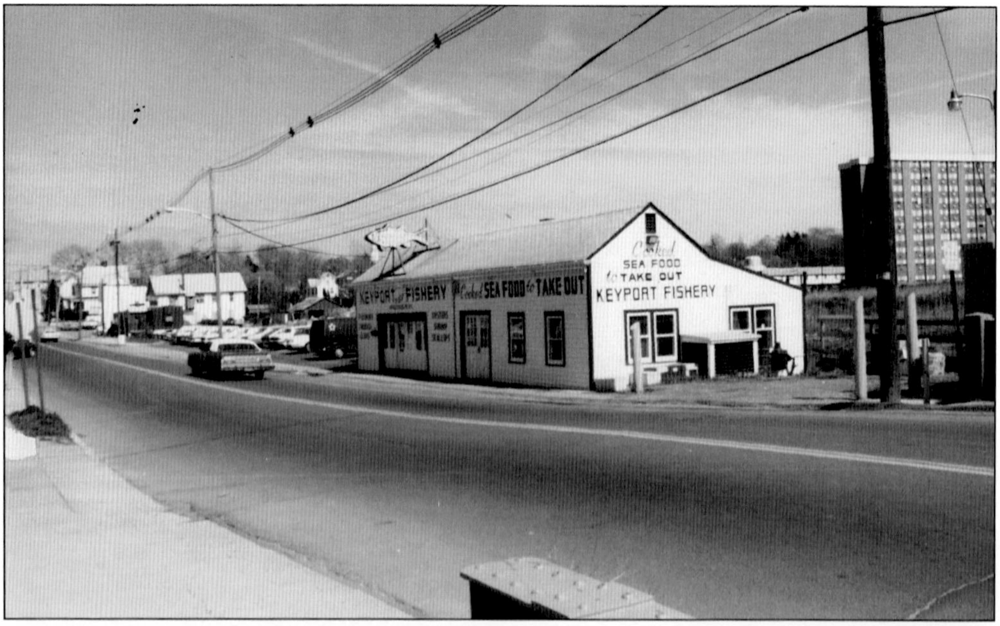

The Keyport Fishery, 1987. A longtime Keyport landmark, tourists know this as the Keyport Fishery, but anyone from Keyport will tell you that it's Wilson's Fishery. Owned by the Wilson family since 1936, the best fresh and fried fish anywhere can be found here. It's takeout only, but well worth the trip, as can be attested by the long lines each weekend.

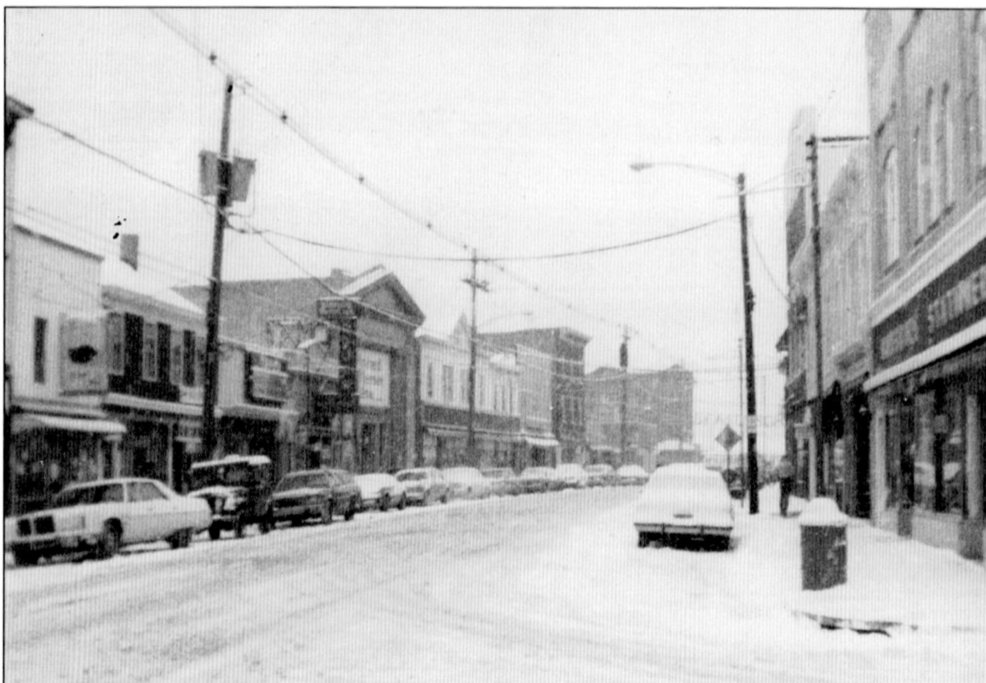

Front Street, 1985. This snowstorm was captured on the author's old 110 camera 13 years ago. By 1998, Newberrys, Bayshore Stationers, and the bare streets had vanished, replaced by antique shops galore, shade trees, and benches to facilitate summertime shopping.

Green Grove Cemetery The old caretaker's house at Green Grove Cemetery has stood watch over the place for well over 100 years. Green Grove Cemetery was organized in 1845 by Wilson Brown, John Sproul, and Alfred Walling. In 1849, 19-year-old Margaret S. Dey became the first person to be laid to rest in the new cemetery. Her headstone was inscribed "Margaret, beloved one, rest in peace."

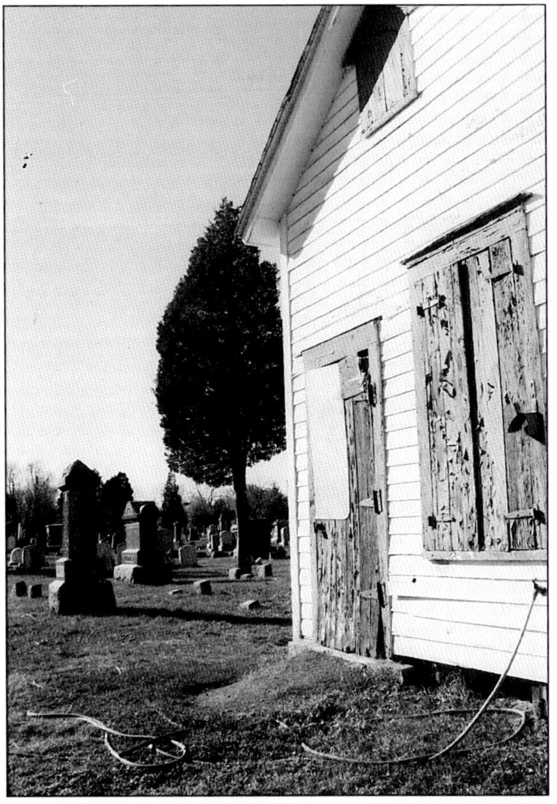

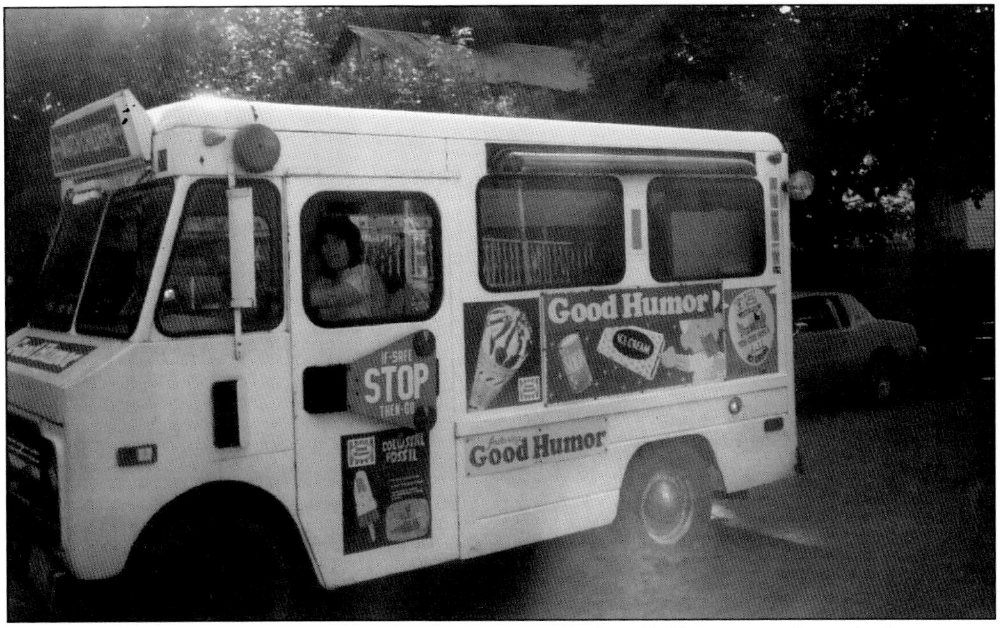

An Ice Cream Truck on Church Street, 1989. With its bells ringing through the summer breeze, the local ice cream truck has arrived once again. Local kids can be spotted darting from pools and houses all along the street, trying to catch up to this frozen treat on wheels. I don't know about you, but I'm going to have a Bombpop, no maybe a Chocolate Eclair, no maybe . . .

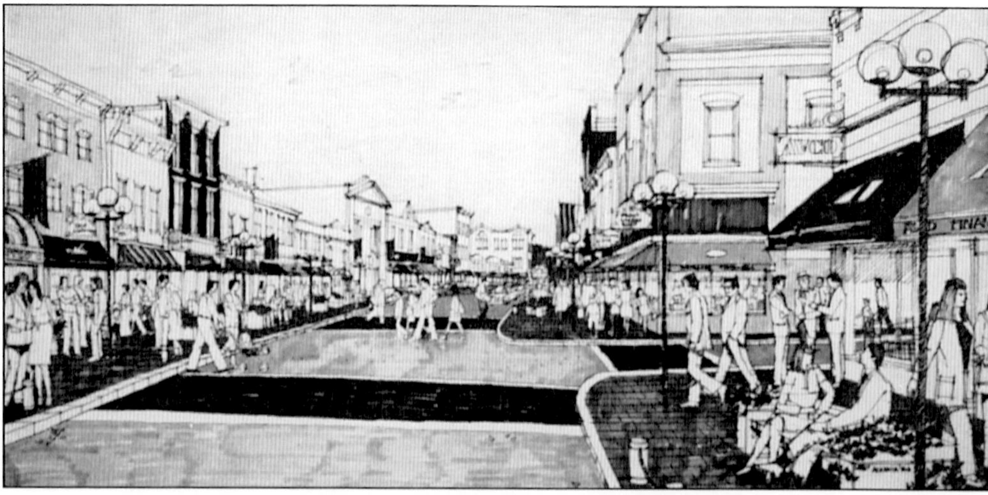

KEYPORT'S MASTER PLAN, 1986. It is hoped that someday this project will come to fruition. Developed in the mid-1980s, little has been done to meet the goals set forth in the master plan. It is interesting to note that the First Street extension, the bayside park, and the extension of the Front Street stores were all proposed as early as 1901 in an edition of the *Keyport Weekly*. The proposal was made by a Mr. E.L. Rapp, who should be given the real credit for Keyport's "Master Plan."

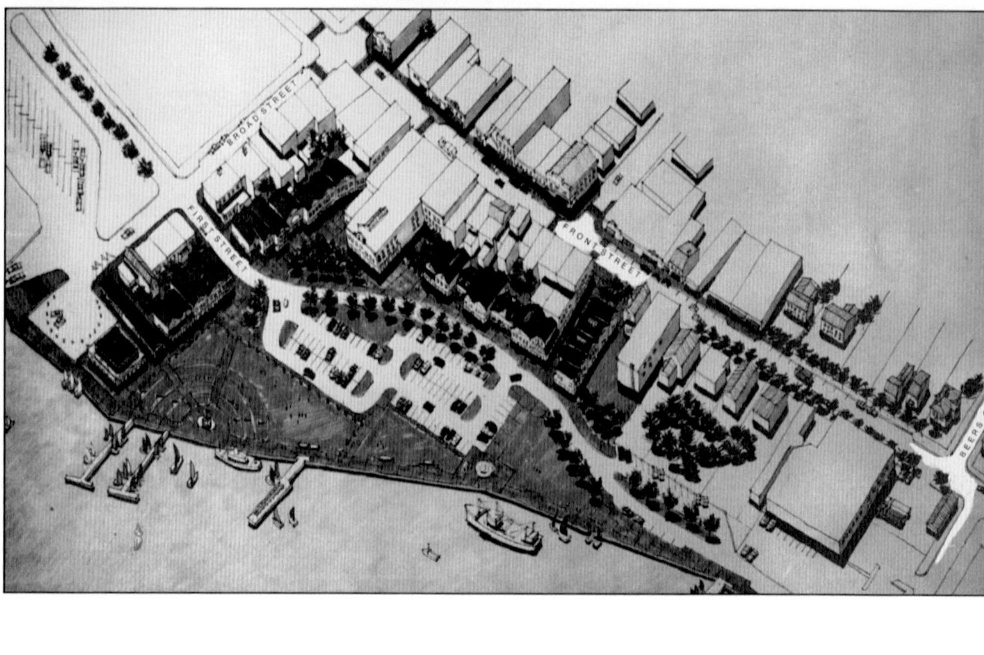

Ten

1991 AND BEYOND

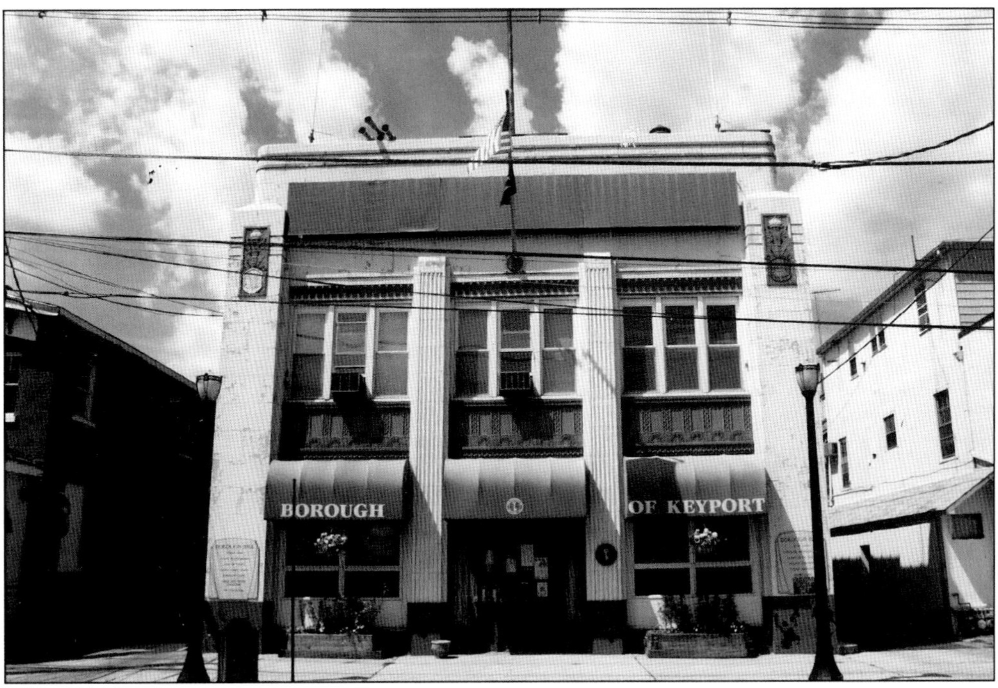

KEYPORT BOROUGH HALL, 1998. Keyport's fourth meeting place was purchased in 1952 from the Jersey Central Power and Light Company. The Art Deco building was the former headquarters for the utility company, which began years earlier in Keyport as an outgrowth of the trolley service. The borough hall is scheduled to be vacated sometime in 1999–2000, as property has been secured on Front Street and plans are underway for the fifth village/town/borough hall to serve Keyport.

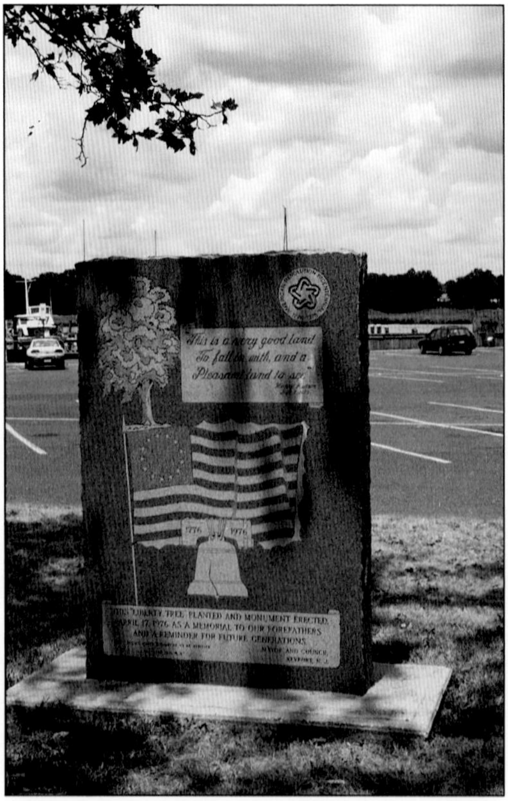

The Time Capsule on West Front Street. Erected in 1976 during the bicentennial, this time capsule is due to be opened in 2076. The impressive monument stands over 5 feet tall and weighs almost a ton. Beneath the monument is a box of souvenirs, newspapers, and postcards from 1976 Keyport.

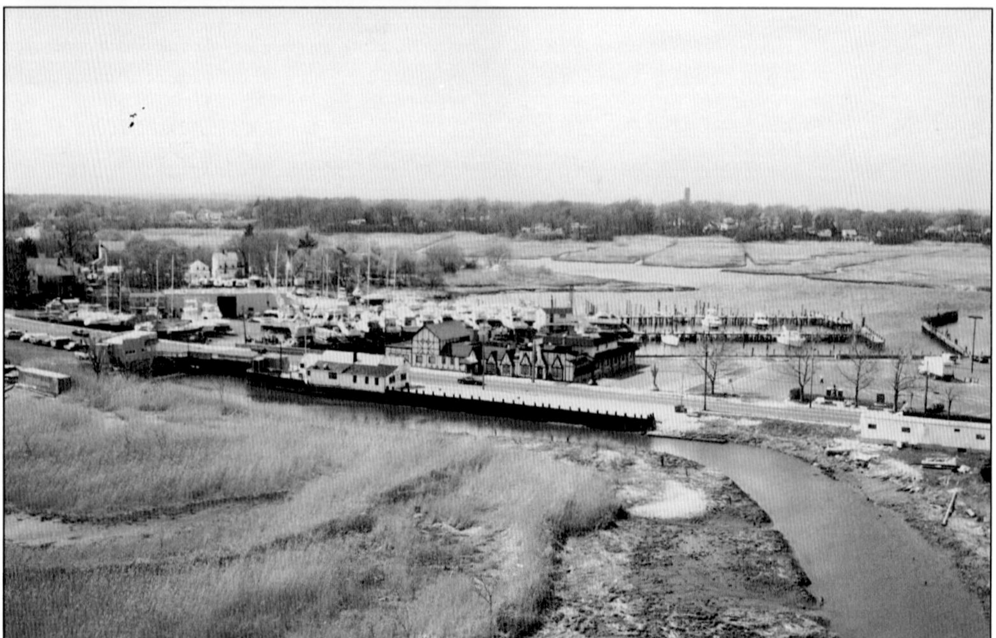

Lupattatong Creek, as Seen from the American Legion Apartments. This view, taken by Jim McTernan, shows (foreground to background) the Keyport Fishery, Ye Cottage Inn, Pedersen's Marina, Matawan Creek, and the salt marshes of Cliffwood.

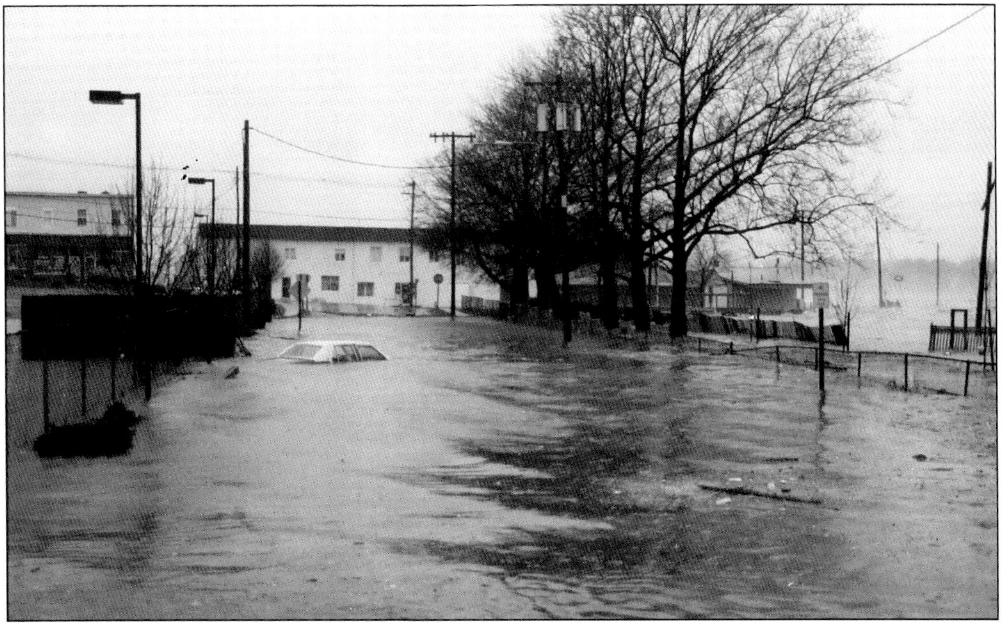

A Nor'easter. Most of the townspeople were awakened by the sound of wind and torrential rains at about 4:00 a.m. on December 16, 1992. By 9:00 a.m. the unforeseen storm had hit the Jersey Shore full force as the bay swelled and reclaimed its former lands. Many people had to be rescued by boats, while others simply sat the storm out. In the top photograph, First Street becomes a lake as a large sedan begins to float away. The water along First Street reached a depth of nearly 6 feet in the hollow. In the bottom photograph, West Front near the creek was just an extension of the bay, as waves caused thousands of dollars in property damage. During this storm the Keyport Historical Society was badly damaged and many important photos and documents were swallowed by the sea.

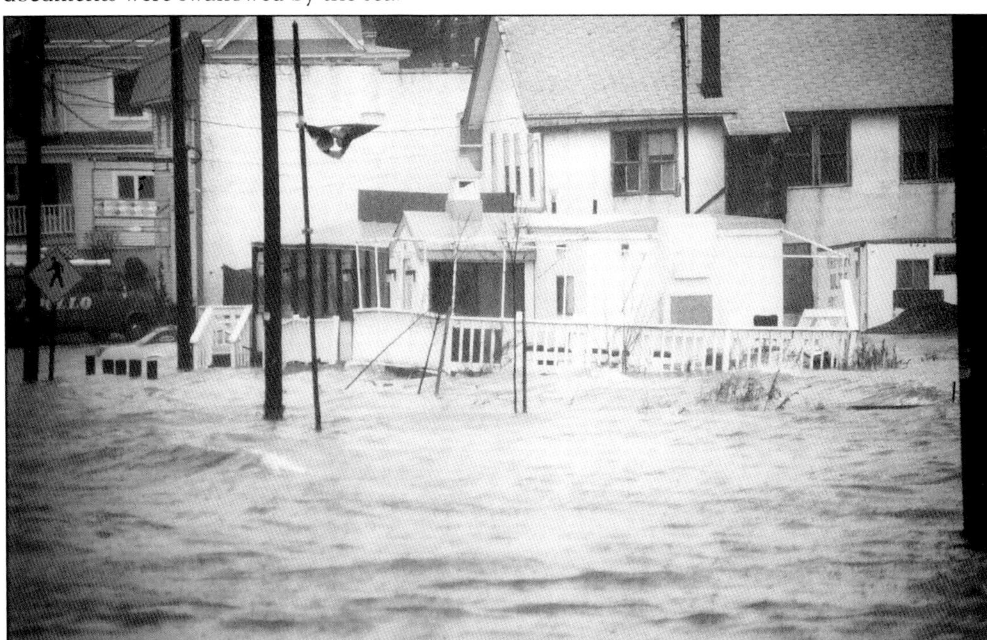

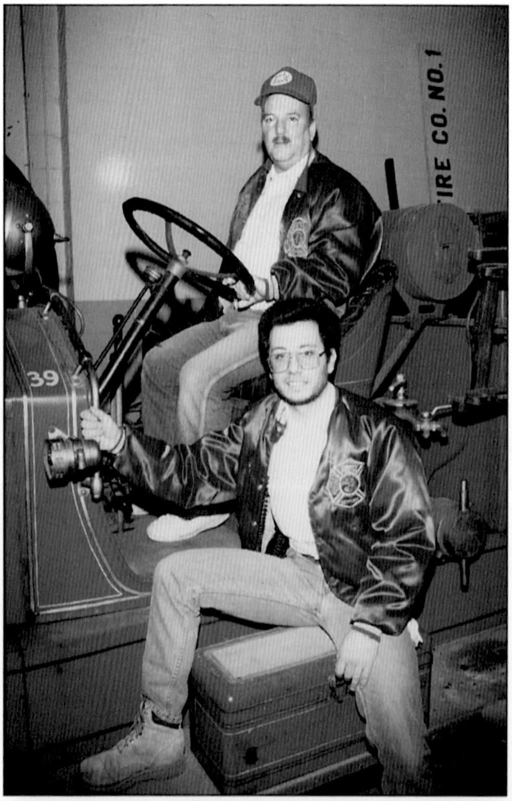

BERT MORRIS AND KEN KROHE, 1996. These two Liberty Hose Firefighters pose on the running board of the 1929 American LaFrance they had just re-purchased from the Flagtown Fire Co. in Somerset County. Former-chief Morris and Chief Krohe could have been no prouder as the old truck was hauled back to her home town, where she had been sold at public auction in 1953. After all those years the truck was still lettered for the Liberty Hose Co. and even had its original ladders and siren intact. It is now used for parades. In the photograph below, Chief Morris and former-Captain John McCleaster are out for a ride on the 29-foot fire truck.

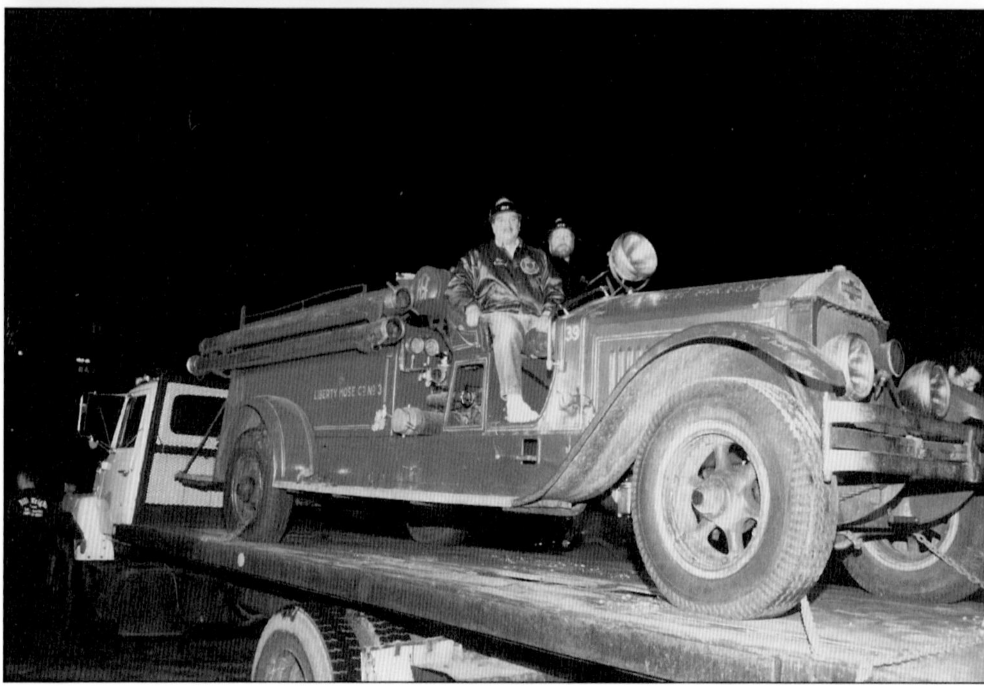

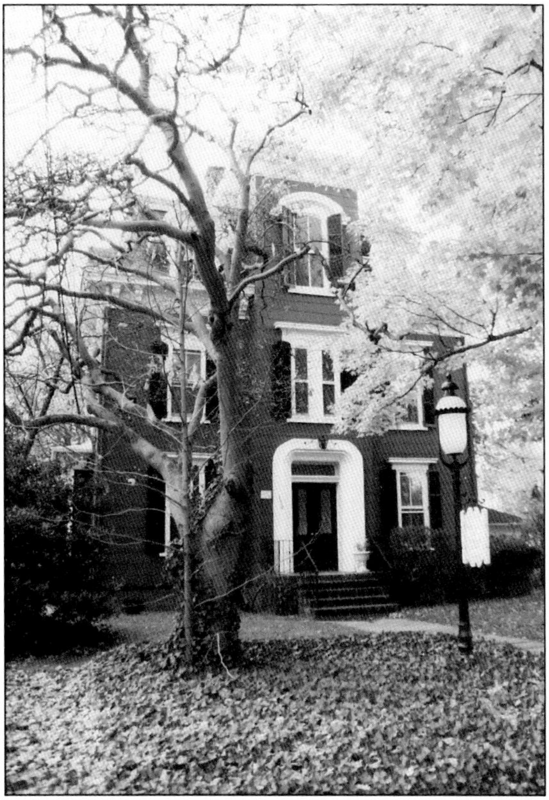

The William L. Conover House. The stately Conover House has been only slightly modified throughout the years. Her original shutters still hang in place. The Magnolia tree to the right was planted in April of 1878 on the occasion of the birth of Conover's first child, Mabel, who married Thomas Burrows in 1902. The house has been the law offices of Kenneth E. Joel since 1946.

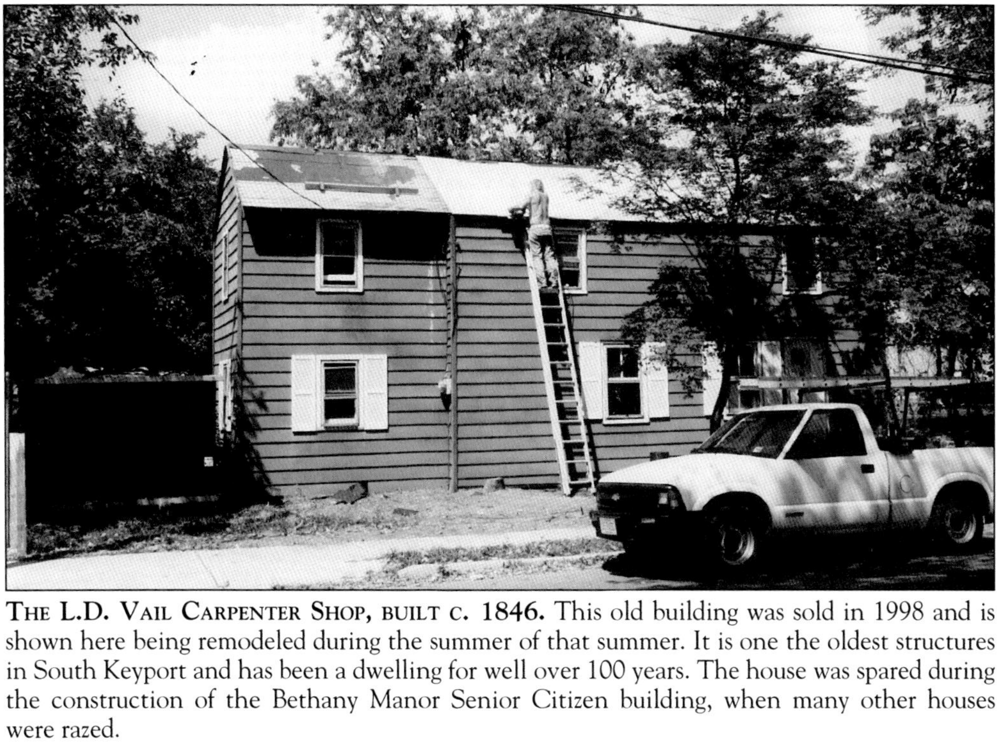

The L.D. Vail Carpenter Shop, built c. 1846. This old building was sold in 1998 and is shown here being remodeled during the summer of that summer. It is one the oldest structures in South Keyport and has been a dwelling for well over 100 years. The house was spared during the construction of the Bethany Manor Senior Citizen building, when many other houses were razed.

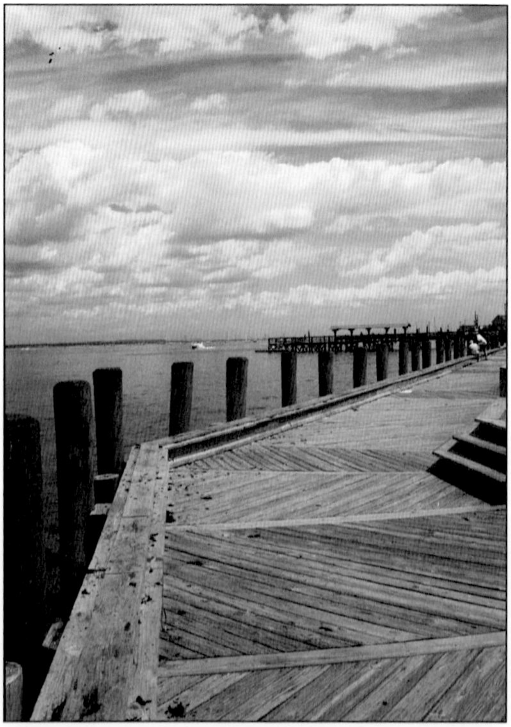

THE BULKHEAD AT FIREMEN'S PARK. By 1993 the new bulkhead and boardwalk was built, replacing the old one which had been in use since the early 1960s. The boardwalk is designed to float in extreme high tides, thereby reducing damage. However, during the 1992 Nor'easter, the tides were so high that sections of the boardwalk floated away and had to be re-installed after the storm.

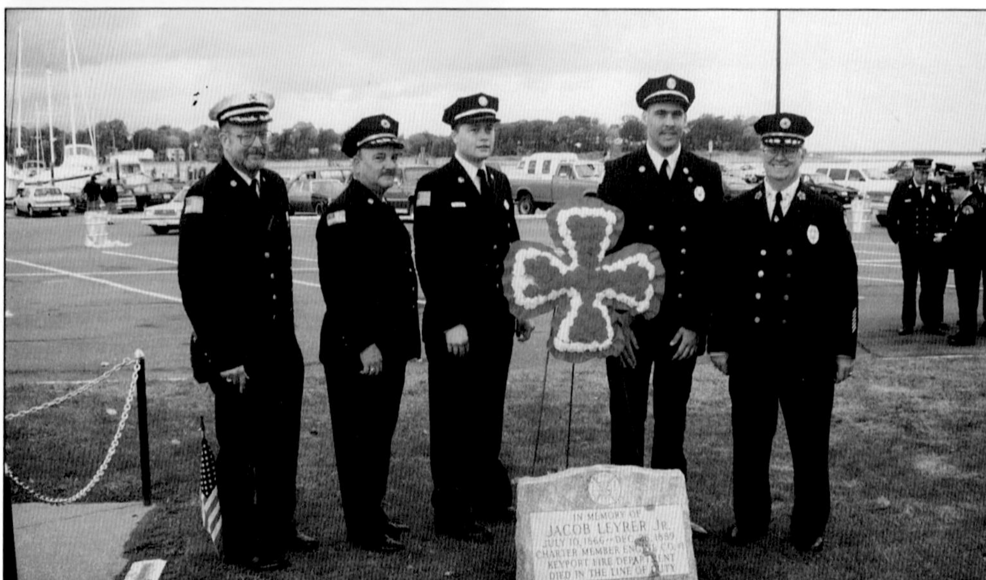

THE DEDICATION OF THE JACOB LEYRER JR. MEMORIAL, 1996. After months of hard work the monument was unveiled at Firemen's Park. The monument honored Keyport's only firefighter to die while in the line of duty. Jacob Leyrer Jr. was burned while attempting to save his own family at their bakery and dwelling, which burned on Thanksgiving 1889. Firefighters from Union Beach, Cliffwood, and Red Bank participated in the dedication. From left to right are Chief Roger Benedict, former-chief Bert Morris, the author, former-captain Jim McTernan, and former-chief James Atkins Jr.

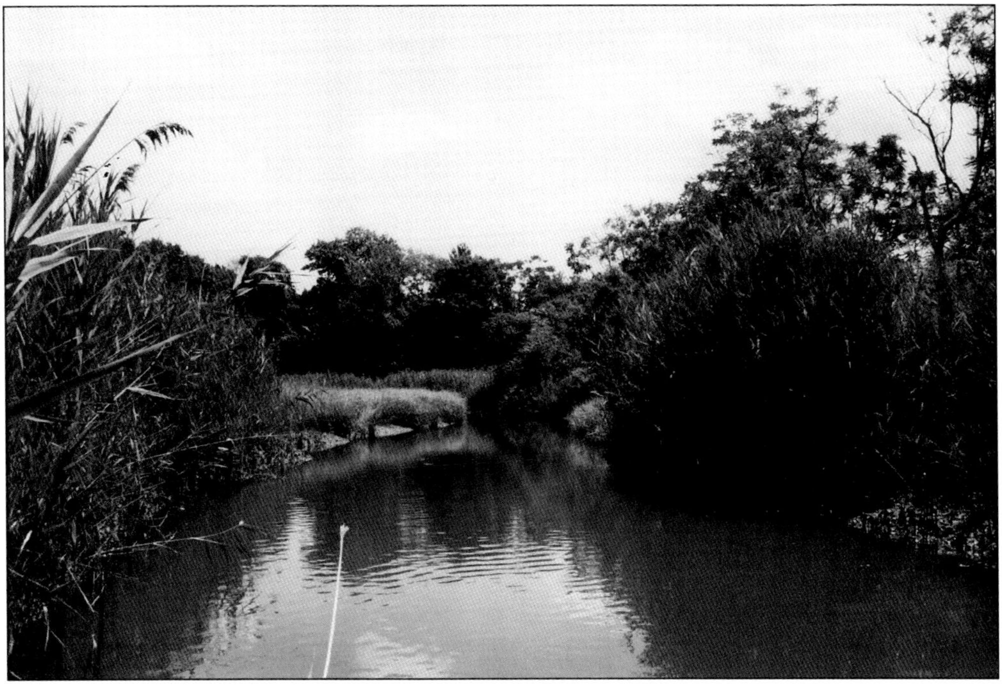

Chingarora Creek near East Third Street.

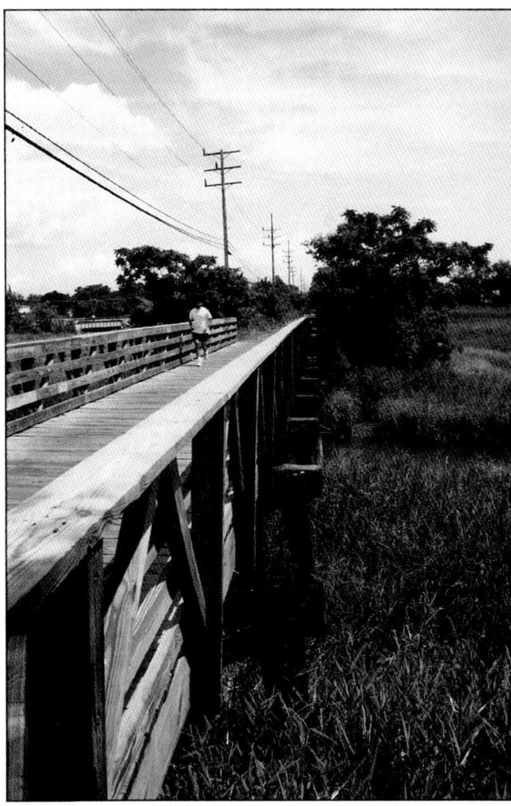

The Henry Hudson Trail. In 1990 the Monmouth County Park System became the sole owner of the former Central Railroad of New Jersey branch line from Aberdeen Township to near Avenue D in Atlantic Highlands. Over the next seven years the tracks and ties were removed, the bridges were replaced or rebuilt, and small parks along the way were developed to tie the entire linear park together. The old rail line is extremely popular with walkers and bikers alike and has turned out to be a very successful venture for the Park System.

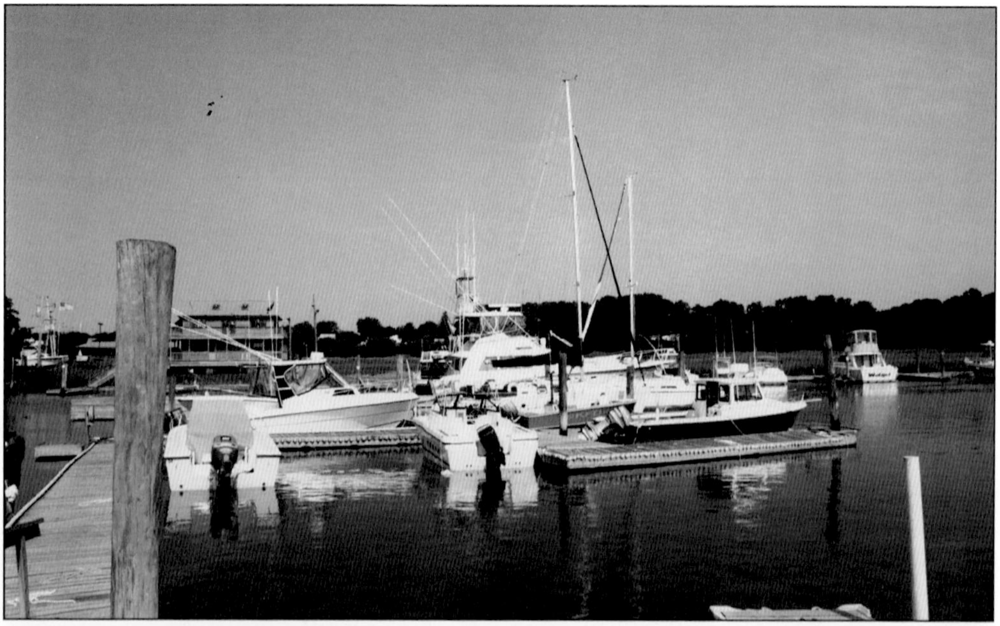

MATAWAN CREEK AS SEEN FROM KEYPORT. This view, taken from the banks of the Browns Point Marina, shows only a small section of the complex series of docks and floats which line Matawan Creek from Route 35 to the mouth of the creek. The area has been actively engaged in boating since around 1800.

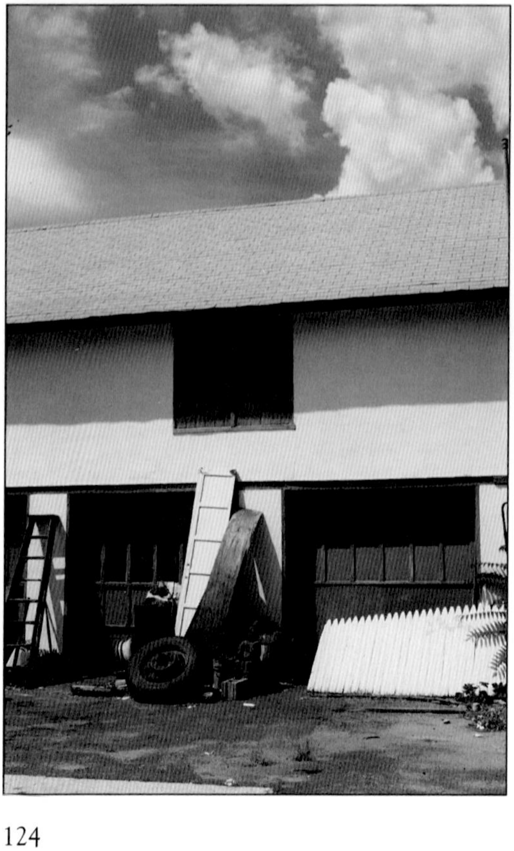

THE KEY PORT COMPANY BUILDING, 1998. It was in this building, long-known as Kapushy's Texaco, that the little village of Keyport was molded. The Key Port Company built this structure on one of the original lots partitioned from the Kearney Estate in 1829. The old building served as the storehouse for everything that was going on in the new town. In later years it became Fred Hoffman's Livery stable and was later purchased by the Kapushy brothers. It is interesting how sometimes things seem to slip in between the cracks of time. Those little loft doors on the second floor are original to the structure and have remained hanging on their original hinges for over 168 years.

The Liberty Hose Firehouse. The old firehouse, which had been built in 1893, was vacated by the fire company in 1948. The hose house was then converted into a single family home. It's currently for sale, and for $90,000 or so it would make an excellent location for a fire museum.

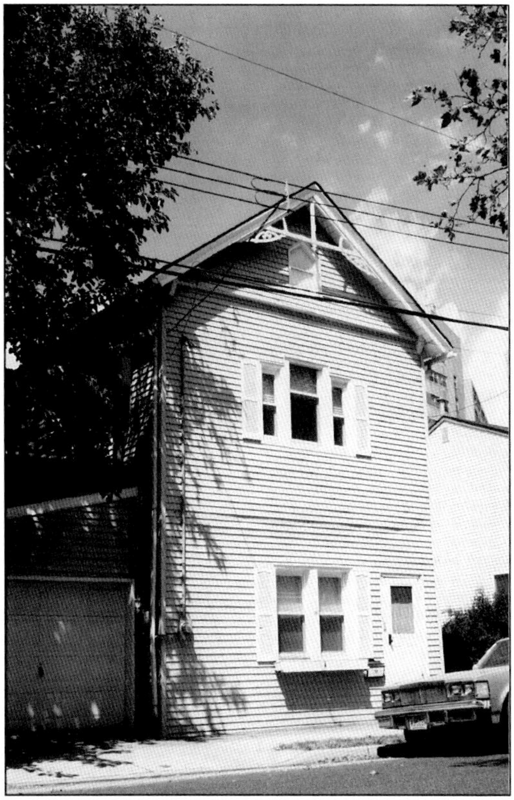

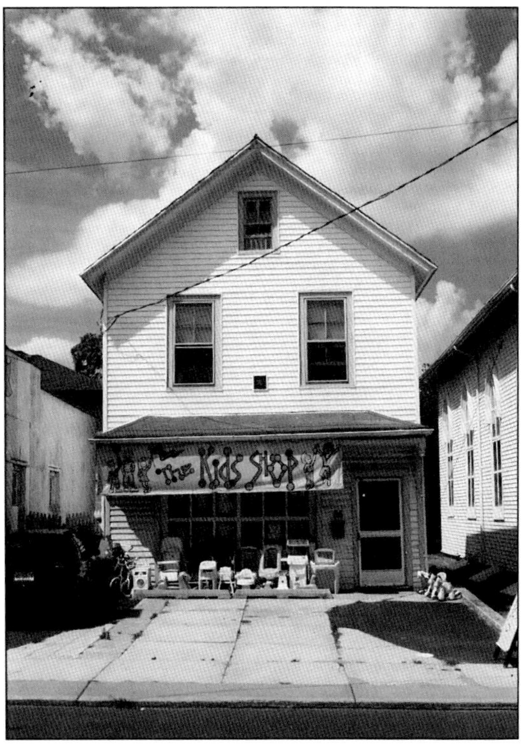

The Raritan Hose Firehouse. Another of Keyport's old firehouses that has been adapted for reuse is the 1900 Broad Street home of the Raritan Hose Co. The building ceased being used as a firehouse in 1969 and is still in its original condition.

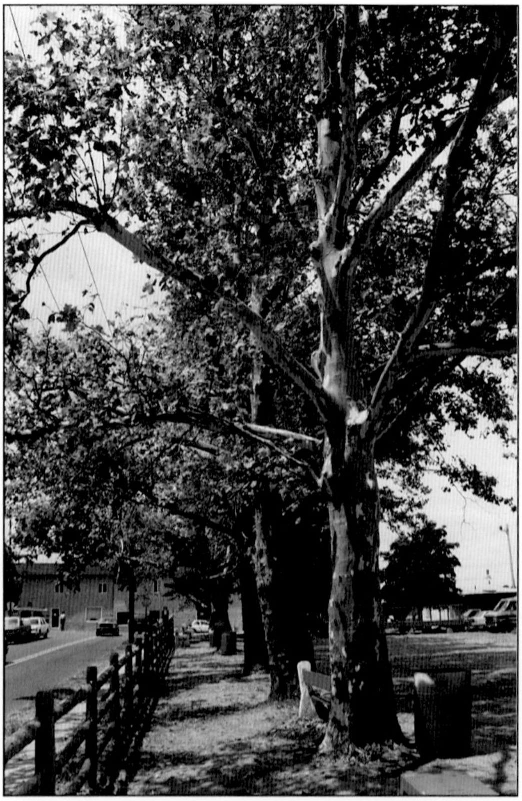

Beach Park, 1998.

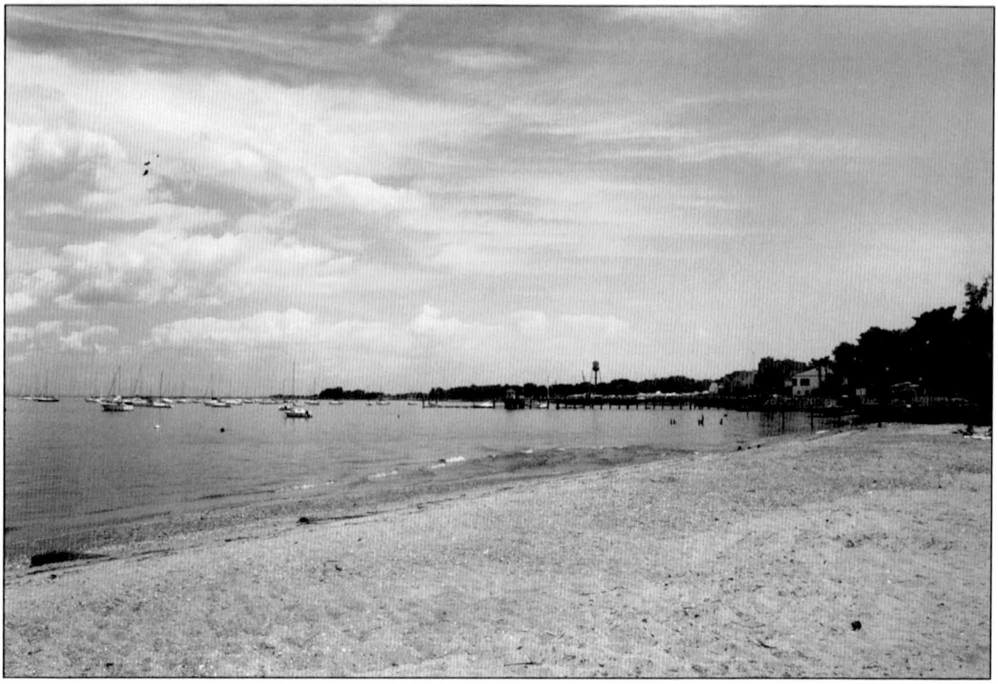

Keyport Beachfront, 1998.

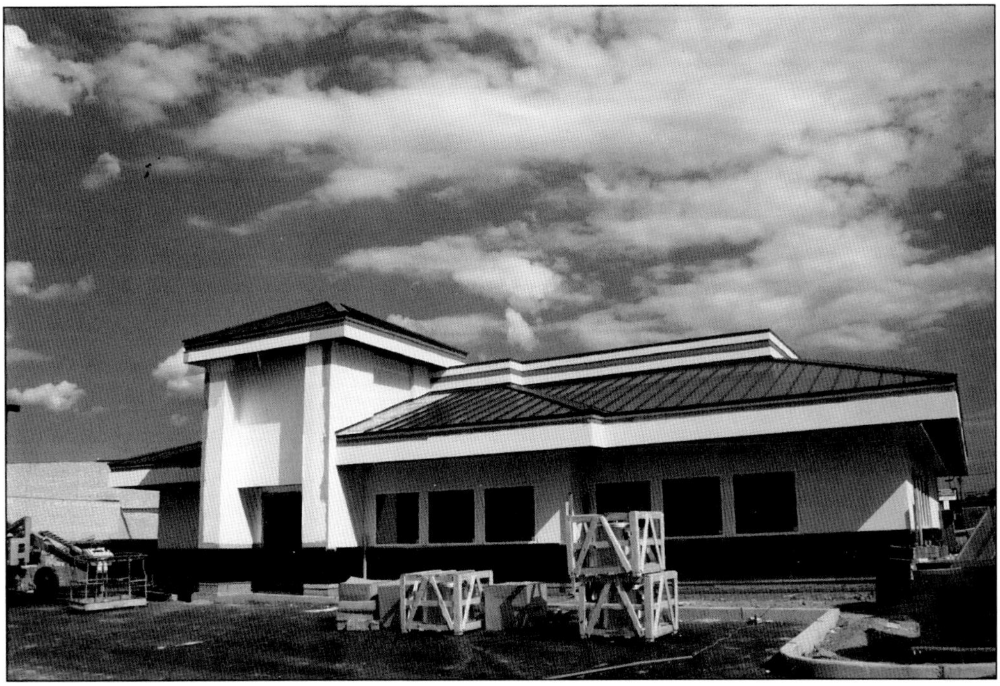

The Keyport Shopping Center, 1998. For the first time in almost 30 years Keyport received its own supermarket and shopping center. Edward's Super Food Store and the IHOP restaurant were both built on the former Route 35/36 site of the Keyport Acme (which disappeared by 1971) and the Howard Johnson's/Ground Round (which closed in 1996). They are a welcome addition to the town and should prove to be an economic boost to the area.

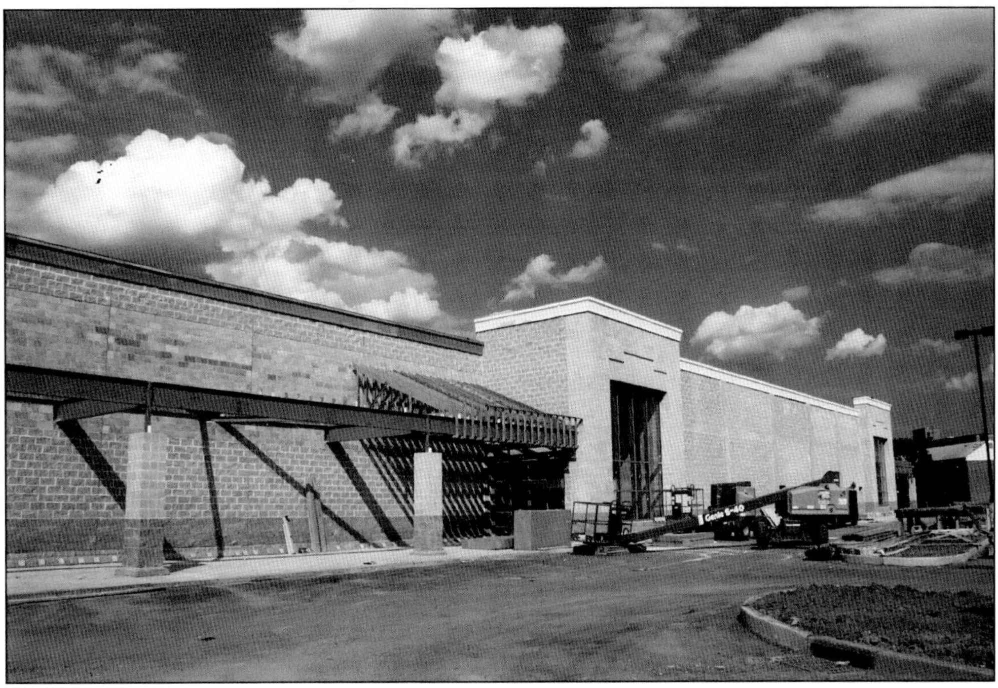

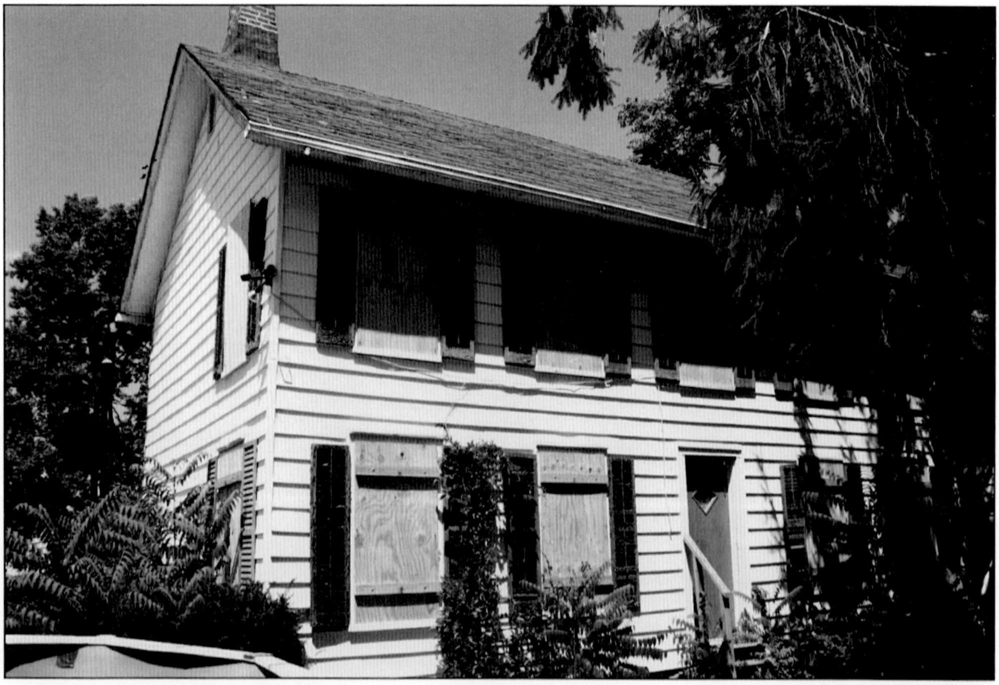

A Sign of Historic Keyport. Built *c.* 1700, this old home, known as "the farmhouse," was purchased by Issac Snyder from the John Sproul estate in 1843. When the house was undergoing renovations later, British bullets were found imbedded in the rafters. During the Revolutionary War this was the only target that Lord Howe and his fleet had along the shore to practice on. Nearly 300 years later this historic dwelling sits vacant and boarded up, awaiting an uncertain future.

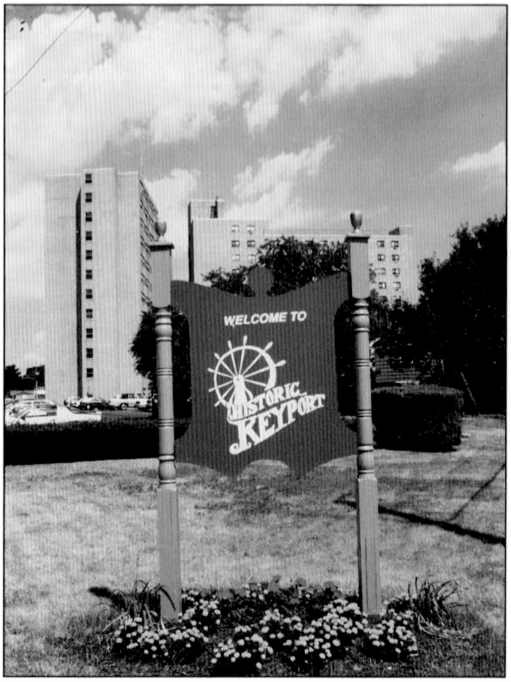

A Historic Keyport Sign. This sign, which stands in stark contrast to the Bethany Manor Apartments in the background, is one of several that greet visitors as they enter the borough. In closing, Keyport has lost so much of its physical and architectural history that when we allow historic buildings like the Snyder House to vanish, we lose the true meaning of what Keyport is. Historic Keyport is only a slogan until the town commits to preserving and protecting our landmarks!